PSYCHO-THERAPY

Isn't What
You Think

Bringing the Psychotherapeutic Engagement
Into the Living Moment

PSYCHO-THERAPY

Isn't What You Think

Bringing the Psychotherapeutic Engagement
Into the Living Moment

JAMES F. T. BUGENTAL, PH.D., D.H.L., A.B.P.P

ZEIG, TUCKER & CO., INC.
PHOENIX, ARIZONA

Published by

ZEIG, TUCKER & CO., INC.
3618 North 24 Street
Phoenix, Arizona 85016

Library of Congress Cataloging-in-Publication Data

Bugental, James F. T.
    Psychotherapy isn't what you think : bringing the
psychotherapeutic engagement into the living moment / James F. T.
Bugental.
        p.   cm.
    Includes bibliographical references and index.
    ISBN 1-891944-13-4
    1. Existential psychotherapy.   2. Humanistic psychotherapy.
3. Psychotherapist and patient.   4. Psychotherapy—Miscellanea.
I. Title.
RC489.E93B84   1999
616.89'14—dc21   98-41823
                                                                CIP

Manufactured in the United States of America

10   9   8   7   6   5   4   3   2   1

DEDICATION

As I enter my later years, I recognize how many and diverse have been my teachers. In the Preface I acknowledge some of them; here I want to add to the roll of those to whom I am forever indebted.

Since this is a book about the amazing business of being alive, I think first of my family. Particularly I want to record the inspiration and support I have had from Elizabeth, Karen, J.O., Jane, and Mary Edith Bugental. Our paths have sometimes diverged but at a deeper level they have brought me courage and support when I needed it.

Four teachers of mine have been particularly important to the formulation of my perspective: Rollo May, George Kelly, Carl Rogers, and Abraham Maslow. I feel pleasure in having known each of them personally and have gained from those associations as well as from their writings and teaching.

My other teachers have been my clients, my colleagues, and my students and trainees. It is a measure of how fortunate I am that they are too numerous to name.

CONTENTS

Acknowledgments

Many Cooks Make a Rich Broth

I want to express my gratitude to those who have contributed to this book. Yet I am blessed with how numerous they are and distressed at how partial is this list. Many others shared their experience to teach me what these pages offer. I hope they will know my implicit appreciation.

I am particularly fortunate in having the help of my wife, buddy, partner, and colleague, Dr. Elizabeth Keber Bugental. It was she who so accurately understood my basic intent in the book that she proposed the very apt title that it carries. Because Liz uniquely knows me, her comments after reading the manuscript often helped me to better express what I wanted to say.

Dr. Myrtle Heery read with a discerning eye, particuarly alert to passages that wandered into irrelevancy. Having taught this orientation many times, she also could identify points at which newcomers were likely to misunderstand.

Dr. Arthur Deikman, himself a distinguished author and psychiatrist, gave me the gift of his broad perspective by asking questions that, although sometimes difficult, were always set in the encouraging context of his interest and support.

Others who contributed uniquely include Dr. Molly Merrill Sterling and Dr. David J. W. Young, my erstwhile partners (before my retirement from the professional corporation). They, having taught this outlook for many years, were unique resources.

The members of my consultation groups and training programs are too numerous to mention individually, but they contributed spirit, eagerness, and prompt trying out of what I offered.

What My Clients Have Taught Me

WHAT IS ALIVE IS WHAT IS NOW

I must try to practice what I preach: I want to convey the importance of the maxim: "What is alive is what is now." Yet I am writing this in the early spring 1998 in my office in Novato, a small town
in northern California, and I know that you, the reader, may be
reading these words in the twenty-first century, in Atlanta or New
York City or Canyon, Texas, or in a library in a small English town
whose name I do not know or in any of ten thousand other places
and times.

I can only reach across space and time with my own experiencing
and with the recognition that you are reaching back, as manifested by
the fact you are reading these words.

More than we like to recognize, this state of affairs is also characteristic of the psychotherapeutic enterprise. We must try to hear
across a chasm of separateness—to hear the client's words, intentions, emotions, needs, efforts, and all else that expresses the client's
unique experience of being alive.

A DISTINCTION FUNDAMENTAL TO THIS BOOK

It is important to distinguish sharply between *experiencing* and *information* about experiences. Experiencing is something going on *right
now,* is a verb. Information, a noun, is inert, may speak *about* life but
is not itself *living.* What is alive is moving, is choosing, is changing,
is breathing, is active in its very principle. What is alive, therefore, is

xii

subjective and is always in some measure unpredictable, incompletely comprehensible, beyond certainty. What is said about what is subjective is, thus, always two steps—extracted from the life flow and put into words, removed from the actual.

WHAT THIS BOOK IS ABOUT

Writing a book that presumes to challenge established views in our field is, in itself, a challenge to the author. I have deep and affectionate respect and gratitude for the people who were my teachers and models and for the wisdom they have so generously shared. Similarly, I am continually nourished and stimulated by those of my own cohort who are so creative and articulate. Another source of promptings to press back my own limits comes from the students, trainees, and practicing therapists who compliment me by coming to me for guidance and instruction. I would not be able to write as I do in this book were it not for all these gifts to me. Nevertheless, I can best do them honor by setting forth the further vision they have lifted me to see.

Based on that fertile source, I have had more than a half-century of training, practicing, receiving and giving supervision and consultation, and teaching and writing about these human enterprises we call "psychotherapy." In brief, what I believe I have been learning is that it is time for us to continue moving on. Such a move needs to be more than simply new applications of familiar principles. It is my intention to reexamine some of those principles themselves.

Here are some key postulates that have generally guided our theory and practice and that I propose to reconsider and for which I want to propose some reconceptions:

- That one's personal history accounts for one's present way of being (i.e., historical causality).
- That understanding the sources in personal history of the life patterns that cause distress will lead to the change or abandonment of those patterns.
- That therapist-developed and -taught (interpreted) views of the clients' life patterns are essential to deep and lasting change.

In the pages that follow I offer fresh conceptions of the psychological phenomena that those assumptions attempt to organize. The proposals offered here are to be viewed as next-generation speculations growing out of the modes generally dominant for the past 25 to 50 years.

I also am confident that, even if these reconceptions are generally accepted and implemented, they will in time need to be reexamined and modified or replaced. Such is the nature of life and of human efforts to understand and work within this mystery that always surrounds, encompasses, and challenges us.

ABOUT THE EXISTENTIAL–HUMANISTIC PERSPECTIVE

Among other characteristics, *Psychotherapy Isn't What You Think* is a further development of the perspective enunciated in *The Art of the Psychotherapist*.[1] Understanding what this volume says does not depend upon familiarity with the earlier statement, but it may be aided or extended when the reader has familiarity with both.[2]

Essentially, the evolution of my understanding of this existential–

humanistic perspective on life-changing psychotherapy may be traced through the books cited. That work has been illustrated in its earlier forms in the two case books (1976, 1980) of the author.

This approach is further described in a variety of other publications.

NOTES

[1]Bugental, J.F.T. (1987). *The Art of the Psychotherapist.* New York: Norton

[2]Additionally, two other books of the author provide background statements that are pertinent: *Psychotherapy and Process* (1987) and *The Search for Authenticity* (1965). New York: Holt, Rinehart & Winston.

INTRODUCTION

The Core Message of This Book

A Synopsis to Provide an Overview

This synopsis is intended to aid the reader's understanding of what is presented in the pages that follow. Having an initial ("high altitude") overview facilitates communication between author and reader. As we move into the chief processes, we are metaphorically coming down to cruising level, whereas the examples and particulars of method may be thought of as "ground level."

Throughout the book, additional aids to our communication will be presented. Each chapter will open with a synopsis to position that material in the broader context of the book as a whole. Endnotes direct the reader to other sources or clarify points or terms that may be unfamiliar.

This is the central thesis that I advance in this book: The difference between a psychotherapy that is chiefly concerned with *information* and a psychotherapy that centers on the *actual experiencing* of the client in the living moment has great significance for life-changing psychotherapy.

Of course, many therapeutic orientations pay attention to both, but in these pages I am emphasizing contrasts. In this spirit, I describe in detail the values, requirements, and processes of giving primary attention to the client's immediate experiencing.

Chapter One illustrates this contrast in perspectives. Chapter Two enlarges conceptually on differences. In the following paragraphs, I will sketch additional contrasts to clarify the distinction.

Information-focused approaches are likely to place heavy reliance on thoroughly prepared case histories, cumulatively descriptive causal scenarios, and carefully administered interpretations of client experiences (complaints, causality, resistance, etc.). They give the past more attention than does the contrasting view. They often tend to see the therapist as the chief (or at least a major) agent of change.

Experiencing-centered therapy gives central place to that which is in fact going on in the client's subjectivity in the living moment. It is concerned with the intentionality, quality, implicit affective tone, intensity, and productivity (i.e., how well it aids further inner discovery and expression) of the client's presentation. It is chiefly in the present tense (i.e., in the immediate moment). Significantly, the client is recognized as the *only* agent of change, while the therapist is chiefly a facilitator of the client's work.

Of course, other perspectives—for example, the newer psychoanalytic approaches—give an important place to the client's experiencing as the site of therapeutic change. However, these approaches often interpret the client's present motivation in terms of his or her history. The view I am taking is that doing so reduces the impact of the work and ultimately leads to less productive excursions into client memories. Underlying all this is a challenge to the widespread belief in personal history as the causal core of human psychopathology. This is discussed in Chapter Three.

Human awareness, whether objectively or subjectively directed, is always in motion. Whether giving attention to an external object (e.g., a flower, a person, a street scene) or an internal object (an emotion, an idea, an intention), that attention is always an evolving process. It is impossible to attend unchangingly. Our eyes, our emotions, and our thoughts are always moving along. This movement takes the form of a *searching* or exploring of whatever it discovers, of its perimeters, of its contents.

In a wider context, a person's consciousness may be thought of as having many levels, ranging from that of which we are most readily aware to that which is in the depths of our unconscious. From this rich reservoir the searching process will continually bring fresh and, often, deeper awareness. Therein lies the potential, through opening and expanding awareness, to change one's experience of life, including life's distresses. (Chapter Four)

For the therapist to be most effective in facilitating that searching, he or she needs to be well grounded in a thought-through conception of his or her role and obligations as well as of the client's rights and responsibilities. This foundation permits wide latitude in style and energy but maintains the ultimate focus on the client's needs and welfare. (Chapter Five)

The therapeutic interview requires sufficient structure to provide continuity and focus for the work, but it must avoid rigidity or allowing form to override substance. This kind of structure transfers significant responsiblity for his or her mode of participation to the client. Likewise, it provides a continuing reference point for the evolution of the work. (Chapter Six)

We learn to identify ourselves and the nature of our individual and collective worlds in terms that come to constitute our identities for ourselves and to others. Thus these self-and-world definitions are at once what make our lives possible and what limit and, sometimes, distort them. (Chapter Seven)

The self-and-world definitions that define us also give us continuity and a sense of identity or substance; yet, because they serve such a vital role in the conduct of our lives, they also resist change. This *resistance* to change is a central feature of depth psychotherapy, and working with it challenges the courage of the client and the skills of the therapist. (Chapter Eight)

Much in our familiar everyday world emphasizes what is overt, explicit, objective. In myriad ways we are impelled to treat ourselves and each other as things. When this emphasis on the objective becomes *over*emphasis, it cripples psychotherapeutic theory and practice. The perspective here advanced emphasizes attention to the client's subjectivity. In turn, such an approach calls for attention to the therapist's own concurrent subjective experience. So important is this thesis that this and the following two chapters are employed in developing it. (Chapter Nine)

Psychotherapists who are limited to what is explicit are critically handicapped. Of course, it is rare for therapists knowingly to so limit themselves, but unwittingly many professionals come close to doing just that. The explicit meaning of words snares us into problem solving, clue collecting, and explanatory interpretations—all of which divert our attention and efforts from what may be being communicated more implicitly. Our clients display much about their inner living in their unconscious speech habits, and particularly in their implicit attitudes toward themselves. (Chapter Ten)

In so much of our current living, the richness, power, and pertinence of human subjectivity are likely to be overlooked. When we take time to consider its place, we may recognize that the subjective is, in fact and ultimately, the realm in which we most truly live. A psychotherapy that would facilitate major life renewal cannot ignore that crucial fact. (Chapter Eleven)

A fictional and synopsized account of the full course of psychotherapy of an individual makes it possible to illustrate in some detail the application of this kind of psychotherapy. This takes the reader over a period of months and through to a successful conclusion, thus providing a richer, more textured understanding of what is proposed. (Chapter Twelve)

A commentary that follows the work of the client and therapist in the sample therapeutic course (illustrated in the previous chapter) brings out more of their interaction and its likely effects. Junctures in the work that are frequent sources of difficulty for therapists are examined in some detail. (Chapter Thirteen)

Setting forth the effective ingredients in psychotherapeutic change makes clear that what is intended is not to heal or cure so much as to coach for improved living skills and greater personal fulfillment. (Chapter Fourteen)

In summation, what I am proposing is a shift in the focus of the healing effort of the psychotherapist—moving it to fostering the client's self-

discovery. It is not my intent to overthrow our more usual psychotherapeutic doctrine; rather, I hope to give it greater power by directing our
appreciation to the client's own actual, in the living moment, experiencing and to how the therapist can facilitate the client's already present
growthful intent.

PSYCHO-THERAPY

Isn't What
You Think

Bringing the Psychotherapeutic Engagement
Into the Living Moment

PROLOGUE

Psychotherapy is not what you think. It isn't the healing of an illness. It isn't guidance from a wise counselor. It isn't the mutual sharing of good friends. It isn't learning about esoteric knowledge. It isn't being shown the error of one's ways. It isn't finding a new religion. Psychotherapy isn't what you think.

Psychotherapy is not what you think. It surprises many people because it is not primarily about your childhood . . . or about what has hurt or traumatized you . . . or about the germs in your body . . . or about destructive habits you've acquired . . . or about negative attitudes you carry. . . .

Psychotherapy is not *what* you think. It is about *how* you think. It calls attention to unrecognized assumptions in how you think. It makes a distinction between what you think about and how you do that thinking. It is less concerned with looking for causes to explain what you do and more concerned with discovering patterns in the meanings you make by what you're doing.

Psychotherapy is about how you think. It is about how you live with your emotions. It is about the perspectives you bring to relating with the people who matter to you. It is about what you aspire to in your life and how you may unwittingly make it harder for yourself to reach those goals. It is about being helped to see that the change you seek is already within you. It is coming to recognize and appreciate the spark of something eternal that is your core.

Psychotherapy is not about *what* you think; it is about *how* you live with yourself right now.

1

A WORD ABOUT WORDS

A person who is sensitive about pronouns will find herself affronted
by this sentence or will he? It is plain that a man doesn't like to be
referred to as *her* and increasingly a woman is likely to resent being
lumped indiscriminately in the generic *him*.

It is a measure of social progress that we have become aware of the
inappropriateness of using masculine words to include both genders.
It is a measure of cultural lag that we, as yet, have found no genuinely
satisfactory way of correcting this lapse.

In preparing this book, I have tried to detour around the problem
by casting all references to persons in the plural (*"Clients* come to
therapists for a variety of reasons"). That works reasonably well
when we are making broad generalizations.

But this is a book about one of the more intense forms of one-on-
one relating and our illustrative excerpts and their companion expo-
sitions become out of phase when we suddenly switch to the plural.

Accordingly, we have chosen an admittedly somewhat makeshift
plan of alternating the genders of our illustrative clients and therapists
chapter by chapter unless some compelling reason dictates otherwise.

1

What Is "The Living Moment"?

Two Samples of Psychotherapeutic Work

There are many possible dimensions that can be used to describe and contrast psychotherapeutic modes. Of these, one of the most fundamental is to compare the focus selected for the therapist's concerned attention.

Probably, the most frequently employed perspective centers on information—information collected from and about the client, information subjectively processed by the therapist, and information given back to the client in the form of interpretation.

In contrast, I propose that switching our focus to the living, in-the-moment experiencing of the client can open fresh vistas for our work and give it greater power to stimulate significant life changes.

In this chapter, I present two fictional protocols of therapeutic interviews with a client we will call "Dave Stern." This pseudonym does not hide any actual person. The interviews are composites that have been drawn solely to provide a somewhat lifelike comparison between two therapeutic approaches.

The first protocol presents work that may be regarded as generally typical of eclectic and humane counselors and psychotherapists who choose to focus on information. The second sample portrays the work of a psychotherapist who focuses on the client's actual, in-the-room, in-the-living-moment experiencing.

THE INFORMATION-FOCUSED INTERVIEW (A)
Client (CL)—Dave Stern; Therapist (TH)—Mark Gillespie

Client has been in twice-a-week psychotherapy for five months. His original presenting problem was persistent episodes of worry and lack of energy. They had become so frequent and intense that his professional career as an architect was threatened. There has been some reduction in the frequency of these episodes, but, when they do occur, they seem as intense as ever.

Today's interview, the 39th, is fairly typical of their work at this point. They have a good alliance, although Dave fluctuates in his ability to invest fully in the work. Mark, the therapist, has been maintaining a relatively low profile, chiefly encouraging Dave to explore his own feelings and his view of himself.

CL-1A: I don't know what to talk about today. It's been better lately, I think, and I haven't had much going on in my life otherwise; so. . . . (*He pauses, looks vague.*)

TH-1A: Do you recall what we discussed last time—how you have a hard time focusing on your feelings?

CL-2A: Yeah. (*Pauses, takes a big breath.*) Yeah, well, I was just wondering whether you thought I should—I mean, whether I could—cut back to once a week now.

TH-2A: Is there some reason this idea comes up right now?

CL-3A: Well, just that it costs a lot, and my office isn't bringing in as much as it used to, you know. And . . . and I think my down times—the worry times—are not as often these days.

TH-3A: Why do you think that is?

CL-4A: Oh, I don't know. I guess it has to do with those things I told you about how my father made such a big deal out of being regular and responsible about work and then I was such a goof-off in college and. . . . You know we've talked about how it seems as though I . . . I was always sort of carrying him around on my back and trying to get him to approve of me, you know.

TH-4A: Uh-huh. And now do you want my approval?

CL-5A: Well, I'm not thinking I'm ready to stop yet or anything. But I thought I might be able just to cut down a bit. Can you see it that way too?

TH-5A: Well, I think that you could come just once a week if that seems necessary, but I'm not sure it's the best time to make that decision. You know there's a lot that we still don't know about what your work means to you and about how that may tie in with your relations outside of the office.

CL-6A: Yeah, that's right. Well, it was just an idea.

TH-6A: I understand, but I wonder whether your impulse to cut back on therapy says something about how you feel about our work or about me?

CL-7A: Huh! Oh, I don't think so. I feel just fine about what we're doing.

TH-7A: Mm-hmm. (*Waiting, expectant manner.*)

CL-8A: Yeah, uh. . . . (*Hesitant, unsure what is expected.*) Well, I don't know what else to say. (*Pauses, looks briefly at therapist's face, then shuts his own eyes and his face becomes intent. Then he looks up with an exasperated expression.*) Well, I don't know where to begin. There's so much, you know, and nothing seems to be high-priority stuff.

TH-8A: Why don't you go back to what you were telling me last time—about where you are with your lady friend these days?

CL-9A: Okay, sure. Well, we went to the beach Sunday, and it was a really nice day. Big crowd there, you know. Everybody wanting to get in some sun time before fall really gets here.

TH-9A: Mmm-hmm.

CL-10A: And I told Nell that she really looked great in her bikini, but I'd bet she'd look even better without it. (*Laughs briefly.*)

TH-10A: How'd she take that?

CL-11A: Oh, she laughed and said something about not rushing things. She's not uptight about sex and things, you know. I told you that sometimes we get into pretty heavy loving.

TH-11A: Is that what you want?

CL-12A: What do you mean?

TH-12A: What do you want with her . . . romantically or sexually?

CL-13A: Oh, I really want to go to bed with her, you know. But there's no big rush about it. I mean, I think it'll happen before too long. She's hinted at that. Why last week when we went to that movie I think she got as hot as I did in the big sex scene, and I thought maybe we'd go back to her place and . . . make love, but. . . . But she said she wasn't ready; so. . . . But it won't be long now.

TH-13A: So . . . ?

CL-14A: So I can wait. Anyway, that's not what I want to talk about. I just remembered what I wanted to tell you: I had another of those awful down times last week.

TH-14A: I'm surprised you only think of it now.

CL-15A: Well, you know, I was . . . I was thinking about Nell and everything. (*Pause.*) Anyway, I was really tied in knots for a couple hours last Wednesday . . . no, Thursday.

TH-15A: Where were you at the time.

CL-16A: In my apartment. You see, I'd just come in from the office and was thinking about what I wanted to do in the evening, and I couldn't decide, and then I began to get sort of sweaty, and then. . . . Oh, I don't know, I just . . . just felt like I was scared or was going to be sick or . . . I don't know. . . . (*Breaks off, sunk in his chair, not looking at therapist.*)

TH-16A Keep going.

CL-17A: (*Rousing himself, sitting up.*) I don't want to get into it again now. I mean, it just takes all of the stuffing out of me, and then I just want to curl up and go to sleep. (*Pauses.*) What should I do, do you think? I just hate these times.

TH-17A: Well, take a minute, get your breath. . . . (*Pauses.*) Now see what you think brought it on just now.

CL-18A: I don't know. (*Almost in a despairing wail.*) I've tried and tried to figure out what causes these damned down times, but I just don't get anywhere. What do you think?

TH-18A: Well, I notice this came on when you were talking about being sexual with Nell.

CL-19A: Yes. That's right. (*Pauses, reflects.*) But that doesn't make any sense. I got over feeling guilty about sex a long time ago. I've told you about what happened when I was in college. And then I had that great affair with Melanie. It doesn't make sense that it would be about being guilty for being sexual. Is that what you were saying?

TH-19A: No, but you know you had the down time right here when you started to get on that subject again.

CL-20A: Yeah, I know. But . . . but. . . . Well, how can I find out if you're right or not?

TH-20A: When you think of having sex with Nell in the near future, what comes to mind?

CL-21A: Mmm, let me see. Well, I think of how she looked at the beach. She's really got great legs and a cute rump. Her tits . . . her breasts are okay, nothing special. I . . . uh . . . I imagine it will be great, and. . . .

TH-21A: What else?

CL-22A: Uhhhh, well, I wonder will we go to her place or come to mine, and does she have. . . . I mean, I don't know whether she's on the pill, and . . . and I think I've still got some condoms in my chest of drawers, and. . . .

TH-22A: Who does Nell remind you of?

CL-23A: Uh, I don't . . . I don't know. . . . I wonder if you mean my mother or my sister or someone like that who's supposed to be taboo, but I don't get any big confirmation or anything.

TH-23A: Uh-huh.

CL-24A: Yeah. Then I . . . I remember when I tried to peek at my sisters when they were taking a bath. You remember I told you about that.

TH-24A: Uh-huh.

CL-25A: And . . . well, I can't seem to think of much else.

TH-25A: Tell me about what you think your mother or father might

have done if they had discovered you peeking at your sisters when
they were naked.

CL-26A: Oh, I guess they really would have been angry. I know
Mom always was so modest . . . overly modest. I never even saw
her breasts.

TH-26A: Did you want to? I mean, did you try to?

CL-27A: Uh. . . . Uh, yeah, I think so. I don't remember very well.

TH-27A: What was your father's attitude about these matters?

CL-28A: Oh, he would have bawled me out for sure, but that's all. He
wasn't real mean, you know, like some of my friends' fathers were.

TH-28A: Do you feel some of those same feelings when you see Nell
in her bikini?

CL-29A: Yes, I guess so. And I think about how lonely I feel sometimes and how nice it is when we're cuddling together and about
how much I miss having someone at home . . . and in my bed . . .
I don't just mean for sex, I mean just to be there in the night with
me. . . . And. . . . (*He pauses, sniffs.*) *And.* . . . You know, I almost
feel like I want to cry. That's silly, I know, and. . . .

TH-29A: (*Interrupting quickly.*) Let yourself have your feelings,
Dave.

CL-30A: Yeah, well . . . I do feel sad and kinda lonely. I guess, I'm
always going to miss Jessie [*his former wife*]. Anyway, maybe Nell
will want to come to my place, and I. . . . (*He is silent, sunk into
himself.*)

TH-30A: Stay with that. When you think of Nell coming to your
place, what do you think about it?

CL-31A: Uhhh. (*A long sigh.*) I don't seem to have a lot more right
now. I guess, it's my loneliness, isn't it? I mean, I don't usually let
myself dwell on it, but. . . . Well, there it is. I think what I need to
do is be more assertive with Nell, don't you think so? I mean, no
strong-arm stuff, just let her know how much I want her . . . or
someone. Oh, I wouldn't say that to her, of course, but really that's
it. And there's no use just sitting around feeling sorry for myself, I
just got to get off my ass and get someone to be with. Right?

TH-31A: Sounds right to me.

CL-32A: Do you think that's what's behind the down times? You know, the loneliness, the wanting someone in my life more?

TH-32A: Did you notice you got this idea right after talking about your family's attitudes toward sex?

CL-33A: Yeah, maybe so. (*Pause.*) I mean, I'm not sure, but it seems like it might be connected. Except that's not really a new idea. I know that, like you said last week, I got mixed messages about sex from my parents. . . . Now, ever since the divorce I've wanted someone in my life. . . . Oh, damn, I don't know.

TH-33A: I think that your feelings for Nell have some way become entangled with your feelings for your family—perhaps especially your sisters . . . and your mother.

CL-34A: Hah! (*Pause.*) I don't know. . . . Yeah, I can kinda see what you mean, and yet. . . . Do you mean I wanted to be sexual with one of them?

TH-34A: When you think of the loneliness, what comes to mind? What is it like when you're alone in your bed and you get this feeling?

CL-35A: Just miserable, I'll tell you. I mean downright miserable! (*He falls silent again.*)

TH-35A: Is that feeling one that you remember having any other times? Take a minute, and try to find some previous occasions when you felt that miserable.

THE EXPERIENCING-CENTERED INTERVIEW (B)
Client (CL)—Dave Stern; Therapist (TH)—Mark Gillespie

Client has been in twice-a-week psychotherapy for five months. His original presenting problem was persistent episodes of worry and lack of energy. These had become so frequent and intense that his professional career as an architect was threatened. There has been some reduction in the frequency of these episdoes, but when they do occur, they seem as intense as ever.

Today's interview, their 39th, is typical of their work at this point. They have a good alliance, although Dave fluctuates in his ability to invest fully in the work.

CL-1B: (*Sighs heavily.*) Whew! It's good to get here. (*Pauses. Moves to the client's chair somewhat hesitantly.*) I was thinking maybe I ought to use the couch today, but at least I'll start out in the chair.

TH-1B: Mmmm-hmm.

CL-2B: (*Settling deeper into the big chair.*) Okay . . . (*Sighing.*) Okay. . . . (*He shuts his eyes, obviously relaxing physically.*) I'm surprised. There's still a lot of tension in me today. Give me a minute or two more.

TH-2B: Take your time. You're doing what's important. [*Teaching client to give priority to getting truly subjectively centered before trying to talk.*]

CL-3B: I've a feeling that the tension is in my back . . . back and shoulders. . . . (*He is quiet, tuned inwardly.*)

TH-3B: Listen to it.

CL-4B: (*After several minutes, he stirs a bit.*) Just a restless feeling . . . a wanting to get going, to do something. . . . I know now that that's a signal . . . a reminder to me. . . .

TH-4B: You're listening to what's going on inside you. Take your time.

CL-5B: Wait a minute, let me get down further. (*He slumps in the chair, sits motionless.*)

TH-5B: (*Very softly.*) It's your time . . . your life.

CL-6B: (*After a minute or so of silence.*) I'm sad, really sad right now. I mean, I want to have someone . . . someone to love . . . and to love me. (*Quiet, breathing deepening.*) Ever since Jessie (*his voice breaks abruptly*) and I split. . . . God! I'm so lonely. So lonely. (*Again he is silent.*)

TH-6B: (*Quietly.*) So lonely.

CL-7B: (*Stirring abruptly, sitting more erect.*) Damn! I didn't think I was going to get into that again. Will that stuff never end? Enough already!

TH-7B: You want to just turn it off, huh?

CL-8B: Oh, yes, I do! I've been mooning around about her and our marriage for a year now. I really don't see. . . .

TH-8B: (*Quickly.*) And you're determined **not** to see.

CL-9B: Oh, c'mon, Mark, you've got to admit I have done my time on that . . . that divorce.

TH-9B: I might agree with you if you didn't demonstrate so often that you still have work to do there.

CL-10B: What do you mean, I demonstrate it?

TH-10B: You just did it a minute ago, and you're doing it in a different way right now. Can you let yourself recognize that?

CL-11B: (*Sobering.*) Yeah, yeah. So when will I be through with it? What do I have to do? Go through the whole miserable thing over and over again?

TH-11B: That's the question only you can answer.

CL-12B: You're not much help. (*Half-mocking, half-serious.*)

TH-12B: Depends on what you want help with.

CL-13B: (*Bitterly.*) Getting past all this misery. Getting rid of those endless regrets. Getting to feel good about myself again!

TH-13B: (*Quietly.*) Getting away from what's really going on inside you.

CL-14B: (*With intense feeling.*) I made such a mess of it. I blew it! (*He pauses, reflects; his face changes.*) And she was no damned angel either. It wasn't all me! She'd never admit it, but it was her fault too. (*He is quiet, but clearly struggling internally.*)

TH-14B: Stay with it! You're doing your work.

CL-15B: (*Voice tight, face intense.*) I hate my "work." I hate feeling this way, being all torn up inside, going back and forth, feeling guilty and feeling blame for her. Will it ever end?

TH-15B: (*Echoing.*) Will it end?

CL-16B: Maybe I just will always feel some regret, and I ought to just accept that and get on with my life without bouncing back to my damned divorce every five minutes. Isn't that really what I should be doing? Come on (*urgently*), level with me: What are my chances of ever getting past all this shit?

TH-16B: You seem to be trying to turn this into some kind of theoretical argument.

CL-17B: (*Sobering and speaking earnestly.*) No, of course not.

TH-17B: You must be really frightened of the feelings you have about the divorce.

CL-18B: Yes, in a way, I suppose. But really, Mark, do you think I'll ever get past all this misery? I mean, surely there's some way we can finish it off and get on without going over and over the whole dumb mess.

TH-18B: (*Speaking in a very level tone and right into the client's face.*) I hear you trying to be reasonable now, and yet I hear also how much you want in some manner to get away from the pain and sadness that are in you. I don't blame you, but I'm not going to join you in trying to deceive yourself.

CL-19B: I knew you'd say something like that.

TH-19B: That's my job.

CL-20B: Yeah, I know. (*Long pause.*) Okay, I know it, but I hate it. So let's see, where was I?

TH-20B: The more important question is where are you now?

CL-21B: (*After several minutes of silence.*) Jessie, Jessie, when will I let go of you? I know I messed things up between us, but. . . . We could have worked it out. I know we could have. . . . But you said you didn't want to try any more. You gave up on us . . . on me. (*He falls silent and is near tears.*)

TH-21B: It hurts so much.

CL-22B: (*Voice dead; defeated silence.*) You gave up on me, Jessie.

TH-22B: (*Silent, waiting, very present.*)

CL-23B: (*Drawing in a big breath and releasing it noisily.*) Yes, Jessie gave up on me, on both of us. It's so hard to let myself know that.

Somehow I always told myself that in the long run we'd work things out. In the long run, we'd be together, but. . . . but we're not . . . and we never will be again. Damn, damn, damn!

TH-23B: (*Intent manner but no words.*)

CL-24B: That's what so hard . . . so hard to let in . . . to really let in. It's over . . . with Jessie and me. It's over. It'll never be all that we . . . I . . . both of us dreamed. Never.

TH-24B: Never.

CL-25B: (*With a long sigh.*) Never.

TH-25B: (*Silent, waiting.*)

CL-26B: (*He is silent for several minutes, face blank, body slumped, eyes unseeing. At last he stirs and speaks.*) I didn't realize how much I kept that secret hope that one day we'd get together again, one day we'd revive our dreams, one day. . . . (*His voice drifts off.*)

TH-26B: One day. . . .

CL-27B: I don't want to give up that hope, but it's too late now. It's gone. It's dead.

TH-27B: (*Echoing.*) Too late now.

CL-28B: Yes. (*He is silent, several tears well from the corners of his eyes. He makes no effort to dry them. At length, he sighs heavily.*) Yes. Too late now. Yes. If I give up that hope. . . . I've been holding onto it. Did you know that? (*He doesn't wait for a reply.*) Did you know that I was holding onto that hope? I didn't know it. But I was! I was holding onto that hope as though that would make it come true!

TH-28B: (*Softly, but firmly.*) You held onto it, to the hope.

CL-29B: I did. I held onto it. Right now, I'm holding onto it, but I know I've got to let it go. . . . That really scares me!

TH-29B: Really scares you. . . .

CL-30B: (*Silent, very inwardly attuned.*) Hmmm. (*He takes a long, slow, deep breath.*) Yes, it scares me, but. . . . but I also feel something else, in back of the scare. (*Silent again, begins to sit up, but then falls back with another sigh.*) Scared, but. . . . but there's just a little edge of something else. . . . of. . . . It's like excitement or . . . anticipation or. . . .

TH-30B: (*Softly but urgently.*) Take your time. . . . Slow. . . . You're doing your work. (*Pause.*) You're looking at what you have avoided seeing for so long.

2 CLARIFYING THE MEANING OF THE *Living Moment*

Psychotherapy Needs to Focus on Client Experiencing

Psychotherapy is, by its very nature, a statement about how the human being is viewed. Thus it assumes some measure of changeability and implicitly or explicitly carries a vision of the nature of psychological well-being and psychological distress.

The view about our human potentialities I present here is generally an optimistic one, but it is, at the same time, insistent that the "work" of self-discovery and self-deliverance (from psychic distress or pathology) is demanding, time-consuming, and—in the final analysis—only to be accomplished by the person who is the client.

This is not to devalue the importance of the therapist's contribution. It is to put that service in perspective.

For many generations, the human experience was comprehended chiefly in one or both of two paradigms: the religious and the moral. The two often existed in parallel, although one or the other was likely to dominate. The religious emphasized spiritual and other worldly influences; the moral insisted on inborn rank or class transmitting a code of ethics and behavior without which a person was thought to be no more than an animal.

Freud typifies the best-known exponents of a changed view of human nature. Following the model of the emerging and productive physical sciences of the eighteenth and nineteenth centuries, he proposed a strictly historical causality as a way to make the subjective

15

objective and thus available to a detached "scientific" approach. For
most of this century (which is now ending) that perspective has been
dominant, especially in approaches to ameliorating psychological
distress.

However, since World War II there has been a growing insistence
that the mechanistic approach to humans is limited and distorting.
Two related elements in this development come from existential philosophy and humanistic psychology. The present work is a contribution to this refreshing transition.

The existential movement initially emphasized the isolation of
each individual in an indifferent universe, regarded human experience as unexplainable, and stressed freedom of choice and responsibility for the consequences of one's acts.[1] It had its roots in some part
in the general European disillusion following World War II.

As the existential outlook came to America, it was joined to the
humanistic outlook that was more traditional on these shores. Rollo
May[2] was especially influential in this conjunction, which has tended
to reduce the pessimism of the initial existential position. As a psychoanalyst and psychotherapist, May taught a more optimistic and
health-evoking view, which has come to be seen as the
existential–humanistic orientation—and is the perspective of this
book.

What is a client or patient?

A person, obviously. A person in some kind of need. A person seeking help. So far so good. But. . . .

What is a person seeking help?

The physical body that comes into my office. The perceptual, cognitive, hearing, and speaking system that got the person here and
now has him or her going through the rituals of introduction and
getting seated.

But only a perceptual, cognitive, hearing, and speaking system?
No. Also an active subjective receiving, processing, and responding to what is going on in the room.

Is that all now?
No, there are also thoughts, feelings, and intentions about things that went on in the past and things that may go on in the future.

Now is that the complete inventory?
No, probably not, but it is enough, and more than enough, for us to get on with our work.

"To get on with our work." But what is that work?[3] Which elements of that array are to be involved? The answer "all of them" is at once too prompt and too incomplete. It dodges the complexity and extensity of all human life, of any human life—thus making the answer of little help. What we must do is select some elements for primary regard while giving discerning but less attention to others.

PROPOSING A CHANGE OF THERAPIST PERSPECTIVE

The most familiar rationale of psychotherapy may be summarized—even oversimplified—in capsule form in something like the following terms.

A carefully developed relationship provides an opportunity for the client and therapist to reexamine the former's life history and life assumptions to discover where they fail to accord with reality. Then this information is sensitively presented to the client with the intention of bringing about changes in the client's comfort and/or satisfaction in living.

This process consists mainly in the therapist's collecting information about the client's history and present life and, at the same time, making observations of the client's unwitting enactment in the therapy room of his or her way of being in the world.

The therapist, having more experience, education, and training, and being removed from the day-to-day exigencies of the client's life, can recognize client patterns that are handicapping or injurious and can then bring them to the client's attention in a disciplined and sensitive way. The healing effect is thus furthered by the carefully selected and sensitively timed input of information from the therapist to the client.

In even more of an oversimplification, we can further summarize this process as one in which information about the client is accumulated, processed, and selectively fed back to the client by the therapist. Of course, the client is an active participant and partner in this process, but the key ingredient is the therapist's wisdom and skill in working with information about the client, including cues to the client's transferring assumptions from other settings into the therapeutic engagement.

In this collecting, processing, and feeding back of information, the sensitive and skilled therapist pays attention to both *content* and *process*. This can be represented in simple graphic form:

Observations from my own practice[4] and from many years of training, supervising, and serving as a consultant to a range of psychotherapists have convinced me that there is another dimension that has rich therapeutic potential but that has not sufficiently been the direct focus of our attention. This is *the client's experiencing in the immediate moment.*

Of course, many experienced and effective psychotherapists pay attention to and give feedback to clients about what those clients are manifestly experiencing concurrently. Doing so makes available a further dimension relatively independent of the content of the conversation (which may be about the past, present, or future).

Such therapist actions are often a part of process feedback (i.e., calling their clients' attention to the manner of their participation in addition to content), which many therapists recognize as facilitating more client self-exploration and disclosure.

What is different in the present proposal is the shifting of the therapist's principal attention from *information about* the client to *the client's actual in-the-moment experiencing.*

The intent of this shift is to intensify and expand the client's subjective activity and consequent awareness. When subjectivity is thus brought forward in the client's consciousness, it increases in range and in pertinence to the client's inner experiencing and processing. In turn, that increase helps the client to discover ways in which she is self-defeating and thus releases the client's creative (or self-healing) potential.[5]

This proposal calls for a major realignment of the therapist's professional concern, and it adds what I believe to be a powerful dimension to the earlier diagram:

THE LIVING MOMENT AS A LOCUS FOR THERAPIST ATTENTION

What is truly in the therapeutic room, what is most directly (almost tangibly) available for the work, is the *present (i.e., living) moment,* the client's and the therapist's being in this very *now*. Their work must be centered on what *is* actually living rather than on what *was* or what *may be.* Of course, there are thoughts and feelings about the past and about the future, but—and this is the crucial point—while they are *about* the past, they are actually occurring in the present. An example:

Client: When I was in high school I was very idealistic.
Therapist A: What form did that idealism take?
Therapist B: How about nowadays?

Sometimes therapists reply as did Therapist B, thinking to get more in the present, and, of course, it does so content-wise, but present-tense content may not be genuinely *actual,* and Therapist B's response is still not actually in the living moment. Therapist C's is:

Therapist C: You're dating that as "high school."

As is Therapist D's:

Therapist D: You sound very distant as you say that.

Holding the perspective[6] that what is *actual* is what is in this room, in this "now," it becomes evident that the actual element is that the whole matter is being pushed away and held at a distance in time from the *now* of the speaking. What is truly actual in this client as she spoke is not the idealism or the high school.

> *This is the key point of the emphasis on the living moment, and it is often misunderstood: We tend to listen to* what *is said rather than* how *and* when *the saying occurs.*

Therapists need to listen to the "music" more than to the words. Indeed, that admonition is not simply one for the consultation room. Most of us learn, with varying degrees of discernment, to note the speaker and not just the speech. The glib salesperson can be self-defeating when she presses too hard or too detachedly; the preoccupied reader's vague and irrelevant responses are familiar examples of ill-matched music and words.

What we come to recognize—usually negatively—is that "canned" or shallowly motivated talk is more involved with the speaker's needs than it is respectful of the listener's concerns.

By and large the conventions of psychotherapy have centered on the past, on causality, or on symptoms that are seen as the significant results of the client's history. Thus it can happen that the therapist may be attending chiefly to the past, while at the same time the client is focusing on the future, with the hope that it will be better. Meanwhile the present is regarded by both as incidental.

My intent is to call attention to an often neglected or underappreciated perspective for psychotherapeutic work—what is actually going on in this person living here in the room at this very time. All too frequently, if that point is raised, it is regarded as trivial, as making much out of little. The actual present, being thus taken for granted, receives only passing attention.

When one listens with ears attuned to the living moment, it is striking how often all of us, even with the best will, get lost in *talking about* and overlook what is present and alive but implicit.

Client: I still feel so much sadness—it's crazy to still carry this around with me I know—about Jessie being gone. I have mourned enough, for Christ's sake, why can't I let it go?

Therapist A: You're still missing her.

Therapist B: (*Empathically.*) So sad.

Therapist C: How long has she been gone?

Therapist D: Your feelings are at war, the impatience attacking the sadness.

Therapist A goes for the unhappy emotion; so often this draws therapist attention. Similarly, Therapist B does the same, but with fewer words, encouraging a deepening of the feelings. Perhaps because of the client's ambivalence, Therapist C seeks information with the possible intention of evaluating the appropriateness of the client's irritation.

Therapist D recognizes what is most present in the room, the pull of mourning and the impatience with its still having such potency.

I believe it is that dismissal of the immediate that handicaps and limits the impact of much psychotherapeutic work. The perspective that centers on the true *now*, as here proposed, can, in many instances, provide a refreshing and powerful base for more effective therapy. Much will be gained when the therapist's attention and efforts are directed to facilitating and highlighting the client's full awareness of her immediate experience in the therapeutic moment.

What is here recommended is a refocusing of the therapist's attention and, thereby, of the client's awareness. Whatever content the therapeutic partners address—personal history, long-range hopes, personal values, emotional distress, or current life issues—their attending to the *actual* in-the-moment experiencing of the client will deepen the client's inner exploration and tap the potential for desirable change.

An Aside

Having proposed that, I do not urge abandoning content, disregarding history, or taking similar leave of the usual paths. Instead, I offer a supplement or alternative that can give the work freshness and added power.

In all candor, however, it is my experience that once the client and the therapist become genuinely aware of the what is present in the living moment, such changes as the following begin to occur.

- More immediacy of engagement
- Growing attention to the present life experiences
- Increasing recognition that that which is *not* actual is at some psychological distance

- Therapist's becoming less intrusively active and more a witness to the client's doing more of her own work, making her own journey
- Unexpected changes in the client's self-and-world construct system and emotions with consequent impacts on the client's life outside the therapy room

In brief, sensitive attention to what is actual in the living moment is likely to become more central to the work generally.

Of course, attention to the actual, in-the-moment experiencing of the client is not unique to this presentation. Effective therapists frequently attend to the in-the-moment stance and affect of the client. What may be less familiar is the conviction that the therapeutic course will prove more impactful and the therapeutic results will be more lasting when the client's immediate experiencing—the *actual implicit* more than the *explicit* content experiencing—is the chief realm of therapist concern and action.

Developing and pursuing such a perspective provides a fresh emphasis that invigorates the work of psychotherapy and the general life stance of the client.

A RATIONALE FOR THE EMPHASIS ON THE *Actual*

As is apparent, centrally important in this perspective is the goal of heightening the client's own immediate and subjective awareness. This is in contrast to the more usual purpose of both client and therapist, collecting and selectively attending to information *about* the client and the client's history.

Most clients (indeed, most of us: clients, therapists, and people in general[7]) are chiefly aware of our own being as objects to be observed, directed, reflected upon, planned for, or remembered. That can be necessary and productive in some instances. However, when we are seeking through psychotherapy to have our living bring more satisfaction and less frustration, then objective knowing about one's self is not adequate to the task.

We are very limitedly aware of our own being in the actual moment and as the subjects of our lives. Thus we are likely to think of ourselves as things to manage so that they will be as we want them to be (i.e., not as they actually are). In this way, we become ourselves-as-subjects working on ourselves-as-objects. A splitting of our being that is fundamentally countertherapeutic.

In contrast, my experience as a psychotherapist and as a supervisor or consultant to other psychotherapists has convinced me of an important truth about the human enterprise: *Increased awareness of ourselves in the living moment means increased effectiveness of self-direction and increased satisfaction in living.*[7]

Psychotherapy, at least implicitly, has as its goal evoking and strengthening the client's self-knowledge and self-direction. Our clients so often present as though they were only objects acted upon by forces beyond their knowing or command. Psychotherapy of the actual seeks to rouse the dormant subjecthood of the client and to foster a growing sense of aware choicefulness.

When client and therapist talk *about* the client and particularly about the client at other times and in other places, they are affirming the *client-as-object.* When the client learns to be aware of her in-the-moment being and the therapist aids and supports that perspective, then the *client-as-subject* is being evoked. This is sometimes thought of as "empowering." I believe that is a misleading characterization. We cannot put power in someone else. The client-as-subject is or becomes aware of the immediacy of the client's being and thus can claim her own power, which has been latent all along.

Power, as we think of it in psychological contexts,[8] generally means having the ability to bring about changes that accord with one's own intentions. Clearly, the effective exercise of power will then require self-knowledge and the application of that knowledge in the immediate. Psychotherapy that affirms the congruence of the client's intent and the client's experiencing (whether overt or implicit) contributes to the client's wholeness and, therefore, to the client's feeling of power.

THE THERAPIST'S CONTRIBUTION

The central import of this way of seeing the therapeutic process is that the client will be helped to come into her own subjecthood when the therapist accurately identifies what is *implicitly present but unregarded* within the client's consciousness at each moment. Of course, it is not desirable or possible to provide only that identification, but when it is offered with sensitivity to the client's readiness to receive it, much will be gained.

The key word in the foregoing statement is "identifies." It is set in contrast to "suggests" or "instructs." *Identifies* in this context means shining a light on something that is already present, that is awaiting recognition. Clearly what is required is intuition, sensitivity, and a readiness to set aside other elements of one's agenda. Most of us need much practice and discipline to effect this shift in focus. Even more patience and effort are required to develop skill in this mode of intervention.

I spoke above of what "is implicitly present but unregarded." Reflecting such observations back to the client requires careful and measured input from the therapist. Paradigmatically, the move is from *recognition* ("You sound very distant") through *reflection* ("How often you find that in your thoughts!") to *interpretation* based on frequently demonstrated patterns ("Once again, when you face a difficult choice in your current life, you find your thoughts going back to your mother").

That three-step sequence is only effective when adequate and repeated confrontations are carried out at each step before the emphasis moves to the next. Thus the work may center on simple recognition and identification for some time until the client begins to make such observations independently.[9]

When that happens, this kind of work continues, but is extended to reflections on repeated patterns—desirably just focusing on one or two until they also become readily apparent to the client. At that point, it is often possible to move to other patterns; further, when the first effort has been effective, much less time and effort are apt to be required thereafter. Now both forms of identification—recognition and reflection—continue, but the therapist begins to bring out the persistent patterns and their implications.

This important sequence of therapist input will be effective only when it is patiently paced, when interventions are accurately placed so that client recognition is nearly immediate, and when the client has learned that such therapist input is facilitating not finding fault or giving instructions.[10]

TWO CONTRASTING INTERVIEWS

To illustrate further the difference between usual ways of working and an approach that attends to what is actual (in the living moment), here are two fictional interviews. The first is a reasonably typical first interview with a client coming for psychotherapy.

The Information-Focused Interview (2)
Client (CL)—Betty Black; Therapist (TH)—Jane Norman

Ten days earlier, Betty had called for an appointment, saying that she had been considering therapy for "a long time" and that now she was ready to "get into it." Today's appointment was set up. She arrives promptly, comes into the consultation room and readily takes the client's chair. Now she sits somewhat primly, with her purse set aside and her hands folded in her lap. She looks expectantly at the therapist.

TH-1A: You said on the phone that you'd been considering therapy for some time before finally deciding that now was the time. Would you like to tell me what it is that concerns you? *[Therapist directs client's attention to the past, even though the question is phrased in the present tense.]*

CL-1A: Well, you see I have this habit of worrying things to pieces, at least that's what my husband says. And I . . . I guess he's right. It does seem as though it's hard for me just to take things easy and go on. My friend Barbara seems so lighthearted, and sometimes I think she is lucky, and sometimes. . . . *[Client describes herself objectively and even then she quotes someone else, her husband. Her self-objectification is further emphasized as she needs to use contrasts with another person to portray her own way of being.]*

TH-2A: You wish you were more like Barbara sometimes, eh? When are those times most likely to occur? *["Sometimes" and (other) "times" push the whole matter to an abstract level.]*

CL-2A: I'm not sure. . . . I think more when I've been trying to deal with people whom I don't know very well. . . . At least that's what I think of first right now. *[Betty makes the first allusion to the actual, but does so in a way that dismisses its importance.]*

TH-3A: People like . . . ?

CL-3A: Like at the store or. . . . Oh, I know a good example: I had a terrible time figuring out what to say to the man at the garage when they didn't take care of the car the way they should have. *[Betty welcomes a concrete instance but keeps it in the past tense. Her in-the-moment satisfaction in finding the example is ignored.]*

From here on, I will comment only on exceptional instances or to illustrate other, more actual, in-the-moment ways of responding.

TH-4A: So what did you do?

CL-4A: *(Embarrassed.)* I finally asked my husband to talk to them for me. *(She makes a rueful face.)*

TH-5A: Do you often find yourself getting him to do things like that for you? *[Betty's embarrassment is manifest and actual, and it*

*would be useful to acknowledge it. "It embarrasses you to talk
about it" or "You seem uncomfortable as you say that" would
bring the actual into the work.]*

CL-5A: Well, no. . . . (*Stops, considering.*) Well, yes, at least sometimes. (*Pause.*) Do you think I'm too dependent on him? Oh, that's
not a good question now, is it? You don't know me yet.

TH-6A: No, but I'm beginning to know you. What else would you
like me to know about you?

CL-6A: Oh . . . that I'm . . . I'm very conscientious. If I do say so,
that's one of my good points. Almost everyone who knows me will
tell you that.

TH-7A: Mm-hmm. *[More attention to the actual would likely have
resulted had the therapist said, "You feel satisfaction in that quality, don't you?" or "You have a very different feeling about your
dependability than you had when we talked about your turning to
your husband."]*

CL-7A: I'm like my father that way. His word was his bond, he used
to say.

TH-8A: Is he still living?

CL-8A: No, he died two years ago.

TH-9A: Were you close to him?

CL-9A: Well, uh, yes. I mean he was sort of an introvert, and it
was hard to get very close to him . . . but I think underneath we
were. . . . I'm not sure. *["Even now you are uncertain about
that." Here it is well to pick up the hesitation rather than tying
it so closely to the father since the therapist has only this little
knowledge of what is unspoken.]*

TH-10A: Was it different with your mother?

CL-10A: Oh, yes! We were . . . are very close. She's still living, and
she's really very well . . . for someone in her seventies. *[Therapist
might well have observed, "There's no uncertainty about your feelings there, is there?"]*

TH-11A: Do you have any brothers or sisters?

CL-11A: One sister. She's ten years older. . . .

TH-12A: How do you get along with her?

CL-12A: Oh, fine. (*Pause.*) She was so much older, you know, so it just wasn't. . . . [*"You don't finish that sentence."*]

TH-13A: So there was just the two of you? Did you ever wish there had been more?

CL-13A: Uh, more sisters or brothers? [*Therapist is busy collecting background information and seems largely to be ignoring the client's subjectivity as she responds.*]

TH-14A: Yes.

CL-14A: Uh, I don't know. Never thought about it much.

TH-15A: Were there other family members around when you were growing up, like cousins or aunts and uncles or grandparents?

CL-15A: Oh, sure. My mother's parents lived near us until I went away to college, and we used to see them almost every week.

TH-16A: Did you like that? Were you close to them? [*This seems pretty much a fishing expedition. By now there is no evident thread of concern within the client's protocol for the therapist to follow.*]

CL-16A: Oh, yes. I thought they were just great, especially when I was little. They were always bringing me little presents or taking me places . . . like to the circus or to children's shows. (*There is a wistful quality to her voice.*)

TH-17A: Are either of them still alive?

CL-17A: No, not any more. My grandmother died just three years ago though. I miss her. [*The therapist needs to note whether this feeling is manifest or is simply reported. It is very likely that it is too soon to say anything to the client yet.*]

TH-18A: Did you see much of her in the last years before she died?

CL-18A: Not really. She was so old, and I was so busy with school and then working. . . . You know how it is. [*"How is it in you right now as we talk?"*]

TH-19A: Sure. How about any other relatives?

CL-19A: Oh, there are some distant cousins back in Montana, I think, but I only saw them once, and that was years ago when I was just ten or eleven.

TH-20A: Did you have many friends when you were a kid?

CL-20A: Oh, yeah. Lots of them. I was kind of a tomboy, you know. So I had both girl and boy friends. Then in high school, I was very close with two girls, and then. . . .

TH-21A: Then . . . ? [*"You stop rather abruptly when you think of those girls."*]

CL-21A: Then I started going steady with Rog, and, of course, after that there weren't as many other people in my life.

What follows is an illustration of how the same interview might go if there were more emphasis on the actual, in-interview experiencing of the client.

THE EXPERIENCING-CENTERED INTERVIEW (2)
Client (CL)—Betty Black; Therapist (TH)—Jane Norman

Ten days earlier, Betty Black called for an appointment, saying that she had been considering therapy for "a long time" and that now she was ready to "get into it". Today's appointment was set up. She arrives promptly, comes into the consultation room and readily takes the client's chair. Now she sits somewhat primly, with her purse set aside and her hands folded in her lap. She looks expectantly at the therapist.

TH-1B: You said on the phone that you'd been considering therapy for some time before finally deciding that now was the time. Would you like to tell me how it is for you to be here now?

CL-1B: Oh fine. (*Pause.*) I mean. . . . It's all right. (*A longer hesitation.*) I guess you want to know why I'm here, huh? (*She glances up briefly, but hurries on with what is obviously a prepared statement.*) Well, you see, uh, I have this habit of worrying things to pieces . . . at least that's what my husband says. . . . And I guess he's right. It does seem as though it's hard for me just to take things easy and go on. . . . My friend Barbara seems so lighthearted, and sometimes I think she is lucky, and sometimes. . . . *[She ignores the question asking about "right now"; instead she hurries on to a planned "problem," which she has very likely prepared before coming.]*

TH-2B: Sometimes . . . ?

CL-2B: Sometimes. . . . Oh, I don't know. (*Stops, reflecting briefly.*) I guess I think she's too casual sometimes, but. . . .

TH-3B: You seem to be debating with yourself.

CL-3B: Yes. I am. That's just the way I am . . . too often. I don't know for sure what I think about. . . . Well, about almost anything. (*Pause.*) Is that something you can . . . something you can. . . . Well, I know you can't fix it for me, but can you help me with it?

TH-4B: It is the kind of concern on which we can work together.

CL-4B: (*Nods, head down, thinking.*) Uh-huh. I mean, yes. I mean, I like the way you put that, that we'd do it together.

TH-5B: Mm-hmm.

CL-5B: Anyway, what I want to do is get to be more . . . more spontaneous, I guess you could say.

TH-6B: I see. (*She waits expectantly.*)

CL-6B: Yes. . . . Well, I'd like . . . I mean, I like it that you will help me with it.

TH-7B: Not being alone with it makes a difference to you.

CL-7B: No. Well, yes. . . . I guess it does. . . . In some ways, I mean. . . . (*Uncertain, clearly troubled about saying so.*) *[She is hearing therapist responding in a way she hadn't expected—that is, talking about her immediate experience rather than about her "problem" or her history. The therapist needs to recognize that at this moment Betty is probably feeling alone in the room since her bids for implicit understanding have drawn little explicit response from the therapist.]*

TH-8B: It's a new experience, isn't it, Betty, to have to say all these things? It seems hard to find what you want to say right now. (*Pause.*) Don't push yourself; just say whatever you can of what comes into your thoughts.

CL-8B: Oh. (*Gratefully.*) Yes. Yes, I just. . . . (*Stops, take a quick breath.*) Well, I guess I was thinking maybe you wanted to ask me some questions or something. . . .

TH-9B: Um-hmm. (*Understandingly.*) No, nothing right now. You're doing all right. You've just told me one thing that's going on in you—that you wondered if I had questions. Can you tell me more about what else is happening inside of you in addition to that?

CL-9B: (*She pauses a minute, reflecting.*) I've never thought about it, you know. I mean it's just those little things that. . . . That we start thinking without realizing it.

TH-10B: I understand. (*Expectantly.*) And now . . . ?

CL-10B: Well, I don't know. . . . I mean, I was just trying to think what I should say that would help you. . . . Well, not "help" you, but. . . .

TH-11B: I hear how much you want to do what you're supposed to do. But, Betty, we do things a little differently here, and the way you already are doing things is just fine. It is difficult for most of us to get in touch with our inner processes and then to share them with someone we don't really know yet. You're beginning to get the idea of that already, but it *is* hard at first.

CL-11B: (*She is silent, reflective. Then somewhat abruptly she seems to recall herself to where she is.*) Oh! I'm sorry. I guess I got sort of sidetracked just then. Now let's see, where was I? (*She frowns intently, eyes squinting.*) [*As with many clients, Betty doesn't really grasp what is asked of her. She has become caught up in her inner confusion, but it doesn't occur to her that that confusion itself might be appropriate and useful to disclose. It will take a number of teaching interventions by the therapist before she can let go to share such spontaneous processes.*]

TH-12B: (*Interrupting.*) Wait, Betty, this is a chance for me to explain something important: You got "sidetracked" as you say, but in another way you got on the main track. What came up inside you and was unexpected is a sample of the things in you that are important but don't usually get recognized and so aren't available to our working together. When you find that happening, listen inside and then tell me as much of it as you can.

CL-12B: Oh, I didn't know that. (*She pauses briefly.*) Anyway, I don't think it was very important. Fact is, I can hardly remember what it was now. Something about my sister, I think, but I'm not sure. Shall I try to go back and figure out what it was? *[Betty, as most new clients, doesn't really understand about trusting her own spontaneous processes, and so she sets about trying to reason out what is wanted.]*

TH-13B: No. What you would figure out would not be the same as what actually came unexpectedly. It's all right. What is important doesn't get lost. We'll just have to wait for the next time it comes along.

CL-13B: (*Clearly unsure and trying to learn what is being taught.*) Okay . . . I think I see what you mean. I just wonder about it. I mean, about what I was distracted by and yet, for some reason, I can't remember now.

TH-14B: It's hard just to let it go, isn't it?

CL-14B: (*Reflecting.*) Yes . . . I mean, I can sort of think what it might have been. . . . It seems like it might have been important. (*Suddenly she brightens and looks eagerly at the therapist.*) Maybe it was about my sister and how she was always correcting me. We were talking about her, I remember.

TH-15B: Mmm-hmm. *[Therapist chooses not to pick up on the obvious parallel between the sister who was "always correcting" Betty and the therapist herself who is very likely being experienced as doing similarly. There will be other opportunities, and now it is important to help Betty learn to value and share her spontaneous inner experiencing.]*

CL-15B: There! That's it. I'm almost sure.

TH-16B: You're pleased that you figured it out.

CL-16B: Yes! I don't like to get muddle-headed and lose my train of thought.

TH-17B: "Muddle-headed"?

CL-17B: Yes. That's what my sister would call me sometimes. She didn't mean it to hurt me, just teasing, you know. She liked to tease me, and I. . . .

TH-18B: You . . . ?

CL-18B: I . . . well, sometimes. . . . Sometimes it was hard to accept it that she was just "playing." That's what my mother would say if I complained about Elly's teasing. *(Pause.)* It didn't feel like playing to me, but I guess I was too sensitive. That's what I heard over and over again, "Don't be so sensitive. . . . Don't take it all to heart. . . . Don't be a crybaby."

TH-19B: *(Nods, listening intently, but not speaking.)*

CL-19B: Oh, I don't know.

TH-20B: Sometimes you felt. . . . *(Leaving it open.)*

CL-20B: Well, I couldn't help it. *(Protesting.)*

TH-21B: I hear how unfair it seemed.

CL-21B: Yes . . . it was unfair!

TH-22B: You didn't like being teased that way.

CL-22B: No, I didn't. *(Petulant.)* Well I. . . . Oh, I get so mixed up. It's just that I don't want to waste any time here, and I'm still not very sure what you want.

TH-23B: *(Sympathetically.)* And that makes you feel unsettled right now, doesn't it?

CL-23B: Yes . . . yes, it does.

TH-24B: We may be helping you to discover more about what's going on inside you than you're already familiar with.

CL-24B: Yeah, uh . . . I mean, I guess so.

TH-25B: So of course it surprises you.

CL-25B: I guess so. It seems like a simple thing, but. . . .

TH-26B: Mm-hmm?

CL-26B: I guess I'm just careless when I say things. I really ought to think more before I talk.

TH-27B: For some reason, you're finding fault with yourself now.

CL-27B: *(Briefly startled.)* Yes, I don't know why I do that. I guess I'm just kinda embarrassed, you know. *(Her look expresses a mute appeal to the therapist.*)

TH-28B: I understand, Betty. It's a new experience talking this way with someone you've just met.

CL-28B: (*Gratefully.*) Yes. (*She is quiet, briefly reflective.*) I mean I don't know what to say right now. What do you think I should talk about?

TH-29B: When you're silent, as you were a minute or so ago, you're very likely still doing your work, Betty. (*Pause.*) Right now you find—we all find—it hard at first to tell someone the thoughts you have just inside of yourself.

CL-29B: Oh, I don't know. . . . I wasn't thinking of anything important. I mean. . . . I was just kind of ruminating, I guess you'd call it. [*What Betty is being taught is a difficult lesson for most people—that what goes on in our inner world is important, and particularly is it so in psychotherapy. She still is disparaging of such intervals in herself.*]

TH-30B: I know that is a kind of thinking we don't usually share with anyone else—partly because it is just kind of "ruminating," as you say. But, as you can, try saying some of it. You see, Betty, that's some of the most important thinking you can share with me

CL-30B: It seems kind of embarrassing somehow.

TH-31B: Yes, I understand that, Betty. In a way it's like taking your clothes off in the doctor's office. Here it's not clothes that need to come off, but the social pressures that keep us alone when we do some of our most important thinking.

CL-31B: I never thought of it that way, but. . . . When you say it, it makes sense. But . . . But I don't know whether I can do that.

TH-32B: That seems right. You don't know how it will be to tell your inner thoughts. After you've tried it for a while, it will be easier.

CL-32B: Yeah, I guess so. (*Somewhat withdrawn.*)

TH-33B: It's hard to see the point of all this, isn't it?

CL-33B: (*Eyes downcast, pouty facial expression.*) Yeah, I suppose so. (*Pauses, looks up.*) I don't know why you're making such a big deal out of what I'm thinking to myself. Most of it's a waste of time. (*She looks unhappy.*)

TH-34B: No, Betty, it's not a waste. (*Sympathetic tone, brief pause.*) Can you tell me more about how you feel right now?

CL-34B: I feel kind of confused and. . . .

TH-35B: And. . . .

CL-35B: Well, I know you're trying to help me, but. . . . But I can't see how this will help me to know what I want. (*Her eyes are misty.*) Oh darn! I don't want to cry and waste more time.

TH-36B: How little you value your own emotions! Let yourself have your feelings, Betty. They're important for the work we will do together. Just now you've come on something that has emotional meaning for you. We don't know what that meaning is right now. but we'll take note of it, and perhaps it will show up again later when we can choose to explore it a bit more. *[The therapist repeatedly mixes reassurance with suggestions for the future work they will do together. Betty is obviously experiencing some emotional stress as it is, so this may not be a time to press further.]*

Of course, these abridged interviews have been prepared to highlight differences between two interview approaches. Neither is intended to portray ideal therapeutic work. The contrast in the time frame of the second therapist's attention is the critical point. While the first therapist was collecting information about Betty and her life and background, the second was identifying and calling attention to her manner of living her life in the actual moment. In later pages, I will illustrate other aspects of this important difference.

PSYCHOTHERAPY AS EXPLORING MYSTERY

Psychotherapy is a venture into the mystery that is the essence of each person. That mystery may show through in many life dimensions: time, relationships, events, aspirations, disappointments, and many more. The range and variety of perspectives that are potential for each such human adventure quite preclude any possibility of one person's knowing another completely. Always the therapeutic pair—and often the therapist most consciously—must make selections of what to consider, setting aside far more than can be directly contemplated in their work together.

My purpose is to call attention to the value of giving priority attention to the facet of the client's life that is being lived and expressed immediately during the therapeutic hour, that which is *actual*.

Reprise on the Actual

Of course, the therapeutic partners may talk about the past or the future or the hypothetical, but the root issue is whether such talk is expressing what is *subjectively alive in the now*. In many therapeutic perspectives, it would be unusual to be attentive to that element. In the therapeutic approach here being presented, it is of primary importance.

In most of our experience—in or out of psychotherapy—we are outwardly, objectively oriented, as I am now in thinking about the ideas I want to express, and very likely as you, the reader, are now thinking about what my words convey and how that message squares with your own experience. Making the switch to attending to our own inner processes is often difficult, for both clients and therapists. Thus in this moment, as I review my words and as you read them, it takes a conscious effort for either of us to pause, turn inward, and get in touch with how it is within ourselves right now. Rather, we are apt to remember about ourselves that perhaps we feel a momentary irritation triggered by the suggestion that would have us interrupt the smooth flow of our writing or reading, and very likely we will be anxious to get back to the familiar stance of reading or writing *about*.

That irritation, no matter how momentary, signals how the effort to be immediately aware pulls us out of the familiar—and usually more comfortable—detachment of usual consciousness. But that momentary "blip" of annoyance signals a hidden loss in dealing with our own processes in what is actually an objectifying way. It is a familiar loss and one encouraged by much in our culture. We are taught the merits of being "objective," which comes to mean the merit of making ourselves objects. The consequences are many, and foremost among them is the distorting of our self-knowing, knowing which we need to guide our lives.

Be clear: This is not a counsel urging blind self-centeredness. The totally selfish person is as handicapped as the totally outwardly directed person.

To state it differently, there is much to be gained by a disciplined attention to our own subjectivity as it lives in the moment in contrast to relying solely on remembering *about* it or imagining how it might be (now or at some future time). When we are genuinely in touch with our inner processes in the moment, we are empowered to conduct our lives in a way that will be more as we intend and less produced out of habit or social expectancy.[11]

CONCLUSION

So it is that we must help our clients learn that it is not enough simply to be accurate in observation and faithful in report. Genuine life change demands the actual presence—as near the total presence as possible—of the client in the direction of his or her own life.

NOTES

[1]See A. H. Soukhanov (1992), p.642.

[2]See especially, R. May (1958).

[3]I use "work" often in this book and in actual exchanges with clients. This is an expression of my foundation outlook on psychotherapy. Calling what transpires in our sessions "work" is a way of honoring what the client and the client–therapist partnership do as appropriate, demanding, and productive.

[4]Now closed.

[5]Chapters Four and Eight provide further descriptions of these processes.

[6]See Chapter Five.

[7]As is recognized by a range of views: Chaudhuri (1956), Hillman (1995), Smith, H. (1982), Walsh, R.N. (1976).

[8]See J. Hillman (1995).

[9]"Sometime" in that statement may be six or eight sessions or two or three years.

[10]Chapter Eight enlarges on these methods and describes ways of working with clients who continue to hear therapist input in counterproductive ways.

[11]The importance of immediate awareness to our well-being in usual life and in psychotherapy is described in Chapter Three of Bugental (1987).

3 LIVING IS ONLY IN THE *Now*

Orienting Psychotherapy to What Is Actually Present

In some sweeping generalizations, this chapter carries further
the contrast between a conception of human nature that seeks
to understand and work with humans as things, objectively, and
a more subjectively oriented recognition that the human experience is at root—and whether so recognized or not—that of
continually ongoing subjective processes.

The implications of the latter perspective are far reaching
indeed. A prime example: The latter view calls into question the
validity of our usual major attention to the client's history. Back
of that challenge is a more fundamental questioning of our customary assumption of psychological causality residing in personal history.

This inquiry leads to a reexamination of the familiar and
important concept of "transference." Three further products of
attending chiefly to what *is actually* the client's inner experiencing in the living moment are (1) greater poignancy of the material explored, (2) lessened distracting intrusion of the cognitive,
and (3) more lasting therapeutic products.

Much of our thinking in the fields of personality theory and psychotherapy practice implicitly tends to assume a timeless
realm in which our clients' lives and our therapeutic work are—occasionally and usually regrettably—complicated by changes. Yet a
moment's thought makes evident how unrealistic this static concep-

tion is. In fact, when we get down to fundamental reality, we are forced to recognize that *the only true constant of the human experience is change*—constant change, growth, alteration, evolution, death, decay. Time and its passing need to be more meaningfully reinjected into our metapsychology and its applications.

> *My wife and I love driving cross-country, admiring, photographing, discussing, exploring. . . . Watching for good photo "ops". . . . Trying to capture and preserve it all . . . or at least some of the special places, special times. Treasures to be cherished, to be returned to later, to remind us. The snow on the Tetons. The wild life in Yellowstone. That wonderful young family in Zion. . . .*
>
> *Why do you keep insisting it was in Bryce?*
>
> *Such wonderful scenes: the beauty of the mountains, the unexpected chance to get that moose feeding, the mountain stream finding its way through the tumbled logs, the sun reflected on the lake. The mountains are so big that the camera can't really capture them. Look at this . . . is that from the Grand Tetons?*
>
> *No, it's Yellowstone . . . or—wait!—was it Glacier?*

Sometimes readily, other times reluctantly, we may come to recognize that each living experience is unique. Your moment of awe is not the same as mine, although we were side-by-side as we shared the moment and are together again now as we look at the pictures. Not photo, not panorama shot, not video, not narration—or, for that matter, not even professionally prepared pictures and text—no, none of these, nor any other after-the-event skill or art, can bring back the *actual* experience or make it identical for both of us.

Sometimes, though, the pictures can provide a happy new experience. *A new experience, but not the original experience.*

PSYCHOLOGICAL REALITY—
A TIME-COGNIZANT CONCEPTION

So it is with our memories, with information about ourselves, with reports and documents about us. They can be informative, but they are dated, time-tied to what they seek to portray. Our memories play tricks with what they present as *the actual events.*

All of this is familiar in many contexts, but so often in the psychotherapy office we give it only passing recognition. While we recognize that a woman's portrayal of her childhood experiences with her father is something short of literal truth, under pressure to account historically for her current experience and emotions, we still implicitly assume that portrait to be sufficiently accurate when we attend to the client's account of her current expectations of men.

Psychological Reality Is Only Present Tense

Always the *now*, the ever-moving, never repeatable present. Knowledge about a person's history no matter how obtained is *post hoc* information. It is only a still photo of what was once life in motion. The former life is gone, and what remains is the present telling, at best a simulacrum of the departed life.

An Algorithm of Conventional Psychotherapy

Much teaching about clinical work accords a central place to the case history. It employs an algorithm along these lines:

- Case history explains symptoms and complaint.
- That explanation informs the treatment plan.

- That plan produces interpretations to the client.
- Those interpretation bring about life change.

Is that sequence indeed so? Is it an accurate depiction of how people change, of what countless hours of psychotherapy are based on, of the implicit underlying nature of human beings? The readers must answer for themselves. I, the author, question this traditional formulation.

Therapy based on such a model so easily becomes a detective story.[1] Clues are ingeniously collected, cleverly collated into explanatory scenarios, and eventually dispensed to the clients—who may or may not take them as intended. When they fail to do so, it is obvious that "resistance" is occurring, and that must be overcome so that the healing understanding provided by the therapist can do its work.

What Is Alive Is What Is Now

The flowing, evolving subjective influences are present only in the living moment of the event itself. Our understanding of just what happens (or did happen) at any given moment depends on who is reporting and when the report is made. Thus our grasp of that happening is irrevocably biased and incomplete.

The fact that humans live most meaningfully in their subjectivity becomes manifest when one listens to accounts of the same incident as seen by several different observers.[2] This is a point that often is brought home to group therapy clients when they try to recall and discuss an event they all witnessed only a week earlier.

Mabel: I thought you were so rude to Bill last time when all he wanted to do was to reassure you.

Betty: I just told him what I thought. I can't help it if he thought I was being critical when I was trying to be helpful.

Bill: Oh, that was nothing. I can't even remember for sure what she said. Besides, I didn't want to reassure her.

Wise group therapists soon learn to interrupt debates about either content or emotions in previous sessions. Groups can get caught up into endless wrangles about supposed facts that they all witnessed. Such occasions provide excellent opportunities to teach the necessity of focusing on the immediate rather than trying an archeological expedition for time-buried truths.

At the extreme, we may say that objective events are simply the launching pads from which varied observers take off with their individual interpretations.

Indeed, one of the salient feature of humans is the pervasive influence of their subjectivity. This powerful "search engine" is almost always at work, consciously or not, waking or sleeping, in solitude or when with others. Our subjectivity is not a still camera taking pictures of fixed, enduring objects. It is not even a movie camera dispassionately watching an outer scene unfold.

Our subjectivity is an active agency continually engaging with whatever it is to which we attend, influencing it with much of the already stored past, and storing it further into an environment in which future experiences may continually affect it. Our subjectivity, the core of our living, is fluid, and—like life itself, of which it is a central part—is constantly evolving.

How much more is all this true when, as is so often the case, the events are long past, subjective, and emotional!

The passage of time increases uncertainty about how accurately what was alive *then* can *now* be recalled or reconstructed. What was formerly an apparent fact becomes obscured by the opening of a greater range within which all manner of subjective influences may and do effect changes.[3] A psychotherapy that is past oriented risks spending much energy on what are most accurately recognized as partial truths or, in some instances, as largely currently evoked fictions.[4] Recognition of this reality does not equate to recognizing a conscious intent to deceive.

Recognizing fully the pervasive and powerful influence of the subjective calls on us as therapists to reexamine some of our key assumptions. The following example from a different realm illustrates this point.

When I first began teaching college courses in psychology, I often spent hours carefully planning my lectures down to the last aside and illustration. I was preparing packages of ideas to be dispensed to the students in an objective and authoritative way.[5] In doing so, I tried to be careful to include the authorities in my presentation without contamination by my own thoughts.

My unreflective view was that these packages were supposed to be passed on intact—for I certainly was not deemed (by myself or others) qualified to prepare packages of my own. Instead, in both instances, the packaging of the ideas and the ways of presenting them needed to be put together in advance and then delivered with little change. This was possible because—at least theoretically—what needed to be taught existed independently of the instructor, the class, and the moment of its transmission. The students would later be tested to discover how faithfully they could reproduce the packages.

To be sure, this description is something of a caricature[6] and only limitedly fits my actual experience; yet, sadly, it was accurate for me and still is for some instructors.

My classes, as some students with whom I later developed more informal relations told me, were full of information but prone to induce sleep.

Having survived the first several quarters, I began to feel more confident and began to develop more interest in what I was planning to teach than in being fortified with citations and intellectual rigor. Soon I needed only a handful of notes, and my class sessions became more enlivening for me and, judging by the student participation, obviously more stimulating to my hearers.

In later years, I would think in general terms about what I intended to discuss, amass ideas, invent instructive class activities, and so on. Then when I was actually with the class, I would let all that I had gathered slide to one side, so to speak, and discover what to say even as I said it.

When I did this job well and was truly present to the class, the material became alive—I was alive and not just a tape recorder. Moreover, I was able to respond to class needs more promptly and effectively. Still further—and this surprised me—at times I discovered implications and nuances in my own material (the "packages") that enriched my understanding, as well as that of the class, and provided initiative for my own further contributions to the corpus of knowledge.

The Alive Therapeutic Interview

When a client and a therapist come together for the first time, a unique event occurs. Implicitly—and not altogether consciously—each begins to sketch a pattern for their relation and their work together. I use the word "sketch" to emphasize the preliminary and incomplete quality of their early engagement. This term also recognizes that what they actually do is not fully verbal, or even verbalizable.

Their "sketches" will not be the same, but they will have sufficient overlap that the business of therapy can go forward.[7] Throughout their work together, these sketches will be evolving continually.

The crucial recognition is that psychotherapy is always an unfolding series of unique events, an emergent engagement between living persons, themselves continually in process. Discussions of psychotherapy, lectures about it, and books such as this one I'm now writing and you're now reading are not therapy. They are static, and their meaning depends on who attends to them, as well as on who presents them.

A truly vital and often overlooked truth: Actual and effective psychotherapy—like living itself—is always and only a present-tense event.

Stating the core idea somewhat differently: It is useful to think of our experience—in psychotherapy or not—as always being composed of a never-ending series of "frames," similar to the individual frames of a motion picture. Each frame has various dimensions—explicit, affective, temporal (i.e., memory-based, anticipatory), and much more. We may think of the whole of one's life as such a series. The important, the crucial, difference is that each life frame is gone forever a microsecond after it appears.

Much of psychological and psychotherapeutic doctrine implicitly ignores that transience. Realistically, too often that denial is self-deluding. Because each life is continually in process, what is manifested (enacted, spoken, understood, felt, or similar) at any given moment is a unique "frame" at that moment. Each successive frame is influenced by those before it and, in turn, influences those that will follow.

But recognizing this continual flux of our experiencing does not equate to devaluing it or to denying its accessibility to incoming experiences.

People, whether or not accustomed to introspection, when taking thought to attend to their inner experience, will recognize the unceasing flow of images, bodily awarenesses, thoughts, and feelings.[8] Whether or not this is a familiar experience, if one opens inwardly and without predetermined limitation, what becomes obvious is the continual changefulness of one's experiencing

In becoming freshly aware of this unceasing flow, it is evident that the exact identity of experiencing from one moment to the next or between persons is quite simply an impossibility.

Religious and military orders (Goffman's total environments[9]) typically try to make humans into dependably constant *things* in order to control them more completely. Yet it is manifest to all who are familiar with such organizations how tenacious and pervasive are individual differences. Despite their supposedly identical uniforms and training, Private Jones cannot be mistaken for Private Smith, or Sister Lucille for Sister Dorothy.

Of course, patterns become habits, and these may be repeatedly evident over a long life. Yet those who know the indiviuals over time may occasionally be surprised by how what was so familiar changes. Such patterns suggest how the client has implicitly come to identify his or her own nature and the characteristics of his or her world. Some constancy is necessary and valuable and makes the conversations of therapy possible. There it is evident, in time, how other patterns can become handicapping and disrupting to the client's life. Of course, a therapist is wise to attend to these as they are played out in the consulting room.

Here resides a contrast between a therapy focused on information and one that centers on the actual living moment. In the former, the identified malignant patterns may be traced back to earlier events in the client's life and then shown to the client to explain, and possibly alleviate, current distress. In the latter experiencing-centered view, attention is directed to the pattern's persistence, its effects on the client's current life and well-being, and what sustains it.

Manifestly, there are similarities in this phase of the therapeutic work between conventional modes and the *present-focused* orientation. The crucial difference resides in the therapist's intent—whether it is to teach the client *about* the source of distress or to bring greater immediacy and fullness of awareness to the client's *experiencing* of the pattern. The latter path assumes **the corrective power of vital and concurrent awareness** rather than relying on understanding and catharsis.

The Traditional Perspective

The following is undoubtedly an oversimplification, but its intent is to disclose the underlying "skeleton" of much psychotherapeutic work.

The information-preoccupied algorithm described earlier frequently characterizes psychotherapeutic thinking and practice. Collecting information about the client, distilling that information into conceptions hoped to be potent, and then feeding these back to the client is a familiar pattern. When those "insights" are accurate enough and accepted well enough by the patient, then it is expected that healing or change will occur. The emphasis is on *information—information* obtained from and about the client, *information* processed and refined by the therapist, and then *information* fed back to the client.

And, indeed, some changes do occur. It is my belief, however, that the healing or change agent is the relation (transference[10]) with the therapist, not a fundamental shift in the client's way of defining himself and/or his world. This conviction is supported by the frequency with which "successful" clients resist termination and return to psychotherapy (often with basically the same "complaint" as when they first entered therapy).

Of course, the relation of client and therapist is important, but it is so because that relation is the carrier for the two-way flow of information. The relation may not otherwise be crucially important in the life of either participant. Indeed, were it to become centrally important to one or both of them, some would insist that an error—"runaway transference and/or countertransference"[11]—was occurring.

Understanding This Perspective's
Emphasis on the Living Moment

To make clear why this therapeutic focus on actual experiencing is so crucial, it is necessary to provide a brief conception of how our awareness/consciousness functions. The following set of postulations will structure this presentation.

A. **Life, living, is a continually evolving or changing process.** This life movement is continual and irreversible. Awareness is a primary aspect of living, and thus it is also continually evolving and irreversible.

B. **"Awaring" is a range of subjective experiencing.** From minimal, chiefly bodily, awareness—which may not be fully conscious— to highly focused, intense perception, awaring of some order is present whenever there is life. This view corresponds to what physiologists refer to as "irritability." It encompasses an immense range (roughly from reflexive pulling away from pain to the supreme achievements of artists).

C. **Consciousness is a characteristic of a limited span of the total range of "awaring."** Thus consciousness is an expression— although a limited one—of life itself. What affects consciousness affects awareness and thus affects the life of the conscious being. It follows that consciousness is a continually evolving and irreversible experiencing. This is the crucial point: *Consciousness never remains "fixed" on one content. Rather, consciousness moves continually.*[12]

Perception Depends on Boundaries

It is helpful to recognize that when we speak of "seeing" something— whether through bodily vision or by arriving at an understanding of it, we are implicitly defining it. Definitions of this kind have two aspects: that consisting of its contents or substance and that which delineates its limits, distinguishing what is defined within the infinite openness of possibility.

I see the book on the desk before me.

Seeing the book, I distinguish it from the desk upon which it rests, from the calendar close beside it, and from the envelope that lies on top of it. In other words, I use awareness of the object's edges or limits as a prime means to identify or define it.

I see the point of the argument that my friend is advancing.

Hearing his presentation, I recognize views similar to those I have heard before but concurrently identify what is different in my friend's position right now. He alludes to precedents and contrasting stances, but he also makes clear that he is not simply repeating already stated conceptions.

Moreover, my friend does not just emphasize differences; he also portrays characteristics that are part of his view. Each such point advanced is supported by its relation to other points of our common knowledge or to shared values. As though he were fitting a missing piece into a jigsaw puzzle, he points out the edges or boundaries of the conceptual whole to which he seeks to add and shows how what he offers matches and expands them.

In this process, my friend may be dealing with the whole of some thesis, or he may partition out a subordinate portion for his attention. In either instance, he attends to the perimeters as well as to the substance.

My friend insists that he is not simply repeating the dogma of a political party but that he is advancing an important further implication that he feels must be recognized.

The central point here is that delineation of a viewpoint or quality requires linking it to, but distinguishing it from, other views or qualities. Once again, limits or borders are essential to understanding (or "seeing"). Essential but not sufficient.

When I propose a shift from information-focused to experiencing-centered work, I am drawing on this basic dynamic quality of awareness and consciousness. The agency of therapeutic change is the opening of perceptual boundaries—that is, seeing important aspects of our lives in fresh ways.[13]

The generalization is: Whatever constrains or delimits our perception helps to define that which is perceived. Thus the infant's eyes soon are, for the most part, quite capable of seeing almost everything a year-old sibling sees, but the infant has to learn to distinguish the chair from the dog and to recognize where the edge of the bed is when he begins to crawl.[14]

One's identity and way of conducting one's life can be thought of in terms of such constraints and their complementing substance. Thus are constituted the self-and-world construct systems[15] that form our lives. They are essential to our ability to conduct those lives, but they also limit our power to so conduct them.

The crucial recognition is: What enables also limits.

Each such constraint tends to hold its form—otherwise, any life pattern would be impossible. Ultimately the form of a constraint is mostly arbitrary—*things are as we see them* (not just their physical properties, but their pragmatic and implicatory aspects). It is this combination of enabling and limiting, the self-and-world construct systems, that constitutes our individual characters and determine how we respond to the exigencies of our lives.

Carrying this perspective further, we may conceive that a problem or symptom or complaint that brings someone to psychotherapy is at its root a constraint. The client's distress arises because he feels limited in some way. Seeing oneself as limited not only may lead to choices that increase the sense of one's identity, but also may unwittingly increase the limitedness.

This paradoxical pattern is familiar to psychotherapists who often see clients unconsciously reinforcing the very self perceptions of which they complain.

Carrie is miserable because her lover has left her, and she feels she will never find another man who will really love her the way she dreams of being loved. Because of this conviction she takes little care of her appearance and avoids meeting new people.

Psychotherapy, then, seeks to open out the complaint to disclose the underlying constraints and then, in turn, to open out those constraints. In this way, the client finds possibilities where none seemed to exist before. This cycling of exploration–discovery–exploration is the *search* process.[16]

Opening out a perception means expressing it and its many implications as fully as possible, in the process disclosing the implicit and often unconscious codicils or extensions associated with it. This is a demanding, sometimes frightening, but, in the long run, liberating undertaking. Since ultimately all of one's self-and-world construct system is interrelated, this opening out theoretically is infinite in potential scope. As we open out a constraint and discover its interlocking subordinate constraints (definitions of the way things are seen to be), we continually discover more possibilities.

In brief: Relief of symptoms or complaints is attained when the opening-out process discloses choice where previously only compulsion seemed possible.

> *In psychotherapy, Carrie struggled with her impulse to seek safety in denial and isolation. In the process, she began to risk opening her awareness both inwardly and outwardly. The content of this work was that of bringing to the surface of her consciousness the rage against life, her parents, and herself, which she had acted out by isolating herself. But that content was a by-product of her greater access to her own inner life.*

The Significance of the Living Moment

What Carrie's story dramatizes is how fostering persistence in searching whatever is *actual* in the living moment of the client's self-presentation peels back the layers of a self-defeating and apparently closed pattern to disclose previously unrecognized possiblities.

This whole process is possible only when the work is conducted with constant reference to the touchstone of actuality. What this requires is sensitive attention to the client's implicit *pou sto*. The resistance can take many forms; among the most frequent are the client's adopting a story-telling stance rather than discovering and expressing her immediate experiencing, the client's unrecognized need to justify himself, the client's avoiding painful topics or those that might disclose too much to the therapist. If that touchstone of immediate and genuine involvement is lacking, the opening-out process is ungrounded and may endlessly elaborate (become speculation or fiction, or be preempted by objectification).

Two guiding principles govern this process: (1) The therapist's attention must be quite persistent in its alertness to the client's moving away from what is actual in the moment. (2) The therapist's input must be confined chiefly to observing the actuality of the client's investment and searching, while the therapist can only sparingly supply content.[17]

Saying it somewhat differently: When one explores inwardly, there is a latent universe to be investigated. This is the unique inner universe (self-and-world construct system) in which each of us lives.

The client needs to persevere at all costs in that inward search while maintaining the power and guidance of mobilized concern.[18] So persisting, the client will not seek nor likely find "answers" to life issues. Instead *the issues themselves will change*; their boundaries will become more permeable; possibilities will be disclosed that simply were not accessible before.

All of this is based on the recognitions that:

- We live in a perceptual world, the world as perceived, not some "real," external, or physical world. Of course, our bodies keep us tied to the physical world, but for the overwhelmingly major portion of our lives, it is the subjective world that is our main concern.
- Perception of any object, idea, memory, goal, or whatever is a continually evolving and changing process.
- Each of us is in a separate perceptual world; yet, although it is never exactly or totally shared, we have much in common.

- Our perceptual worlds are composed of definitions or conceptions of "realities"—that is, of what is "good," "bad,"
worth effort, has power, and is essential to life, and what
is deadly and to be avoided.

HISTORICAL DETERMINISM AND AN ALTERNATIVE

Psychotherapy and psychological personality theory (including psychopathology) have been dominated by the notion that earlier experiences determine present phenomena. If that is not so, protest
clinicians and theorists, we would have chaos, no way of ordering
our understanding or planning ameliorative actions. But, although
some would debate this, that insistence that earlier experiences cause
later actions, emotions, or relationships is a matter of faith—not of
evidence-based proof.

The belief in historical determinism is scarcely a century old. It was
a big step forward when it displaced two beliefs that had been regnant
for many generations: religious faith and social station. In philosophy,
literature, and the arts, of course, similar challenges were being
made in the same period. Much of the impetus for these changes
must be recognized as part of a reaction formation that characterized late-nineteenth-century thinking. This pendulum swing sought
to emulate the physical sciences and to eradicate all subjectivity.

It is my belief that the currently regnant objectivist conception of
human nature, treating clients as things to be manipulated by standardized "treatment regimes,"[19] is handicapping true breakthroughs
in the theory and practice of psychotherapy. We have scarcely
advanced in our conception of human nature since Freud pioneered
that extension of rationality and objectivity to the psychological realm
a century ago.

Rethinking the Concept of Transference

A man tells the therapist, "You're always finding fault with
whatever I do. You're just like my mother."
Simple. Clearly a transference. It's even explicit.
Or is it?

The client's mother was 22 when he was born. She was not yet 30
when he started school. He graduated from high school the year she
turned 40, and he lived at home until he finished junior college at 21,
when he moved out to live with his girlfriend. In all, he lived with his
mother (and other family members) for the first 21 years of his life,
and during those years, his mother evolved from a very young adult
into a mature woman.

Which mother does he mean when he likens the therapist to her?
Roughly estimating that 21 years provided 7,665 days (not count-
ing leap years) and that these days may have provided eight hours
each of mother–child contact for a total of 160,965 hours, the
question is: At which hours of which days was his experience of his
mother the model on which his current assertion to the therapist
was based?

Of course, that's nonsense. He means the way his mother was
many times during his life with her. In particular, he means the way
he now selects to remember his mother to make an instrument for his
in-the-moment purpose. So we should cut the estimate in half and
then, perhaps, in half again. Was the therapist then like the mother
was for 40,241.25 hours of the client's life? Still nonsense. Make it
just one-tenth of that, 4,024 hours? Well, maybe.

Having already belabored the point to an unseemly extreme, let
me cut to the chase. A parent—this young man's mother—was and is
many things in her children's lives. Indeed, it is said, with good reason, that every child has a different mother, even though they are all
thought of as the children of the same parents. Some characteristics
are pretty constant, others more fluctuating. But with rare—and usu-

ally psychotic—exceptions, individuals tend to show several facets in any one day (indeed, often in any one hour).

The point is that when this charge is thrown at the therapist, the client has selected from his latent array of images of his mother a particular one that fits his mood/need at that moment. This is not, of course, a conscious process; the selection is the work of the client's needs and emotions in that moment. At another time, in different circumstances, this same client might tell his lover, "You make me think of my mother with your gentleness (or intensity or humor or . . .)" or to his daughter, "You have your grandmother's love of music."

The problem comes when the therapist—on the basis of several angry outbursts—assumes knowledge of the mother's role and influence in the client's life, and then uses that in an attempt to understand the client and in giving the client interpretations.

What I am proposing is not an improved interpretation based on more knowledge about the client and the client's history. As the psychotherapist, my intent is to be a living presence in the client's life in the very moment. Therefore, I respond not to his likening me to his mother, but to his irritation with me or his intent to change the direction of our work—that is, what is *actual* in the immediate interaction. Thus one might respond in any of several ways:

Client: You're always finding fault with whatever I do. You're just like my mother.
Therapist: I'm not your mother; deal with me.

or

So . . . ?

or

You hear me finding fault and so you try to take attention away from what you are doing to yourself.

or

Wow! You want to get into a fight with me and avoid
dealing with the real issue.

or

Et cetera, et cetera. The list is endless.

This is an oversimplified example of the layering of the resistance.
It is not only present where there is a conscious or unconscious intent
to mislead or escape from the therapist. All of us have nested areas of
concern, threat, yearning, and similar subjective nexuses that have
become overlaid by many experiences. They are not necessarily sites
of pathology, although they may be brought into the service of the
resistance at times. A simple example may illustate this.

> *Helen denied vehemently that although she remained single, she*
> *was jealous of her sister's happy family life. Asked what her*
> *main sources of satisfaction were, she readily listed reading,*
> *going to concerts, and being with several women companions.*
> *As she finished this recital, the therapist noted that Helen's man-*
> *ner had become subdued. Tears came to her eyes, and she said,*
> *in a very soft voice, "But I so want to have a baby of my own."*

Helen's enjoyment of the activities she listed was genuine and not
a resistance, but it was brought forward in this particular instance by
her reluctance to recognize a poignant yearning that seemed destined
never to be fulfilled. In other words, it was in the service of the resistance, but it was not itself a resistance.

As we see matters at the end of the twentieth century, it is beyond
question that history does much to provide the raw material from
which we fashion our lives. But two cultural forces—the astonishing
expansion of counseling and psychotherapy and the emergence of a
new concern with the spiritual—have carried us far beyond Freud's
mechanistic vision of psychological causality.

My own belief, molded doubtlessly by those same two forces, is that what we do and what we experience are the products of our immediate experiencing in interaction with our continually evolving (and basically individual) conceptions of our own nature and of the world in which we find ourselves. To express those experiences, we draw on our stores of earlier experiences.[20]

Of course, those earlier experiences contribute to how we understand and name our current experiences. But since they were earlier, they have been undergoing constant alterations—minute, immense, and at all levels between—from their origin until the moment of their present actualization. These alterations arise from our interactions with other persons, with every manner of event, and within our own inner (intrapsychic) living. Thus the "descendents" of an earlier event in one's life will be multiple current sequelae, varying in congruence with or in contrast to the original incident—just as today there are likely to be some hundreds of descendents—each a unique individual—of John and Priscilla Alden.

The bottom line is this: Human beings are most truly subjective presences and processes, rather than objective things solely manipulated by forces beyond their conscious knowing. For many of us, this recognition demands some shift in our image of the human, with a consequent change in our understanding of psychotherapy. That, in turn, calls for a move from emphasis on the objective, explicit, and causative to a focus on the subjective, implicit, and intentional.[21]

PSYCHOLOGICAL DETERMINISM: A POWERFUL IDEA PASSING ITS ZENITH

Too often our psychotherapies tend to be attempts to bring physical engineering perspectives to bear on human beings. Freud envisioned a natural science of psychoanalysis, and many still seek similar goals—and thus the emphasis on description, classification, and objective evidences.

Of course, it is inherent in the managed care movement[22] that there be an emphasis on objectification, explicit formulation, and brief service. The recognition of the subjective I am here advancing is in almost direct opposition to that perspective.

A truly human psychotherapy must celebrate the uniqueness of humankind and of each human individual. We are flames, not buildings—nor are we pigeons, rats, or monkeys. We are changing, not constant. We are not marble statues but alive beings growing—it is to be hoped—toward maturity.[23] We are the despair of those who want sure predictions. We are music that must be played in its own pattern.

NOTES

[1]Indeed, R. R. Kopp (1995) uses that very metaphor.

[2]This is the stuff of which major courtroom battles are made.

[3]Other traditions have long recognized this fluid nature of experiencing. See Jaynes (1976), H. Smith (1982) for examples.

[4]This is the conundrum that our legal systems can never fully solve, and that all too frequently undermines justice.

[5]Many of us who have taught went through a period in which we conscientiously did more or less what is here caricatured, but in time we gained the confidence to continue to be reliable and, at the same time, to be more spontaneous.

[6]It may be that in the "hard" sciences—physics, chemistry, geology, and similar fields—this picture is less a caricature, but even in those realms, I imagine, the wide individual differences in instruction styles bring it close to this image.

[7]See I. D. Yalom and G. Elkin (1974). This is, without doubt, one of the most courageous psychotherapy books ever written.

[8]Some may have difficulty in confirming this assertion. So many of us are so practiced in focusing outward that attending inwardly may seem pointless and certainly unfamiliar. When that is found to be true, it is a valuable undertaking to begin to practice this new skill. Doing so almost always opens fresh perspectives on one's life.

[9]See Goffman, E. (1961).

[10]I see *relation* as the broader term for any connection between persons (or, sometimes, between a person and an animal or object or cause). *Transference,* I would propose, is best reserved for the subset of relationships in which the chief bond is that one person projects on another expectations that initially arose in a prior relationship with quite a different person.

[11]Following up the definitions provided in note 10, *countertransference* is usefully restricted to instances in which the therapist transfers expectations from some other aspect of his or her life to the current client.

[12]Eastern thought has long studied the processes of consciousness and has provided sophisticated insights. See Jaynes (1976).

[13]See Jaynes (1976).

[14]See J. C. Pierce (1985). Piaget's observation that, for the child, self and other are all one may be generally accurate until the child is about age seven.

[15]See Chapter Seven.

[16]See Chapter Four.

[17]Chapters Six, Ten, and Twelve provide details about this core of the psychotherapeutic work.

[18]See Chapters Four, Seven, and Eight.

[19]Typical of most "health maintenance organizations" (HMOs).

[20]Note that this is "to express" rather than "to explain."

[21]The "intentional" is a way of designating the forward thrust of human experience. It subsumes such processes as wishing, wanting, willing, and planning. See Chapter Nine.

[22]The managed-care movement has become a major force in the U.S. health service field as it attempts to reduce the professional's work to fixed time intervals, with very limited opportunities for informal relating—and thus for the subjective to be given attention.

[23]And perhaps beyond?

4 UNDERSTANDING *Searching* AND CONCERN

Two Dynamic Processes Essential to Life and to Therapy

A psychotherapy addressed to the living moment must give a central place to the power of the client's own concern for his or her life and to the inborn human capacity to search within oneself.

"Searching" is a name I give to the process that is the chief form of the client's psychotherapeutic participation. This process is energized and guided by the client's concern. Searching is an inborn capacity of all life. Some of its familiar forms include exploring, speculating, problem solving, inventing, and researching. Searching is a basic and essential life capability implicit in much that we do. The power of searching can be endlessly extended; when it is, the result is likely to be enriched living.

Concern is a force often assumed, but otherwise overlooked. Yet it is the impetus of concern that brings most clients to therapy, motivates their continued participation, and strengthens their resolve to put into actuality in their lives the gains that truly life-changing therapy makes possible. Ultimately the success of the psychotherapeutic venture will depend on how fully the client's concern is mobilized in the therapeutic hours and how well it is focused on the issues that the client confronts in life.

THE IMPORTANCE OF THE PROCESS OF SEARCHING

E ach person's consciousness is a flowing and fluctuating perceiv-
ing process, at times focusing inwardly and at other times outwardly. One form of consciousness is particularly elicited when the
person is in a situation for which a habitual response is not immediately available. This aspect of consciousness is what I here call
searching.

When we talk spontaneously with a friend, when we reflect on
how we will vote, when we change our route home because of heavy
traffic, when we select our dinner from the menu, when we argue the
merits of our favorite team, when we write a letter—all of these and
many, many more occasions evoke what we have learned *already* and
our capacity to search.

Indeed, pause a minute, reflect on what is going on within you, the
reader, this very moment, as you read these words, this chapter, this
book. Notice the many levels: the explicit content, the reaction to
having the focus switched so abruptly, the impatience to get back to
reading, the sense of other activities in deeper layers. . . .

Searching is an inborn, powerful, and life-essential capacity. As
such, searching is a process that complements learning. In other
words, searching selects from the library of learned responses those
most pertinent to the immediate situation. Searching also is necessary
in the development and incorporation of fresh responses.

When we start the car and the left rear tire bumps the message that
it's flat; when an unexpected freeze catches us without fuel for the
furnace; when the library's new policy stops us from keeping the
book we're reading long enough to finish it; when an unexpected
major expense comes up just when the mortgage payment is due;
when the object of our affections doesn't seem to know we exist: in
each of these, and in all the many exigencies of living, searching is our
first recourse for solutions.

Of course, searching will not necessarily produce the solution we want. The flat tire is hopeless and all the service stations are closed; we have to call a cab. We scrape together funds from other planned payments and avoid losing our home; we date the one who is number two on our list, and it doesn't turn out so bad after all, but still. . . .

Indeed, all that we do requires both learning and searching. It is rarely, if ever, that we find ourselves in situations for which there is absolutely no pertinent learning. If that did happen, we would be unable to search. Actually, in any occasion that approximates that extreme, we bring in learned responses from other realms so that we can use this life-essential power. Thus someone from another country, lost in one of our cities, tries to speak her own language even though she may be well aware that there is almost no likelihood it will be understood. So the visitor gestures, exaggerates her speech pattern, pantomimes—always using learned modes in a search for a way to communicate.

Since we use searching all the time, it is so familiar that we rarely recognize that we're doing so. Some of us develop great skill in its use and become known as innovators, inventors, and creative artists, or as con artists, embezzlers, and deceivers. Most of us develop adequate general skill and greater facility in areas of particular concern to us as individuals.

Searching Is Central to Psychotherapy

When Sigmund Freud laid his palm on the forehead of a patient and commanded, "Now some thoughts or memories will undoubtedly come to you, and . . . you must ignore all censorship and express every thought even if you consider it to be irrelevant, unimportant, or too unpleasant,"[1] he was tapping into a power known and used in one form or another by millennia of priests, shamen, physicians, counselors, and many others. This he called "free association," and he made it his "basic rule" for psychoanalysis.

What we call "searching" is a path similar to that same human capacity and to the deeper lying consciousness that it serves. Although we use searching somewhat differently than did Freud—putting more emphasis on the process itself rather than on the content or information that it turns up[2]—we agree upon making it central to our work. We are not unique in doing so; this searching capability is important to psychotherapy generally.[3]

Searching identifies the fact that (as we saw in Chapter Three) the focus of our consciousness or awareness is continually moving. It is literally impossible for a living, sane human being to focus unchangingly on any single object, whether objective or subjective. Impelled by our concerns—which range from the trivial to the truly life-essential—we always move along. And when further impelled by aroused and deeply rooted concern, we move to deeper levels within ourselves.

> The widowed client is overwhelmed with grief and insists he will never again think of anything but his loss, but even as he so insists, he has moved from the grief itself to this insistence on his never changing. And if left to his own promptings, he will almost immediately enlarge on that or move to some other aspect, which in turn will give place to yet another matter.

Sometimes these shifts are startlingly evident; at other times, they are subtle and implicit, as the next example illustrates.

> The client is so preoccupied by yearning for children that she insists that nothing else enters her mind, and she buttresses her position by angrily denouncing the concerns of other family members. When the therapist makes no comment, the client expresses bitter regrets that the therapist is so unfeeling, and these are soon followed by a recital of all the other disappointments the client has had to endure.

Each person's search takes the person on a unique path, but one guided by that person's deep concern. And it goes on continually,

The mind is a mill

waking and sleeping, acknowledged or denied, recognized or resisted. The fact is that all that human beings experience and do emerges from inner/subjective processes in interaction with external experiences. The subjective elements are only partially accessible to consciousness. As Chapter Three demonstrated, therapy that intends pervasive and lasting changes must affect those deeper levels as much as they may be accessible. Searching is the prime means for doing so.

Sri Aurobindo, Indian philosopher, political leader, and guru, said: "The mind is a mill; its function is to grind, and it grinds unceasingly."[4] In the segment that follows, the open-ended and continual "grinding" becomes manifest.

An Imaginary Interview

A-1: *What matters to you?*

B-1: Oh, a lot of things. Like my family, my work, my health, a lot of things.

A-2: *What matters to you?*

B-2: I just told you. (*Pause.*) I guess you want me to answer again, huh? Well, let's see. . . . Well, right now the thing that matters most is that I've been feeling a little under the weather lately.

A-3: *What matters to you?*

B-3: Again, huh? . . . Yeah, well my health, like I said, and then that makes me think of how much I want to be able to take the trip we planned for this summer. Don't want to be laid up then, believe you me.

A-4: *What matters to you?*

B-4: You see, we're going to go back east to visit my son and his wife. They're expecting, and it's probably going to be real soon, so we want to see the new member of the family, and . . . and it's sort of . . . sort of important to me. I'm not as young as I used to be, you know. And a new baby in the family kind of reminds me of my age. So . . . so I want to make that trip, and. . . .

A-5: *What matters to you?*

B-5: Yeah, yeah, I know I stopped myself, didn't I? Well, all right then: It matters to me to see that new child if I can because I'm not . . . not going to be around forever, you know. (*Pause, tone changes to a somewhat forced lightness.*) Imagine me as a grandfather!

A-6: *What matters to you?*

B-6: (*Abruptly sober, intense.*) It matters to me to be with my son . . . and his wife and youngster. I wasn't always such a hot father, you know. Worrying about the business and all. I want to try to talk with him and tell him I'm sorry. (*Pause.*) Well, damn! I didn't expect to say that. Hardly let myself think it. But it's true anyway.[5]

In our imagined conversation, only by conscious effort did "A" simply repeat the question. "B," freed of this necessity, found an unending succession of answers within, and those answers took him to ideas, feelings, and memories that were unexpected when the process began.[6]

Now let us imagine another protocol. In this instance the subject, a man, is setting himself to the task of keeping only one thought in mind:

I'm just going to think this thought: "I have only one life to live and I better get on with it." I've only one life to live, and I better get on with it now. . . . Oh, I just added that now. . . . Damn! Well, now I'm going to just think that thought, I have this life to live and I better. . . . I mean, I have only this one life. . . . I have only one life to live, and I think I'd better get on with it. Did I say "think" before? Oh, well, I have only one life to live, and I better get on it. Somehow that seems different, but. . . . I have only this life to live, and I. . . . I got distracted, my daughter's pulling on me to explain almost everything. . . . Oh, oh, . . . Maybe there's life after. . . . Oh, well, I've got better things to do than this nonsense. . . .

A Way of Thinking About Our Minds

As the searching process continues, it brings into awareness material that emerges from less conscious regions or layers of consciousness. Freud's geography of conscious, preconscious, and unconscious provides a way of thinking about this. I will adapt it a bit for our present purposes.

It will be useful to reconceive those three zones as *focal-verbal, intentional-preverbal,* and *proto-conscious.* As an image to aid our thinking, we will roughly compare these three to the layers of water in an ocean. In the same way, these areas are not sharply defined, but blend into each other along their perimeters.

The Top Layer

The focal-verbal top layer consists of conscious thoughts that are in, or very nearly in, words. It is from this area that we most readily draw when someone asks, "What's on your mind?" or when, in a familiar situation, we spontaneously take part in conversations. This surface zone is quite small relative to the other regions, but it is the one of which we are most readily conscious.*

Sitting in the stalled car with the flat, we try to remember where the hand pump is in the garage chaos, but nothing comes to mind, except anger at the poor-quality spare the salesperson persuaded us to buy. That makes us think of other purchases that weren't successful either. "Damn, how I hate to have to make deals in areas where I feel so dumb!"

---

*It is important in reading this geography of the subjective to remind oneself from time to time that (to extend the metaphor) we are drawing lines on the water, creating a fictional representation of what may be speculated about but is not directly observable. Some such "as if" framework is an essential aid to thinking about our human capacities.

The Middle Layer

The region beneath the verbal is much larger and more complex. It can be thought of as the *intentionality* layer of our awareness. It is made up of the intentions, impulses, purposes, and values by which we guide our lives, but that characterization must not be read too narrowly. Memories, anticipations, bodily sensations, fantasy, relationships, and much more are part of this domain as well.

This intentionality stratum is a maelstrom of impulses interacting and influencing each other. Some are modifying, some are reinforcing, still others are contrasting or even antagonistic: Some are fairly stable, whereas others are just emerging. We cannot begin to be aware consciously of all that is going on at any one time.

Indeed, even to be aware of thinking our thoughts or of beginning to put them into words (not the same thing) can be a subtle and complex activity. Moreover, as thinking, listening, and speaking occur, further changes continually are injected into this region.

This vast intermediate level may be thought of as the site of inner, purely subjective processing. Thus this is the wellspring of the emotions that accompany deep sharing with another person. Then, depending on the nature of our relationship with that other person, that impact may vary in content, affective tone, and pervasiveness. Many other influences enter at this stage. Among the most prominent of these are our reflexive awareness as we listen to ourselves and our projected or actual sensing of other persons' hearing and reacting to what we say. From such awareness come our reactions to whatever they actually do say.

The top of this intentionality layer, as might be expected, is material that is just emerging into the verbal area and thus is in the process of being translated into words. Deeper are feelings and impulses that are never fully verbalizable, which include promptings of which we may be only dimly conscious ourselves. This portion of the intentionality layer "bleeds" into the deepest area, or proto-conscious region, of our subjectivity.

The Deepest Layer

The deepest region of our consciousness is not susceptible to direct observation. It is here that our bodily maintenance processes, our most primitive impulses, and our irrevocably unconscious emotional needs and activity reside. Here, too, is the site of whatever paranormal or extrasensory capacities we may have. We can sense in ourselves, and in those we know most deeply, something of the nature of this region, but its contents may be only indirectly inferred, as by their very nature they are beyond full verbalization.

In psychotherapy we seek to foster a kind of osmosis in which material from deeper levels is drawn to the surface, as in the "Imaginary Interview" on page 67. The continually moving quality of consciousness, guided by a deeply felt sense of concern, will bring about that movement and make deeper materials more accessible.

Searching as a Basic Human Capacity

We know now that Freud's "basic rule" tapped into a capacity that all human beings share. This is a faculty for exploring in and beneath the verbal layer and thus for aiding clients to discover more of what is important within themselves than they would know if only direct questions were employed. It is evident that this process evokes a dynamic movement of materials toward the intentionality layer. Sometimes, indeed, some material from the deepest level becomes accessible at the verbal level. Concurrently, more may be evident implicitly to the trained and sensitive observer.

Survival Implications

Stepping back for a moment, I will put what I have been describing into a different context, that of the human need to arrive at solutions to problems. The maintenance of life itself—whether in primitive living circumstances or in our modern technological world—is dependent upon how we deal with the difficulties and problems we encounter, as well as on the opportunities we discover and the successes we achieve. This impetus is inborn; it is worth noting that one of the main human activities at times when effort is not required to sustain life is recreation in the form of games, puzzles, sports, or artistic expression. All of these are forms of the life-vital search process.[7] Not only is this process necessary to our survival, but it can be rewarding in itself as well.

Continually, all life is confronted with the need to respond; in some species, this need is taken care of, so far as we know, chiefly by instinct and reflex. In many species, including the human, much of the need is handled by conditioned responses, habits, and social custom. But the higher up the phylogenetic scale we go, the more often does the need to respond in largely unpredeterminable ways occur. Thus the search process, a characteristic of all life, is particularly the vehicle for human action.

THE IMPORTANCE OF THE EXPERIENCE OF *Concern*

It is obvious, by and large, that what energizes and guides the search process is not random impulse. Searching has purpose and power. To identify it, we use the concept of *concern*. It is a familiar word ("I was concerned that the bank failure would jeopardize my savings," "She acted out of concern for the children," "It's no concern of yours; let it be"). However, we will give it a very particular meaning.

To grasp the nature of concern, it is useful to pause in one's reading and reflect:

What really matters to me in my life right now, at this minute?

Take time to identify one or two definite answers (but not more). "Taste" the sense of concern. Doing so, one is likely to discover that it almost always has the three qualities described below. Getting a genuine sense of these three is important to understanding why this subjective experience of concern is so powerful.

Qualities in the Concept of Concern[8]

When one "unpacks" the usual meanings in the word "concern," three qualities are likely to be the most prominent:

1. There is an implication of *some degree of anxiety, worry, unease, or stress.* It signals that something in one's life needs attention, is not as one wishes, is troubling—perhaps only slightly, perhaps stronger.
2. The experience of concern *looks toward the future.* We are concerned about what may happen, not solely about what did happen,[9] what we may do or not do, what is necessary or required in the future—the next hour, tomorrow, the rest of one's life.
3. *One's own sense of power* (or one's struggle against powerlessness) is importantly involved. The emotions when we feel totally powerless (e.g., knowing that we will die eventually) are quite different from those when the concern is about some impending circumstance over which we do have, or hope to have, some control. It is what one may do or not do, what will be expected or necessary for one to carry out in some way.

Concern and the Mobilization of Searching

Concern is the process that arouses, energizes, and guides searching. Thus it is both a compass and an energy source. Without it, searching would be reduced to random and purposeless activity.

Concern may be about anything in one's life—relationships, recognition, achievement, aging, money, health, loneliness, and so on through all the aspects of living.

A moment's reflection will make obvious the potent inward mobilization that is likely when one's feelings of unease are joined with anticipations for the future and a sense of one's own powers. It is this combination that is central to the mobilization of the capacity to search and that guides the process. Concern energizes the searching, and it helps the searcher recognize what is and what is not pertinent to his or her initiating life issue.

We may feel concern about almost any topic—our health, the way our children drive, the international situation—but unless those three characteristics are present within us, the emotion may better be thought of as simple worry, rumination, exasperation, or anxiety. It is only as we begin to assess our own capacity to respond at some future point to that which troubles us that it is useful to invoke the concept of concern as we are employing it here.

Four Dimensions of Concern

It is helpful to conceive of therapeutic concern—that is, the kind of subjective motivation that will empower the work of searching—as having four important dimensions: pain, hope, commitment, and inwardness.

Pain is a way of designating the discomfort, stress, and/or anxiety that are often the most impelling forces in bringing the client to psychotherapy.

The *pain*, may, of course, take various forms; for example, worry, an inability to perform usual activities satisfactorily, withdrawal, or irritability. This dimension is expressed in the unease so typically experienced when we "taste" our concern as suggested above.

Hope is present in the seeking for change, relief, or a better life experience. Hope is often suppressed by the anxious patient because it is too frightening to contemplate discovering that one's situation is unalterable—that is, beyond hope. Yet it is almost always true that hope, although denied and repressed, is present. Without it, the client would not come to the consulting room.

Commitment is related to hope and may be as difficult to enlist. Yet, manifestly, some commitment is essential if the work of therapy is to go forward. Usually this means regular sessions, prompt arrivals, appropriate payment when it is required, and, above all, a willingness to engage in the work—telling about oneself, answering questions, risking disclosures.

Inwardness, the readiness to look within oneself and to forego the temptation to blame others or circumstances, is, at times, difficult for the client to accept as essential. Until there is readiness to look into one's emotions, memories, aspirations, and all else that resides within each person, the work will be badly compromised.[10]

In psychotherapy that addresses itself to the living moment, inwardness is particularly important. The client who needs to dwell chiefly on external events and other people is manifestly avoiding the actuality of being in psychotherapy to change his or her own life experience. Generally, the major significance of this detour into other realms is that early therapist attention needs to be given to redirecting the energies acted out in this resistance.

It is important—even reassuring—to recognize that there is an underlying orderliness to what may superficially appear to be chaotic.[11] It reassures us so that we can be more open to "wild" or embarrassing or other unexpected impulses when we engage in searching. Indeed, it is not unusual to recognize that motivated impulses that at first appear irrelevant may, on more careful examination, provide creatively fresh paths. As long as we remain in touch with our root concern through all its permutations, we may confidently allow—even encourage—the free ranging of our searching awareness.

Despair and Searching

In *The Flies*, Sartre[12] has Orestes say, "Human life begins on the far side of despair." What a strange idea! Or is it? Is it possible that despair—that sense of ultimate failure and futility, that dreaded falling away of all hope—could have a positive, hopeful aspect?

That is exactly what depth psychotherapy, a therapy that seeks to work beneath the verbal layer, teaches us. The search process takes us to one after another of our ways of dealing with life. When the impelling core concern is strong, we move along this tortuous trail with urgency, often with pain and anxiety, and always with demanding intensity. We struggle with our own resistances to thinking the unthinkable, to discovering what lies behind the veil of unknowing. But there are some times when the search seems to yield no resolution, when each briefly promising path ends at an abrupt cliff's edge. Our seeking becomes more frantic. Something must be done. "Something's gotta give."

This is when despair can mobilize deeper searching to produce major life changes; sometimes it is the only thing that will make such revisions possible. Despair arises when one feels hopelessly caught in a threatening or otherwise unwelcome situation. Often clients only come to psychotherapy when they are already despairing, having exhausted all other routes to dealing with their concern. As desperate as such clients often are, their despair, itself, may prove productive in the therapeutic effort, in the searching that must be done.

To alleviate despair, our searching extends its range, considers desperate extremes and frightening possibilities, even seems to have escaped the bounds of good judgment, good sense. Now we begin to know—yet fight to keep from knowing—the bleak face of our despair.

What has happened, although often we do not recognize it at the time, is that we have searched to their (apparent) limits our present ways of defining who and what we are and what the nature is of the world in which we live. We have found no answer that does not involve a kind of suicide,[13] a killing (of the way we have lived). We are confronted with the prospect of making fundamental changes in the way we see ourselves or in the way we conceive the world. Thus, trying to avoid change, we come to the point of despair, of believing that we have "no way out."

Relinquishment, long avoided, is the price of escape from despair. To let go, to give up, to surrender—such hard words, so bitter. They may be all they seem. Sometimes they hide surprises.

Mandatory Quality of Genuine Concern

Here is a point too infrequently recognized: *When a person does experience a genuine life concern, that person does something about it.* This is no longer a matter of choice; deeply experienced concern demands some action, implicit or overt, desirable or not.

Of course, just what that "some action" is becomes the critical issue. It may or may not be a wise or desirable action; nevertheless, there will be some product of the concern. We do not—cannot—remain inert when fully gripped by a genuine sense of life concern.

Genuinely mobilized concern *always* results in implicit responses, overt action, or both. What that action is—if there is no immediately available and familiar pathway—will be, first of all, that we intensify our searching efforts.

To be sure, there are preformed solutions to many problems—in the simpler instances the auto club will send help, we can get a loan, and so on. But in other instances there is a period of drastic, desperate concern before the solution is seized. That period is when we are searching more deeply. Sometimes it turns up a satisfying answer. Sometimes it seems as though there absolutely is no possible answer of any kind.

Wrong!

There is always a response to any life-significant concern that we genuinely experience. This is not some kind of Pollyanna-ish optimism. The answers we arrive at can be productive solutions or they can be violent and destructive, and even increase the problem. *But we will do something.*

We run on the flat and make a mess of the tire and rim, but we get there. We chop up an old table and make a fire to ward off the freeze. We beat up the head of the library board. We make a new and tighter family budget. Whatever we end up doing, *we always actually do something.*

HOW CONCERN EVOKES THE SEARCHING PROCESS

How do we arrive at what we will eventually do when we are truly concerned? When someone risks opening awareness as fully as possible and saying what is disclosed there, the path is not predictable, but it is still being importantly guided nevertheless. That guidance comes from a deeper level than the conscious, verbal awareness; it comes from the mobilized intentionality. For example, the respondent in the "Imaginary Conversation" on page 68 uses the remembrance of a past experience ("I wasn't such a hot father") to fuel and direct his current (and future) concern.

When we give that kind of attention to our lives and persist in saying (or writing[14]) what comes to mind without interrupting it with criticism,[15] then our deeper-lying needs and conflicts push toward the surface and awareness. This is a powerful process—it is, of course, searching. It is used in various ways by all depth psychotherapies.

It is important to recognize that the searching process can bring one who is troubled and strongly motivated to an unforeseeable range of possibilities. By no means are the options that searching may present assured to be socially approved or personally desirable. Mobilized distress is powerful in part because it can transcend the usual and accepted limits of thinking and possible action.

Despair as a Change Agency

When one is forced to confront the necessity of letting go of a cherished part of who one believes oneself to be or of what has always been the way of one's world, a crisis of existence is encountered. Letting go of what up to this time has been lived out through that threatened aspect can call life itself into question. When the questioned self-percept is centrally important, it is experienced as such a rejection of what one has been that it can seem equivalent to a suicide. Or, in some instances, it makes actual suicide seem a preferable course.

Further, to relinquish the possibilities for the future that consciously or implicitly have been linked to that part of oneself is a murder of the self one expected to be; it is killing off one's hopes for the future.

Sally had dreamed of being a wife and mother from her earliest years. When she married Tim, it was as though she were coming home to a life she had been waiting for all her life up to then. They were happy, and their two children fulfilled deep yearnings in both of them. Then Tim and both children were killed in an automobile accident. Sally seemed so brave through all the funeral arrangements, but a month later, she tried to throw herself in front of a speeding truck.

Pete had had a highly successful career as a newspaper reporter and columnist. His writing was being widely syndicated, and his royalties were beginning to promise a whole different lifestyle. Then his world collapsed when he was accused of plagiarizing large parts of his recent columns. He was fired from the paper and blacklisted in every other publication outlet. When he finally entered a detox program six months later, his life was in shambles and his health was seriously jeopardized.

Myron was the pampered and beloved son of older parents. Blessed with superior intelligence and abundant financial backing, he had coasted through college, taken an undemanding job in an uncle's firm, and settled into a comfortable life routine in suburbia. Then he contracted an illness that left him largely paralyzed, and he had to go through extensive, painful, and only partially successful treatment. For nearly a year, he was depressed and nearly unreachable.

There are, of course, other times when the familiar paths simply are no longer possible. Then we may experience the terrible but freeing effect of despair. It is a liberty dearly purchased—often with what we thought we valued most. But it is a freedom not otherwise to be found.

After several years of psychotherapy, Sally found employment as a clerk in a library. In time she went back to college and earned a degree in library science, and developed a lasting and satisfying career in that field. She never regained the sense of wonder and delight she had known as a wife and mother, but she did find a measure of fulfillment and peace.

For Pete there was a long road back marked by repeated failed attempts to return to writing, attempts that won only rejections. He reacted to each disappointment by again resorting to drugs and alcohol to obliterate his sense of loss. At last, ill and destitute, he gave up that career path and, with the help of psychotherapy, achieved modest stability in retail sales.

Relatively abruptly, Myron became more accessible to his family and friends, terminated his employment (which had been left open for him), and thereafter devoted his financial resources and his own energies to working with those fighting the illness that had struck him and to helping other victims less fortunate than he.

The confrontation with fundamental existential issues, such as the stories of these three people exemplify, throws one's whole being into question. That questioning is one form of the basic human capacities for feeling concern and for engaging in searching.

Death Thoughts and Dangers

It is not surprising, when we understand the nature of despair, to discover that the despairing person is likely to have thoughts of death, of suicide, or of other violent actions. In fact, often there is a "death" that must occur, a violence must be done to some of the ways that person has been in her or his life and in the world up to this point.

To change fundamental parts of our ways of defining ourselves and our world is to kill one whole path of possibility. Is "kill" too strong a word? It may seem so to us, sitting apart, writing or reading. To the despairing person, it is agonizingly accurate.

Despair is the ultimate incentive to full use of the searching capacity. Despair is focused and intense concern. For some, despair is the essential trial through which they must pass if they are to make major life changes.

CONCLUSION

The searching capacity is a product of our reflexive awareness, our awareness of being aware, our consciousness of our own being. This means that the focus of our concern is continually evolving, never the same. Then this same reflexive evolution may go on for as long as the sense of concern empowers it.[16]

It needs to be emphasized again that the outcome of mobilized concern is an action of some kind, overt, verbal, or implicit—achievement, retreat, violence, aiding another distressed person, suicide, psychosis, gaining a fresh perspective, illness, invention, life change—

and that that action itself then feeds back into the process, changing our perception of the situation and our next responses to it.

The group process known as "brainstorming" is, of course, another way in which this basic human capacity may be tapped. In science, the arts, and many life areas, searching is implicit and basic to creativity.

However, as emphasized earlier, searching is by no means solely a conscious process. It is a continuously present, if unnoticed, part of our everyday living. A gossiping group easily finds material to fill hours. Storytellers build on each other's accounts. A research staff bounces ideas back and forth, seeking and finding fresh ideas. In any scientific field, and in the arts generally, the chain of connections from very humble beginnings of discovery and invention to quite complex and sophisticated modern products is a record of composite searching by many contributors.

Essentially, creativity is the exercise of this capacity. It is not the sole possession of a limited number of geniuses; it is within the scope of all of us.[17] To be sure, some are more gifted in using this talent in music, some in graphic arts, some in literary pursuits, some in solving mechanical problems, some in relationships, and others in still other fields. But aside from giftedness, we all can learn to use this capacity better. Indeed, the range of possibility is, so far as one can tell, infinite.

NOTES

[1] Freud spoke of this way of tapping into this human capacity as "free association," and his biographer, Jones, calls "the devising of this method one of the two great deeds of Freud's scientific life."

[2] Our assumptions about psychological causality, as is described in later pages, also make for important differences with the classical psychoanalytic conception.

[3] Eugene Gendlin (1978) has developed a systematic way of accessing this same potential; he calls it "focusing." Martin Buber and John Wellwood (1982)

approached this process from another direction and gave it the name "unfolding." I prefer the term (which has some history in American psychology) "searching."

Of course, it is unimportant just which term is used to characterize this native power we all share, but the searching power-and-capacity itself is life-crucial. In simplest fashion, we can recognize searching as an inborn mode in which we operate when we need to act in some way but do not have readily available a previously learned and satisfying way of doing so.

⁴Aurobindo.

⁵It is important to recognize that in the kind of therapy from which these observations are drawn, this dynamic process is employed in a much more flexible form than the mechanical repetition ("What matters to you?") in the dialog example. However, experimenting with that limited form (with a nonclient who is cooperative) will demonstrate that the quoted example is reasonably representative.

⁶The sample interview is condensed, of course, but it is very like what might occur had the process gone on for 20 or 30 minutes.

If the reader is tempted to experiment with this, two suggestions need to be considered: First, select a partner who is aware and accepts that personal matters may be disclosed, and second, ensure a situation of privacy and confidentiality.

⁷Tragically, it is this area that is likely to be the first curtailed by those who review public budgets for education and the arts, as it is seen as impractical.

⁸See the discussion of *concern* and the interview segments illustrating working with it in Bugental (1987, pp. 201–225).

⁹To be sure, sometimes we use the word 'concern" in a past reference (e.g., "I was concerned that I failed that test"). When the past is the source of concern, there is an implicit, but perhaps not always verbalized, present or future element ("So I know I must get in more study time before the next test").

¹⁰Based on J. F. T. Bugental (1987, Chapter 11).

¹¹In the appendix, the first axiom of this form of psychotherapy says that "everything is everything," and the second is "whatever the client does is the work." This is a way of insisting that whatever the client does is motivated and is, therefore, part of the work of psychotherapy.

¹²Jean-Paul Sartre, *The Flies*.

[13]Or actual self-destruction.

[14]For those who write anything at all with some degree of comfort, writing may prove a facile mode for searching. The written products, once they have facilitated the handling of whatever issue is involved, can be discarded or saved for later review. They are not the most important results; that recognition characterizes the freeing up of one's inner resources.

[15]Easier said than done, of course. Efforts to suppress self-criticism are counterproductive when one is learning to use searching. Instead, with practice, one learns to take note of the critical impulses and then to open awareness to what else is present.

[16]Those familiar with chaos theory will recognize that this process is similar to (or perhaps even the same as) the iterations that characterize processes in that field.

[17]See T. Sarason (1990).

5 *Pou Sto*: A Place to Stand[1]

Thought-Through Assumptions Empower the Work

Consciously or not, psychotherapist and client are likely to bring seriously contrasting expectations to their engagement. While often these will apparently accord satisfactorily, at other times, they may be subtly or obviously ill matched. A primary responsibility of the therapist, and one important to the progress of the work, is to think through her own anticipations in advance rather than abruptly discovering, at some critical point, differences requiring attention.

It is not suggested that this perspective be explicitly announced to the client in advance of an occasion that might require it. Rather it is the therapist's own forethought that enables her implicit manifestion of this steadying perspective all along.

Archimedes, announcing the power of the lever, is reported to have said, "Give me a place to set my lever, and I will move the earth." That place to set the lever is called a *pou sto*. A pou sto is a place from which to exert power, a place to ground one's work, a base of operations. It needs to be solid, well founded. The psychotherapist needs a firm pou sto.

The therapist must give thought to having clear perspective for her engagement with the client. This means that the therapist needs to have given thought in moderately specific terms to her intentions, limits, and availability—that is, to what she will or will not do, will

85

or will not say, what responsibility she will or will not accept. Additionally, the therapist needs to consider what she will expect of the client, what she will not accept from the client, and with what flexibility she will hold these expectations.

It is also important to recognize that rigid and unresponsive adherence to the pou sto is neither desirable nor therapeutic. The therapist who has developed considered stances in relation to these issues will usually be able to recognize when variations or exceptions are appropriate, responsible, and truly therapeutic.

A familiar example of contrasting pou stos is the difference between the posture of a professional whose only task is to establish a formal diagnosis for administrative purposes and that of a colleague who is trying to facilitate a client's self-exploration. The former is apt to be more detached, directive, and observant of objective aspects of the client (e.g., involuntary movements, grooming, and rationality of thought). The associate will be employing empathy, support, and openness to whatever directions the client's needs take.

In other words, once again the stress is on what is *actual*, rather than simply a concern with the transmission or receipt of information.

AN EXISTENTIAL–HUMANISTIC POU STO

I propose the following sample positions to demonstrate the kinds of issues that constitute a pou sto. Other therapists may address these matters differently as is congruent with their understanding of human nature and of the modes of psychotherapeutic practice. However, it seems to me that the issues themselves are likely to be intrinsic to any therapy.

Each of these points is partially illustrated by the phrases that follow it. These I propose as carrying a humanistic outlook into effect.

The Embracing Conception

This is the assumption on which these specimen phrasings of the pou sto is based:

How the client uses the hour is a valid sample of how the client conducts his life.

The client brings his way of being in the world to the therapist's office. Despite any needs to dissemble, excuse, or blame, the raw beingness of the client in the room is the only valid sample of what we will call (in Chapter Seven) the client's self-and-world construct system—that is, how the client implicitly defines himself and the nature of the world in which he lives.

As the client is encouraged to *search* inwardly (as described in Chapter Four), he will demonstrate how he sees his own nature and what he sees as the important opportunities, obstacles, and requirements of life in general. He will also encounter difficulties in letting his searching process freely disclose whatever it contacts. These difficulties are likely to be significantly related to the client's distresses in the larger compass of his life.

In other words, the difficulties the client experiences in trying to use the hour optimally are probably expressions of ways the client structures his life generally, that is, they are elements of the client's self-and-world construct systems. As the client is helped to recognize and explore these stresses at length during the hour, those obstacles to full living will tend to be reduced or overcome.

With this framing perspective, we can now examine the proposed elements of the pou sto as they define the therapist's and the client's positions.

The Image of the Client's Authentic Situation

The client is a person in the midst of his own life trying to make sense of what he experiences, trying to guide what he will do, trying to be more fulfilled and to have less pain. He is talking to the therapist because he wants to be more able to be truly in his life and to accomplish his purposes more readily. When talking to the therapist, another person, a client knows at some level that the therapist is in a very similar situation. At that level, the client also knows that the therapist is neither all-knowing nor all-powerful.

How does the client talk to the therapist? Does he talk in line with this reality, or is there implicit in what he says some distortion from this reality?

It needs to be obvious that a central place is given to a division of responsibilities and that the client's autonomy is a foundation element. At first glance, that seems a matter of course. The fact is, however, many therapists, with the best intentions, gradually are drawn into trying to guide their clients' actions, attitudes, and values. To an outside observer, it can seem only human decency or fellow feeling to make "suggestions." Yet it is these well-intentioned efforts that so easily get translated into implicit instructions or even requirements.

The pou sto I propose here counsels against this temptation. Experienced therapists often learn (to their dismay) how readily they can foster a dependency that encumbers the work and gradually evolves into a very different relation than that they had intended.

The Image of the Authentic Therapist Role

The therapist is here to aid this person in his efforts to find greater fulfillment in his life. She can do this best if she confines the bulk of her efforts to noting how this person pursues fulfill-

ment, how well the person uses all his resources, and how the person defeats himself. She does not know—nor can she ever know—all there is to know about this person; he will always know more about himself and his own life than she can or does. She does not know how he should live his life or make his choices. She has enough to do just trying to manage her own life, so she cannot in conscience try to manage this person's life as well. She can, however, provide him with a trained awareness and a disciplined manner of intervening—both focused on how he uses his capacities for himself. These are no small gifts to give, and she will give them gladly.

The central focus of the therapist's stance is the client's self-governance, the ways in which the client is self-defeating, and how the client uses his own powers for his own best interests. Here is the core of the attention to the *actual*, for the therapist seeks to identify *in the living moment* the ways in which the client ill serves his own fulfillment. "In the living moment" is, of course, the crucially important element. Only when that is accurately timed—in terms of the client's accessibility—will the client be helped to make the internal journey that can lead to lasting changes.

Summarizing the Principal Significance of These Images

Psychotherapists are not consultants on how to live. We can be consultants in how people use their own capacities to better guide their own lives. We can be coaches for clients doing their own life work, using their own innate capacities.

Transference and the Pou Sto

An important benefit of having a well-thought-out pou sto is the basis it provides for noting and assessing the transference of the client and the countertransference of the therapist. The following examples will make this more evident.

When a client asks me to advise her on whether to quit her unrewarding job, to marry her persistent suitor, to make up with her estranged sister, or any of the many troubling decisions that each life encounters, she is seeking to make me into something or someone I am not: an all-knowing seer, a benign and supernally wise parent. When a client rages at me for not endorsing some contemplated action (about which the client is, usually, uncertain himself), when a client beseeches the therapist to intervene with someone in her extra-therapy life (someone whom she feels will not heed her own efforts), and when, in any of a myriad of other ways, a client tries to have me step beyond the role appropriate to this pou sto, then it is clear that a transference is occurring.

It is equally helpful to use the measuring rod of the pou sto to assess the therapist's own reactions to her clients.

> Susan wants so much to win the therapist's approval of her efforts to be a "good client" (actually, she wants to be seen as the therapist's "best client ever"). A first impulse might be to at least give her some personal approval. She is certainly likeable, and Ben, the therapist, does value how well she uses the therapeutic opportunity so far. Yet he could subvert all her gains if he yielded and said, "You really have done an exceptional job in therapy, Susan; indeed there are very few I see who have done as well." That's what she really wants, but to say that is to confirm her lifelong seeking for an approving father—that is, an authority to fall back on when, as happens so often, she doubts herself so much as did her actual fault-finding father.

Also, she probably wants to avoid having to confront her own unrelenting superego (patterned on her father).

So the therapist needs to say, "Susan, I can see how much you want my approval, and I'm glad you feel pleased with your progress, but I am not thinking of it in measurement terms. I hope you'll look inside yourself and see what is going on there to bring about this urgent wanting from me." It is likely that she will still hear him as her critical father, but that takes some stretching since she also has experienced that the therapist has not frequently acted in that way.

Thus the work may move to the next phase of disclosing this transference.

This instance demonstrates how transference and countertransference often have links. Although it is not always so, it seems as though in many instances in which one is aroused, at least some complementary impulse is stimulated in the therapeutic partner.

In work as intense and intimate as depth psychotherapy extending over months and even years, there are many temptations to utilize countertransference actions and words. Among the most obvious that I have experienced personally are impulses to intervene when a parent tries to justify the brutal treatment of a child, invitations to intimacy from an attractive woman, my yearning to set straight a narrow and self-righteous employer victimizing her staff, and (in some ways, for me one of the hardest) the repeated impulse to comfort a newly widowed spouse.

It must be understood that withholding the impulsive act or words described is not the same as being indifferent or removed from compassion. I will try to illustrate this with a greatly oversimplified example.

Marta was left abruptly by her fiancé and lover, Gil. She had looked forward to their marrying, and the shock of his aban-

doning her has filled her with overwhelming grief and sup-pressed rage. She is weeping now, head down, tears flooding, not speaking. Her hand reaches out blindly to me. After a minute's delay, I take her hand and gently press it, then release it.

"You're so full of pain . . . and disappointment," I say.

"Yes, oh, yes, I am," she sobs. The hand comes out again, but this time I don't touch it.

I wait several minutes, then, "It's so hard to realize that the life you planned with Gil is gone."

More sobs. She cries for a while, and then turns her face up to look at me. "You understand how it is for me, don't you?" There is an implied appeal, which somehow feels as though it seeks more than simple understanding.

"You've told about your pain, but if there's more you want me to know, tell me that too." This is responsive in a limited way, but it is not what she seeks.

"Would you just hold me for a little bit?" she looks up at me through her tears.

"Maybe sometime, Marta, but not right now.[2] There's some-thing more you want right now, and my holding you might get in the way of your finding out about that something more."

In this example, both transference and countertransference are present. Marta is seeking more than a therapeutic exploration of her grief; she wants immediate and personal comforting. Although I feel an impulse to comfort her more overtly, I measure that out very carefully. My pacing, tone, and actions seek to give her some of what she seeks, but they also set limits and recall her to our work.

To be clear and explicit about these situations generally,[3] I had no objection to taking her hand, but I wanted it to be deliberate and suf-ficiently delayed to forestall any assumption on her part that it would become an impulsive and regular part of our work. I have held the hands of women—and men—at various junctures in our work together; it can be supportive and helpful, but it needs to be a considered action. I have let my own tears of empathy be seen when they were there, and it was consonant with the status of the alliance and the immediate context of the moment. I might even have held Marta for a bit if I had felt that she was asking only for that. What I didn't want to encourage was a seeking that in less conscious ways might be for a replacement for Gil.

My emotions are valid parts of the work when they arise from the work itself, but not when they are brought in from my outside life. That is a neat formula that, in all truth, has only limited utility in the complications of actual therapeutic encounters. Nevertheless, it is a starting point for the responsible therapist's assessment of his or her own experience and how much and in what way it will be brought into the work.

CONCLUSION

Psychotherapy that is more than simple support or advising launches client and therapist alike on a vast ocean of possible content, emotions, and relationships. It is this great range of possibilities that makes it possible, in some instances, for major and lifelong changes to result. But it is also this same potential range that permits—and at times even fosters—destructive and harmful outcomes to occur.

Graduate training programs for counselors and psychotherapists, as well as posttraining continuing education, are means for helping professionals clarify and attain stability about their stances in these extreme circumstances. State laws and professional association codes of ethics are attempts to carry this control further. But no training, laws, or codes can displace the need for therapists to inquire deeply into their own needs, impulses, and values, and to arrive at a pou sto that will be a steadying influence for themselves and a support to their clients' ultimate gains from therapy.

It is important to recognize that the pou sto is not a set of prohibitions. More significant in the long run is the recognition that life-important work can only be accomplished when there is a meaningful structure within which that work can go forward. The total lack of such a structure (and its limits and opportunities) is not freedom; it is chaos. So it is that a considered, broad, and practical part of the therapist's equipment is a well-thought-out pou sto.

NOTES

[1] Material pertinent to this chapter will be found in Bugental (1987, Chapter 12).

[2] This is a difficult situation for the ethical but truly caring psychotherapist. It is discussed in the last chapter of my *Intimate Journeys* (Bugental, 1990).

[3] A discussion of therapeutic deprivation and therapeutic gratification can be found in Bugental (1987). See also Bugental (1972).

6 INITIATING THE THERAPEUTIC PROCESS

Helping the Client Begin to Appreciate the Living Moment

The foundation for the therapeutic task is the pou sto,[1] the considered basic position of the therapist. It is present implicitly in whatever goes on in the interview hours. The existential–humanistic perspective builds on that foundation in structuring the interviews that will carry the work forward. That psychotherapy work needs a carefully thought-through setting if it is to be both as spontaneous and as impactful as desirable. Spontaneity does not war with structure; it depends upon it. Without it, simple chaos results.

It may well be argued that the psychotherapy of a given individual begins when that person first hears about the fact of psychotherapy as an option. It goes forward as information and hearsay about the process are gathered from all sorts of sources—novels and movies, friends and neighbors, jokes and horror stories, reading and academic references, and much else. It is probably safe to say that no one comes virginal to the first actual therapeutic session.

Of course, how and what the potential client first learns about the psychotherapist he will consult is likely to be especially influential. Female or male; young, middle-aged, old; of what racial and religious background; demanding, lenient, or flexible; expensive, moderately priced, or low-fee; and so on and on. Many of these details will wash through, of course, but some, usually particularly significant ones, will cling. Knowingly or not, they select whom the client will call, how readily that client will cooperate in finding a first interview time, and what expectations will be brought to that conversation.

By and large, most professionals' offices tend to be similar. I am proposing here that that model is not the ideal one for therapists prepared to work with the *actual* experiencing of the client.[2]

THE PHYSICAL SETTING AND ITS EFFECTS

The recommended waiting room is not typical of most such settings. It is comfortably but simply furnished with several armchairs, several straight chairs, and one "two-seater" settee. There are a few subdued prints on the wall. There is no radio or sound system, nor are there magazines or other reading materials. A simple button-switch allows the arriving client to signal his presence to the therapist.

At some point, therapist and client may have occasion to talk about this rather Spartan setting. This discussion might arise when it becomes known that the client has brought reading or other materials to occupy herself while waiting. One way that discussion might go is illustrated here.

John Doe arrives promptly, presses the button that signals that fact to the therapist, and then sits in one of the armchairs. He takes a magazine from his pocket, crosses his legs comfortably, and reads. When the therapist comes to the door, John hesitates, obviously finishing a thought in the article he's reading. Then he moves quickly to follow the therapist to the consultation room.

TH-1: I notice you had a magazine when I came to pick you up.
CL-1: Yes. Have to do something to kill the time when I'm early. You sure don't provide anything in there.

TH-2: That's intentional, and when you bring something to do with the time, you are robbing yourself.

CL-2: Really? I don't get it. What am I supposed to do, just twiddle my thumbs until you get ready for us to go to work?

TH-3: Evidently you see that you can only work on yourself if I'm with you.

CL-3: Well, when you put it that way. . . . No, I suppose not, but I have lots of time to myself, so I don't need to sit there being bored.

TH-4: You're equating being with yourself with being bored.

CL-4: Not really. (*Pause.*) Well, what do you think I should do in the waiting room?

TH-5: C'mon, John. You know why you're here, and you know how we work. You answer that question.

CL-5: Umm, yeah . . . I suppose I could be thinking more about myself and why I'm here.

TH-6: You know now that when you come in to this office, we usually have to spend some minutes in helping you just really get here and inside yourself.

CL-6: I get it! Why not use that time in the waiting room so we could get to our work sooner in here?

TH-7: Why not, indeed?

CL-7: Got it! Sure that makes sense. I'll try it out next time.

TH-8: Good. But while you're thinking about this, what do you do when you leave here after our session?

CL-8: Head for the car and get back to the office. . . . Oh, oh, I see where you're headed.

TH-9: What do you see?

CL-9: Well, why don't I take a few minutes for decompression sort of? I mean, it wouldn't be so bad just to stop and let things simmer a bit, would it?

TH-10: You get the idea. That's another reason we don't encourage talking and visiting in the waiting area.

Of course, the client is bright, well motivated, and highly responsive—as is usually true of hypothetical clients. In actual practice, therapists will find that some argue this point, some agree but soon forget, some simply go through a ritual-like self-centering that has little apparent effect on their presence in the actual session (and it may complicate that work as the client comes in with a prepared topic, which prevents true working presence), and some actually use the suggestion to good effect.

THE FIRST POST-INTAKE INTERVIEW

After the intake interview[3]—which, of course, is or should be therapeutic also—the next session is (in the minds of one or both participants) the beginning of the actual psychotherapy and particularly important. This importance resides in its central task of introducing the client to a way of using the hour that is likely to be different from what the client is expecting—indeed, from what many in the general culture expect. Table 6.1 summarizes these contrasts to usual expectations.

TABLE 6.1

How This Work Varies From Usual Expectations*

The client must be helped to discover:

- That the therapist generally will not be collecting information by questioning the client.
- That the client must learn two essential skills: to attend to his or her own inner in-the-moment and subjective experiencing and to share this with the therapist as directly as possible, while receiving relatively limited input from the therapist.[4]
- That the client must learn the crucial difference between

*These points are illustrated in the sample interview segments later in this chapter.

thinking about and describing himself or herself, on the one hand, and discovering her or his immediate experiencing, on the other.

Introducing This Way of Working

When the intake interview is conducted, as illustrated in the second protocol in Chapter One, the therapist will usually have some impression of the client's readiness to accept and use the characteristics listed in Table 6.1. How these are then further brought out depends on the sophistication of the particular client and the emotional pacing that client can sustain—which varies from the totally naive person who is "coming to the doctor to be told how to solve her problems" to the collegial (literally or not) sophisticate who readily drops into *apparently* self-directed inner exploration.

In either case, one generally may expect that to establish the optimum therapeutic alliance, there is demanding work yet to be done.[5]

That work has several aspects. The primary one is the monitoring of the client's emotional tolerance for what may seem a new and unsettling way of being helped. When a new client arrives in a state of tension or anxiety, confronting that client with instructions to participate in an unexpected way may elicit even greater distress. In such an instance, the therapist will need to use his clinical sensitivity and empathy to modulate the transition. Particularly helpful in such a case is encouraging the client to tell her story in her own way with the therapist making only occasional observations of the actual experience of the client as she talks. For example, consider this client's complaint:

CL-1: I haven't been able to get a good night's sleep for a month or more. I'm so tense at night that I just can't let down.

TH-1: Um-hmm. In fact, it seems as though there's some of that tension in you right now.

CL-2: That's right. There sure is. It's just always with me. I sure hope you can help me.

TH-2: Your hope is still there too.

CL-3: Yeah, but it doesn't do me any good. Like I was telling you: At the office it's starting to get to me, and that's really bad. Why just the other day. . . .

TH-3: I'm going to interrupt you briefly to point out that the fact that the tension *is* in you right now is important to our work. It means we are not limited to just *talking* about your tension; instead, we can work with it right here in the room.

CL-4: Yeah, I hadn't thought about that. So how do we do that, that working with it right here?

TH-4: You're working with it when you tell me how it is inside of you right as you talk.

CL-5: It's miserable. That's how it is.

TH-5: Uh-huh, and let yourself just listen to it inside of you. Then tell me whatever comes into your awareness.

CL-6: Yeah, well like I was telling you, it's really getting so I can't concentrate at the office. The other day. . . .

And so the client is back to *telling about* herself. If the anxiety is strong, it is best to let her get some catharsis so that she will be more accessible to the necessary teaching, which must soon occur. That instructing will be an attempt to teach her to recognize the difference between *actually* discovering her experiencing and simply reporting on what she has experienced previously or what she has thought about her distress.

Among other client patterns that require the therapist to modulate the pace of introducing attention to the actual in the moment are the demanding (sometimes hostile) person who tries to insist that something must be done either immediately or in the way the person wants to do it (CL-B1), the inert overly passive client who seemingly lacks any ability to find something to say (CL-B2), and the excessively talkative individual who continually talks with little or no attention to therapist interventions (CL-B3).

CL-B1-1: I told my husband I was coming to see you, and he just hit the roof! I mean, he was so mad that I thought he might break a blood vessel. His heart's not the greatest you know, and when he gets going on something, there's just no telling what he will do. It seems as though he's getting worse, and. . . .

TH-B1-1: You're telling me more about your husband than about yourself and what. . . .

CL-B1-2: (*Interrupting.*) Yes, well, you really ought to know what I put up with. Sometimes it just gets to be too much, like when he came home in the middle of the day when I was trying to do the washing and arrange for the PTA supper. Honestly! There he was expecting me to drop everything. He doesn't seem to think I have anything to do and. . . .

CL-B2-1: I don't know what to tell you. It just all seems so hopeless.

TH-B2-1: That's telling me something—that it seems hopeless to you.

CL-B2-2: (*Silent.*) Well, it does. I don't know what else to say. Why don't you ask me some questions?

CL-B3-1: It has been weeks since I've had a decent night's sleep, and it just plays hell with my work, and so I'm getting farther and farther behind on everything, and I can't see any way of getting caught up ever! It's just so. . . .

TH-B3-1: You are just flooding me with information without either tuning into yourself or . . . letting me. . . .

CL-B3-2: (*Interrupting.*) Well, it's a serious situation. Why only last week I was trying to talk to Mel Wilson, he's my main contact, and sometimes he. . . .

For any of these patterns, frequent but simple identifications of the most readily recognizable ways[6] a client avoids becoming more deeply involved are likely to be helpful. If that goes reasonably well, then gradually these resistances can be disclosed more promptly and coupled with occasional, very simple structurings. But for all these and other similar patterns, therapist sensitivity and pacing are the essential keys to how to help a client discover more of her own inner processes.

Following are some examples of the kinds of resistance identifications and subsequent structuring that can be helpful if appropriately adapted to the individual client.

- You are under so much stress that it's hard for you to use what I tell you. Yet if we are to alleviate that stress, we've got to learn to work together.
- It's clearly very hard for you to talk about what is important to you. I'll wait with you until you can get to something that really matters to you today, but meantime just try to learn to attend to your inner experiencing as it is going on right now. Then, when you can, say a bit about it.
- I'm going to interrupt you for a minute. (*Speaks very firmly.*) I want you to just be quiet and try to see what is the underlying thing you want me to know right now. (*Pause, then speaks more strongly.*) No, you're starting too soon and without really checking inside. I value your chance here to make your life different and I'm going to keep interrupting you when I think you're just telling me *about* yourself but not really listening inside in the very moment in which you are speaking.

One additional client pattern needs to be addressed: the client who frequently feels reprimanded. Even when the therapist has accurately reflected the client's *actual* experience, explicitly or implicitly, it is evident that the client hears that reflection as pointing to a fault.

TH-B4-1: You sound angry as you say that.

CL-B4-1: Well, I think I have a right to be angry!

TH-B4-2: You hear me saying you don't have that right?

CL-B4-2: Well, it sure sounded that way to me. (*Aggrieved tone.*)

TH-B4-3: (*After first checking within whether indeed he did feel critical of the client's response and not finding such a reaction*).[7] I've just taken a moment to see whether I did feel critical, and as best I can tell, I did not. Will you check inside also and see where your feelings are now?

CL-B4-3: (*Quickly.*) No, I don't.

TH-B4-4: You answer so quickly. You seem to find it difficult to take the time to really listen inside yourself.

CL-B4-4: Now you're finding fault with me again.

TH-B4-5: It seems hard for you to hear my efforts to help you as anything but finding fault, doesn't it?

CL-B4-5: See! There, you're doing it again.

TH-B4-6: Yes, that time I did find fault, just as I am right now. You've lost the thread of your own experiencing in order to try to accuse me. It's a demonstration of how you can lose track of your own life at times.

Now, of course, those structurings are utterly useless if used verbatim or if injected into a conversation without earlier efforts to bring the client to participate more productively so that there already is a conversational context.

Assessing Client Readiness for Therapist Interventions

As with all therapist activity or inactivity, one must proceed with sensitivity to two crucially important variables: the state of the *therapeutic alliance* between client and therapist and the *context* into which any therapist action or nonaction will enter. Beyond these, therapists of equal skill and sensitivity vary widely in their personal styles, and that is very much as it should be. Psychotherapy is, at its root, the artistic product of two human personalities engaged in a life-changing enterprise.

Some therapists prefer to engage in a bit of direct teaching early in the first therapeutic interviews, in a sense setting the scene or the "ground rules" and providing a reference mark to which they can return as needed. Others prefer to do this teaching only in the moments when it is most pertinent. Much can be said for each mode. Perhaps the best resolution is to go back to the issue of client readiness and let that decide the timing.

An Example of Early Structuring
Client (CL)—Arnold Ames; Therapist (TH)—Helen Forrest

Arnold is 37 years old, a licensed counselor,[8] and is presenting great grief over the loss of his lover to AIDS. He says he can't find meaning in his life, but denies suicidal thoughts, and feels he is not being as effective with his counselees as he was formerly.

The first interview brought out that he has twice had relatively brief therapy experiences that he characterized as "helpful but too shallow." He wants to be helped to "work more deeply, to get to the real sources of (his) melancholy."

CL-1: I was thinking on the way here this morning that I ought to tell you more about how my mother babied me. I think it probably had the effect of making me too self-centered. Does that seem likely to you?

TH-1: Arnold, I want to do two things right now as we start a new phase of our work together. First, I want to answer your question, and second, I want to talk about how we need to work together.

CL-2: Okay, fine. I just thought it seemed like a good idea of what might be back of a lot of my stuff, you know.

TH-2: Yes, I understand, and I'm glad you're thinking about our work's needs. Yet, here's an important point. I think it's a very logical possibility, but that, in fact, is the trouble: It *is* chiefly logical and it *is* only a possibility.

CL-3: Oh, I know. But it might be a lead. . . .

TH-3: (*Interrupting.*) I'm going to interrupt you to talk about leads like that and to use that to tell you more about how I think we can do our work together most effectively.

CL-4: Yes, please do. It was just an idea, and. . . . (*He cuts himself off with a sheepish grin.*)

TH-4: You're a counselor, Arnold, and you know as well as anyone how many possible explanations there are for almost anything you or I might do. (*Moves quickly to continue as Arnold is getting ready to speak.*) So we can't rely solely on logical possibilities. We need to get at a deeper level where we'll *know* and not just *figure out* about patterns that we have and act on.

CL-5: (*Reflecting.*) Yes, I see what you mean, but how do we do that? I mean, I'm willing to try anything, but I don't know. . . .

TH-5: Take a minute and look inside. You're puzzled, a little intrigued, and probably somewhat skeptical that you can do whatever it is I'm suggesting. Is that fairly accurate?

CL-6: Yes, except it made me think of how I always had trouble in sciences in school, and. . . .

TH-6: (*Interrupting, with a smile.*) You just thought of that, didn't you? I mean you didn't have to work out that thought. It just spontaneously emerged because you were feeling something and thinking about it.

CL-7: Well, yes. You see, when somebody tries to explain something to me, I'm always kind of afraid I won't get it, and. . . .

TH-7: (*Coming in quickly.*) Yes, and that link-up between what happened right now just came to you the same way. Again it was just there for you.

CL-8: You mean, I didn't have to think it up? I just knew it all of a sudden. (*Intrigued.*) I never thought about it that way. Yes, it's like it was just something I knew.

TH-8: How different that was than your speculation about your mother babying you!

CL-9: That's true, but you see I knew what I was thinking and feeling here a minute ago, but I don't know about. . . . Wait a minute! Let me see if I can get a feeling about Mother and her way with me. (*Both are silent for a minute or two. Arnold closes his eyes, and his face portrays concerted effort. Then he opens his eyes and speaks slowly and uncertainly.*)

CL-10: Well, I think that's probably so, but I'm not real sure, you know. I kept getting sidetracked, worrying whether I was doing it right and. . . . And what you were thinking and whether I interrupted you too much, and. . . .

TH-10: Arnold, what you're dismissing as "sidetracks" is exactly what I want to help you recognize and value. These are live awarenesses that just emerged in you out of what you were concerned with. That's what we want to help you identify and talk much more about.

CL-11: Yes, that's so, but why couldn't I get a clear feeling about this question of Mom's babying me? It certainly seems like it's important, and. . . .

TH-11: The point is, Arnold, you need to be into yourself, not testing yourself in order to get that level of understanding. You were into your desire to find something significant, but not into your whole relationship with your mother or with feeling babied or whatever might have brought the awareness you were seeking. Moreover, and this is important, you have to take time to get into yourself rather than just trying to flip the pages of your subjectivity and find it all spelled out.

CL-12: (*Disappointed.*) Well, how do I do that?

TH-12: You're doing it right now. There's no "how to." It's your natural way of being inside. When you start out, it helps if you first get really centered in yourself. Then you listen to what matters to you at the moment rather than dictating to yourself as though you were some machine.

CL-13: (*Uncertainly.*) Yes. . . . I guess so, but. . . .

TH-13: What is in your awareness right now?

CL-14: I don't know. I mean, I'm not sure I get what you just told me, and. . . .

TH-14: That's all right. When you tell me about not being sure you understand me, you're doing your work. When you can't find a quick answer, you have a chance to find a deeper and less familiar answer.

We'll leave Arnold there in his vague sense that something strange and unexpected is being asked of him. That, by the way, is a very accurate perception—although Arnold would find that fact even more surprising. It is useful at times to tell a client, "Confusion is your friend. It means you're not using your familiar habits, and so there is an opportunity for you to see and react freshly."

That reassurance often has the net effect of increasing the client's confusion. Progress!

NOTES

[1] As described in Chapter Five.

[2] Of course, the therapist may not always be in a position to determine the nature of the reception room—or even the consultation room. Still, having in mind the image of the ideal presented here may suggest some possible adjustments. More important, it will convey the value orientation of the work to be described.

[3] As illustrated in the second interview in Chapter One.

[4] Some counselors and therapists, patterning their work on what they take to be the "psychoanalytic" style, are chiefly and continuously silent in their work with their clients. It is my observation that this is likely to demonstrate a poor understanding of both psychoanalytic method and the use of silence. Therapist

silence has a wide spectrum of interpersonal meanings and impacts. Among these, several will serve as illustrations: At times it may provide a very supportive medium for the client's own work. At other times, it may be a challenge or a reprimand to the client. And, of course, sometimes it is a demonstration of the therapist's lack of empathy and limited skill.

[5]In not a few instances, in which the client is also a colleague with his or her own way of conducting interviews, there may be as much or more difficulty than with the truly naive client.

[6]Technically, such client efforts may be termed *resistances*, but it is important to recognize that these are only incidentally obstacles to the therapeutic work. More fundamentally, clients ward off inner searching because of some threat to their ways of conceiving themselves and their lives. See Chapters Seven and Eight to understand more about these processes.

[7]It is absolutely essential to be very straight at such a juncture. If there was some element of fault-finding, the therapist would do well to say, "I've just checked inside and you are right, there was some element of fault-finding in what I said. That's not what I want to feel, but it does occur sometimes. However, I now want you to check inside also and see what you can find there."

[8]Using a counselor as an example of a client is intended to demonstrate that this way of conducting psychotherapy is likely to be as unexpected to many professionals as it is to clients.

7

THE NECESSITY FOR SPACE SUITS

Our Self-and-World Construct Systems

One way of thinking about the underlying nature of depth psychotherapy is to conceive of it as a thoroughgoing review of one's implicit vision of one's own identity and the character of one's environing world—a review conducted in the hope of attaining a more satisfying subsequent life. Of course, the degree of thoroughness of this review will vary widely, but even the most abridged therapy, which attempts to do no more than make some limited and surface changes, will involve some amount of such a survey. In this chapter, the perspective is that of psychotherapy undertaken to facilitate significant and lasting improvements in the client's experience of his life.

One of the most remarkable feats of recent years, to my mind, was the repair of the Hubbell space telescope, that astonishing orbiting eye-in-the-sky. Here's how I recall the story.

The space telescope is a very large and complex instrument circling the earth. After it was first placed in orbit, it was discovered that the original lenses were not performing as required; therefore, it "had to be fitted with new glasses," as one reporter put it. No simple task!

The Hubbell telescope, as I understand, is about the size of a railroad boxcar, and it is hurtling through space at something like 17,000 miles an hour. Imagine being asked to catch a boxcar moving at that speed, and not only to catch it but to maneuver it into the

109

cargo hatch of the shuttle! Fortunately, a docking tool had been developed to simplify this challenging task.

But the docking tool didn't work!

And so the task for the astronauts was to catch that orbiting box-car *by hand* and then fit it into the hatch. While it is true that there is no weight in space, it is equally true that there is indeed inertia. That means that if a hand were caught between that speeding tele-scope-boxcar and the wall of the hatch, there would be instant destruction of the hand and of the person attached to it.

Yet the astronauts did it! They avoided disaster and corrected the optical fault.

They caught the telescope, pulled it from orbit, carefully put it in the hatch, made the replacements, took it from the shuttle, and restored it to orbit. An almost unbelievable accomplishment!

Now we are provided regularly with pictures and accounts of vis-tas human eyes have never seen before. Our knowledge of the uni-verse in which we live is growing immensely from the discoveries made possible by the rectified Hubbell telescope.

This science-fiction–like triumph was the product of many factors, among which is one that is particularly pertinent here: the space suits. Those cumbersome looking suits of late-twentieth-century armor protect their wearers and thus make the impossible possible.

These suits make possible the work of the astronauts, and *these suits limit what the astronauts can do.*

Space suits provide limits, as does the umbilical that supplies air and nutrients—and as does the solid shell of the shuttle. An astronaut in a space suit may be able to do amazing things, but that astronaut in a space suit cannot scratch an itchy nose! The space suit makes some things possible, to be sure; but, equally surely, it also makes some other things impossible.

This is a fundamental truth that is so easily forgotten: *That which enables also limits.*

This truth is reemphasized by another component of the space pro-gram, the "free fall" experience. If a person is put in a situation of zero gravity and cannot touch any surface (another person, the wall, floor, ceiling), that person in the suit is totally helpless. "Free" indeed! Similarly, a person in a space suit and outside of the vessel without a tether of any kind, although only a few feet from the craft, would also be completely and fatally unable to help himself.

It is only when there is something to push against or pull on that some degree of movement becomes possible. Once again, a similar lesson: *Total freedom results in total helplessness.*

EVERYONE MUST HAVE A SPACE SUIT

Neither you, the reader, nor I, the writer, could survive without our space suits. If we were to remove them, literal insanity and disaster would be the inevitable result. When we try simply to change them, we are modifying and possibly endangering that which makes our lives possible, that which makes them work as well (or as poorly) as they do.

A metaphor? Of course. An exaggeration? Not at all.

Surrounding each of us at every moment—at this moment right now as I write and this other moment *right now* as you read—is space, empty space. This is not the space of the physical universe but that of psychological possibility.

You could put the book down in disgust and refuse to read further. You could stop and make notes for future reference. You could throw the book through the nearest window—very likely without opening it. You could keep on reading.

There are more possibilities, of course. You could get up and walk out of the room in which you are now, keep walking out of the building, down the street, and perhaps end up at a friend's home. You could do all of this, but instead of going to a friend, you could take a gun out of hiding, hold up a motorist, steal his car, and leave the country forever. You could. . . . You could do any of a literally infinite number of things.

(Since you're still reading and I'm still writing, we've chosen to continue, at least for the time being.)

And space all around us: In the next moment you may receive the message that a distant relative of whom you can't remember even hearing has died and left you $100,000, or the message may be that, for no reason you can imagine, the police have surrounded the building in which you sit at this very moment and demand that you give yourself up. A holdup man may suddenly enter your room, or it might be your best friend or a total stranger who will totally change your life—or a call to dinner just as usual.

Both within ourselves and all around us are space, emptiness, possibilities beyond calculation. Yet each moment we consign many of those possibilities to oblivion as we, consciously or unconsciously, choose those that we will make actual in the next moment, and then choose again, and then again, and. . . .

Space all around us, space that is open until we choose what we will do or will not do. Possibility always at hand, in each next moment and beyond it, still more possibility—endless, infinite. Mostly we don't notice it; mostly we follow familiar patterns, but there are always other possibilities.

Why don't we carry out some of the other possibilities? Because it would upset our plans, too many people, our own lives.

I'm committed to finish writing this (or reading this).

"Committed" but not forced—still a choice. *Oh, but I am "forced" by my wanting to get through this, by my sense of responsibility, by my wanting to. . . .* (i.e., by my choices still).

Or we say, "I'm not the sort of person who would ever steal a car, or do any of those other things you suggested." Still choices. And, of course, those choices come from how you define yourself. But the possibilities are still there.

"Anyway, you can't get away with robbing people and running off, or if you try it, you'll get caught and punished." More expectations: what is possible, what the consequences might be. Always our own conceptions give rise to possibilities, often implicitly, even those we pronounce impossibilities. Is this a world in which one can murder enemies? Must one pretend a casual attitude when bitterly opposed? Is money more important than character? Is it smarter to get an education or to get a start in a career? What is it good to look for in a spouse? How can I make things work out better for my son than they did for me? Will the present political system lead to better times or to civil disorder?

The ways in which we define ourselves and our worlds are parts of the space suits we wear. If we defined ourselves differently, if we conceived what is valuable differently, or if we saw other dangers, we would, of course, act differently. The questions are endless, and we answer them over and over without realizing how our answers are drawing the constraints and identifying the possibilities that constitute our space suits.

This is in no way to deny the very real forces pressing upon us at all times. It insists, however, that how they actually affect us is a product of that external force in combination with our inner values, attitudes, and needs.

Gravity's pull is beyond denial, but we walk upright, fly great distances (even to the moon), erect tall towers and buildings, and climb sheer rock faces.

"Thou shalt not kill," we are taught, but we arm and train our police and the military; we execute murderers, and we spend millions to create, show, and enjoy spectacles in which fictional killing is featured.

The newspapers and newscasts tell us about those who have different space suits than most of us: the daring astronaut, the embezzler, the Nobel scientist, the serial killer, and all the astonishing range and variety of human lives.

So much of what makes up our space suits came to us without our recognition of what was happening or our feeling any choice about the matter. "I'm a man," and that means different things than does "I'm a woman." And those differences are different again in other cultures. But even these definitions are changing—perhaps more for women than for men, but worldwide for both genders. The possibilities for such changes have always existed, but the cost of adopting those changes has changed.

Experiences of great danger and the imminence of death (e.g., in war or a natural disaster) or occasions on which we have more sense of choice but know our lives may be forever changed (marriage or divorce, depth psychotherapy, graduation from the highest level we will ever attain, becoming a parent) share a common and crucial element: Major life changes call on us to become aware of our space suits, of our ways of defining ourselves, our worlds, our views of what is good, what is bad, what has power.

And often, but subtly, they call on us for awareness of what may be, strangely, even more difficult to become aware of: our ultimate choicefulness and the nearly limitless openness of possibility.

Recognizing our openness can lead to creativity or to madness. The creative arts and the best of scientific efforts are space voyages into the surrounding emptiness. Most stay close to the familiar earth; occasionally one ventures farther (note the expression, "Far out!"). The difference between the two is the difference between moving in an incremental way from what is well accepted as contrasted with making an abrupt leap—into a bizarre, creative, or an otherwise unexpected life. (This may happen in a divorce, in quitting a long-held job, in moving on short notice to a new city.)

What this means is that every truly creative step—in the arts, in science, in relationships, wherever—is a leap, a venturing into the unknown. And there are no certainties in that darkness. Disaster may be as possible as is success. Indeed, that is often the mark of a truly creative step. The creativity may reside in the very fact that the outcome is not predictable.

Reason and science have taught us that possibility is space, literally and figuratively. Possibility is infinite. At first thought, that sounds great: "School's out—there's nothing to stop us!" However, further confrontation with the emptiness of possibility and of space may change the emotion. Now we see that it is too open, and we are driven to seek the shelter of probability, the fort of predictability. "Possibility" is an inviting word, suggesting innovation and discovery, the thrill of creation. But the other face of possibility is terrifying—formlessness.

The universal dread of death is in no small part the threat of having no identity, no palpable reality. Existence without form is inconceivable. Our self-and-world construct systems give us form and thus identity, potentiality, experience, and investment in being.

If certainty is denied us—as increasingly we recognize it is—then we try to form structures: rules, laws, contracts, customs, traditions that in their dependability approximate it. The need for some environing stability is as fundamental as is the frantic seeking for air when we are smothering. We must know that the room in which we sit will be constant, that tomorrow will be another day, that the persons we love will be there for us, that our usual ways of talking and listening will still serve us, that the coinage of our country will be valid, and so on, and so on.

When the environing structures collapse as in war-torn areas, or when a government is overthrown, or in a place in which a major natural disaster has hit (cyclone, earthquake, fire, or similar widely shared cataclysms), terror, heroism, and apathy may result, and we are confronted with how vulnerable, arbitrary, and temporary are the structures with which we furnish our lives.

On a more individual scale, the sudden desertion or death of a spouse or parent, the loss of long-held employment, the unexpected but total bankruptcy of a family accustomed to financial stability—these and similar personal disasters make us suddenly aware of how unthinkingly we have counted on our ways of seeing our worlds and of identifying ourselves as permanent.

The Self-and-World Construct System[1]

The questions with which our living confronts us do not wait for us to research our responses in order to make them the best possible;

instead, we always act on tentative answers. "You have no choice; you must place your bet," Pascal is reputed to have said.

Although they are pro tem answers, with our aging they become more firmly parts of our way of being—become, in fact, our *personae*, our ways of expressing ourselves, furthering our own interests, relating to others, protecting ourselves and what we value. Maturity means, among other conceptions, having a fairly stable way of being oneself in the world. By that time, many of our answers are so firmly established that they frame the very thoughts with which we seek to consider the issues. Thus they become self-confirming. "I am a man. Men are realistic. Therefore, I am, or must be, realistic."

This whole process is more implicit than verbalized and much of it is only partially conscious and even more is completely unconscious. Only as we age or as life circumstances (e.g., tragedy or vital losses) compel us do we reflect and begin to recognize the life assignment to which we're already largely committed.

Growing up, becoming the actual person in one's own life, consists of developing a reasonably stable set of definitions of who and what one is and what the world is. In our subjective living, we are engaged lifelong in this task of creating our worlds and defining our places in them. From many sources we assemble the materials for this monumental, literally life-structuring work. Our parents, siblings, relatives, friends, teachers, the media, and much else contribute materials, but each person alone—and with but little consciousness—weaves his or her own unique design for existence.

And, of course, contingency may intervene without warning and call into question much that seemed assured, or demand that we undertake extensive revisions—think of the handsome movie star thrown from his horse who has become totally paralyzed, the obscure poet whose work abruptly has won a Pulitzer prize, the young mother astonishingly balancing a career and three children whose husband has been killed in an auto wreck, and so many others as detailed in each day's news.

This design is the way we answer the crucial questions of existence:

Those about the world, such as: What is important in living? What will bring satisfaction? What will bring pain and frustration? What has power to make things happen or to change the way things are? How important are such matters as relationship, money, position, family, age, beauty . . . ?

Those about one's own self, such as: What do I really value, want in my life? What is threatening, undesirable? What powers have I to influence what happens to me? How should I be with the people I value so they will welcome me? How can I change myself to bring more satisfactions and fewer disappointments?

And so on and on.

Our answers gradually grow more stable and become our maps for conducting our lives. They are constructions of our awareness and are only partially conscious, but they give us a sense of identity, continuity, and purpose. They become familiar to those who know us; indeed, they are the very stuff of their knowing of us. ("Josh is always so thoughtful; Brad is someone you can't really count on; Jeanette brings such cheeriness; Helen is so pessimistic.")

It is this circumstance that points to one of the central necessities for depth, life-changing psychotherapy: to support the client's reexamination of his way of being in the world and his efforts to revise or broaden the self-and-world constructs that have directed his life. It may sound like an intellectual task; it is anything but.

This self-and-world structure that we have gradually grown is so central to our lives that it is often considered the essence of life itself. "Self-sacrifice," even when reaching the ultimate of death, means refusing to yield some elements of the way one defines oneself or one's world in order to preserve other elements—the brave person who undergoes torture rather than betray his or her country, the defiant homeowner who is arrested for trying to stand off the sheriff who seeks to evict his family, the youngster who accepts punishment rather than tell the whereabouts of a runaway friend.

As is evident, one's self-perceptions range from the superficial and transitory ("I love to play chess these days") to the more central ("I've always been a tough competitor") to those so at the core of one's being that they are synonymous with it ("I'm ready to die before I will betray my buddies").

It is important to recognize that these self-and-world perceptions are not as isolated as my citing them separately suggests. One who dies for one's buddies does so because of a variety of self-and-world percepts. They might be something like these:

> *I'm my father's son, and Dad was always so gutsy. . . . The world is a tough place. . . . I've got to be tough now. . . . I've never been any good at dealing with threats. . . . Words are not very powerful. . . . I'm not going to be a quitter now . . . like I sometimes have been. . . . God is on our side. . . . These bastards (enemy soldiers) are mean and will never let me go.*

Over the years, they become integrated into an embracing fabric. Thus when one aspect of it is inquired into—as in psychotherapy or in deep sharing between friends and lovers—it will inevitably lead to other aspects. In a long, deep conversation, one often finds oneself talking about matters far from where the conversation began.

That fabric of defining percepts, as we've seen, is the self-and-world construct system, the central subjective structure of a life. We weave the webs that eventually hold us, give us form, make our lives possible and limit them as well. When we search (as described in Chapter Four), we bring to consciousness portions of these webs and may implicitly—and even without awareness—demonstrate still others. It is the psychotherapist's role to identify some of those elements of the client's self-and-world construct system so that the client has some chance to reevaluate them. Such elements have become almost invisible because they are so integrated into the client's way of being alive; only an empathic "outsider" can shine a light on them. A very brief example may illustrate this.

CL-1: I have told her that I just won't put up with that kind of treatment any longer. I really have no choice. I know myself, and I'm afraid I'll crack if she continues.

TH-1: You sound very troubled.

CL-2; Well, I am! I just never have been able to tolerate her sarcasm or anything like it. I want. . . .

TH-2: You keep emphasizing that you've always been this way.

CL-3: Of course! That's just the way I am. Why wouldn't I emphasize it?

TH-3: It seems so important to insist that's the way you've always been. Important to whom?

CL-4: (*Pause.*) To me! (*Pauses, reflects.*) Well, to you. (*A longer pause.*) Well, what does it matter? It's just the way I am. (*His voice is much less certain.*)

TH-4: What is happening inside of you right now?

CL-5: Well, . . . Well, I don't know. You've got me all mixed up now.

TH-5: That's because you're giving yourself a little more room. Stay with being mixed up, and tell me whatever comes along.

Of course, this is a greatly oversimplified example of a client's beginning to learn to listen within himself. Now he may be able to get back of his insistence that this attitude is "just the way" he is. Where it will take him and how soon he will be able to reassess his self-perception, we cannot guess at this point.

It is important to recognize the difference between client self-report ("That's just the way I am") and what was actually *in the living moment* in the room, that is, his insistence that he was as he was and could be no other way. It is important to attend to a client's oral report about the client's self-and-world construct system, but it is at least equally essential to be aware of what is *actually* being lived out in the moment.

Of Freedom and Limits

This realm of space and danger and opportunity instructs and surprises us with the implications and possibilities that are revealed. As an example: So often we see such words as "openness" and "freedom" as near synonyms, but recognition of the uncompromisable necessity of protecting astronauts from the total openness of the vacuum of space may cause us to reexamine that equation. Conceptually, it is a short step from that shift in perception to the realization that the openness of possibility in all aspects of our lives, while encouraging innovation, may also lead the unwary to catastrophe.

At times we may recognize the ultimately fragile nature of the social contract that holds our worlds together. While it makes possible, in some measure, our living as we wish, it also restricts possibilities in other ways.

If no limits exist or are enforced in a society, everyone is helpless. A major freeway without lanes, speed limits, or exit markings would be a death trap. Without structure, chaos results, and such a commonplace matter as going to get food or trying to communicate with someone no more than a block away can become a hazardous journey or an impossibility.

We have seen these very circumstances being enacted at a ghastly cost in societies in which civil order no longer enforces limits—during the French Revolution's Reign of Terror, in some modern African nations, in the Balkans, in riots in our own major cities. Total freedom leads to total danger for everyone.

Within the individual, a similar state of having no enduring structure leads to inertia, madness, or death. The individual who has no clear self-definition, who does not know and live out his values, who does not have a sense of a social role, can become irrational and show gross disturbances, such as "running amok," breaking down and needing to be taken into protective custody, retreating into catatonic stupor, or otherwise losing the ability to maintain life in the world.

Milder, but still quite distressed, levels of a damaged self-and-world system are often produced in the wife who has built her life around her husband and then is abandoned by him through divorce, desertion, or death. Similarly, men and women who have based their identities chiefly on their work may evidence disorganization of varying degrees of gravity when they or their positions are terminated or even when retired with adequate benefits.

For some the ink blot of death seems to present the ultimate destruction of any self-and-world construct system. Two quite contrasting responses to this interpretation have occurred repeatedly in human history: despair, withdrawal, and madness, on the one hand, and inspiration, renewed faith, and creativity, on the other.

Yet total control as exemplified in dictator-dominated nations generally ends up being devastating for the individuals subject to it and even, in the long run, for most of those exercising that domination. Our century now ending has witnessed the misery, destruction, and ultimate futility of totalitarian regimes in many parts of the world. The root cause of the failure of such attempts is the unrecognized but inexorable and continual thrusting out for change, for the new, the more, which is fundamental in human nature. This drive, it may be recognized, is the *searching* impulse in yet another form.

The self-and-world construct system provides ways of coping with the openness of possibility. When a person has some stability in self-identification, knows generally what he can and cannot do, has a sense of relationship to other people in general and to a chosen few others particularly, has some purpose, has a sense of place (geographic and social), then that person may make use of the degrees of freedom that are available without needing to test the limits continually.

We must have our space suits to survive in the openness of space, in the limitlessness of possibility. We must have a sense of our own capabilities and limits and of how to carry out our lives in the world in which we find ourselves. Yet too constricting a suit, too limiting a life conception, is life destroying and makes humans into things. And there is something deep in the human psyche that rebels against being made into an object.

In Praise of Limits and Death

It is in our nature to stretch, to reach out, to search, and to test our limits. Yet it is also in our nature to feel the terror of absolute limitlessness. Indeed, one may propose that creativity itself is an exercise in modifying the balance between openness and limitedness—as we change the limits, we propose new definitions of our lives' spaces, of what is possible, of how we define ourselves.

Death, as the essence of unformed possibility, thus may be thought of as our unrecognized partner in whatever we bring into being that will remain when we are gone—artistic works, engineering achievements, geopolitical creations, our own children.

Death, the ultimate limit, is our customary conception of an ultimate limit. Yet the fact of death is an incentive to conceive beyond death—whether by spiritual or religious conceptions of an afterlife or by creating works, physical or conceptual, that are likely to continue once we, their creators, have died.

Understanding the central and essential role in our lives played by the definitions and limitations composing our self-and-world construct systems is manifestly a central process in depth or life-changing psychotherapy.

NOTES

[1]See Bugental (1987, pp. 193–195, 238–240; 1990, pp. 325–328).

8

LIFE STRUCTURES: VITAL AND LIMITING

Understanding and Working with the Resistance

We have seen how necessary are the space suits that protect astronauts from the vacuum of space and the metaphoric space suits that protect us from the endless openness and pull of possibility. Without definitions of who and what we are and of what the world is and how it is constituted, we would be helpless— as helpless as are infants physically and otherwise because they lack self-and-world construct systems.

The development of such structures is the most important task of life. We call it "maturing," yet that work goes on lifelong, and, if we are wise, we never become so fully mature that we can neglect it.

Our society provides many bulwarks against the tides of possibility, and even those who follow "antisocial" paths unconsciously depend on them. If everyone could print money, counterfeiting would be useless. If honesty were not the expected norm, communication and commerce would become even more of a shambles. If force were the only limit, we would live below the level of the great apes, and no further culture would be possible.

Just as laws, social conventions, and contracts protect and constrain us, so do our self-and-world construct systems. The societal forms are walls against the always-potential flood of anarchy, of formlessness. They resist the chaos that is latent in all human association. Our personal self-and-world construct systems resist the chaos that is possible in both our individual and our collective living.

PROTECTING OUR SPACE SUITS

Just as we need our space suits to protect ourselves from the catastrophic possibilities of absolute openness, we must protect those space suits so that they can fulfill their literally vital function. The ways in which we define ourselves and make sense of the world give form to our lives. By recognizing such elements as gender, age, degrees of relationship, education and special training, vocations, avocations, and similar descriptive dimensions, we identify ourselves and each other.

Today in our country we are engaged in trying to free ourselves from the influence of some apparently similar attributes—gender, race, and skin color. Some see these efforts as opening up important possibilities for everyone; others insist that this attempt will result in loss to themselves and others.

There are many hazards and many temptations to change or damage our space suits. The ways in which we define ourselves and our world are both enabling and restricting. Thus we may see them as defenses against chaos and social disarray while at the same time we recognize that they function to limit our possibilities.

We defend our ways of defining who we are and what is the world in which we live, and sometimes our defenses actually prevent our growing and changing. Thus while the *resistance* is important and worth defending, it also has elements that can be self-defeating.

My self-concept, an important element in my space suit, makes me debate whether to take advantage of a tax loophole really intended for those less fortunate than I. Yet I am tempted, and defensive excuses come readily to mind, "Everybody does it. . . . No one would ever know. . . . It's only this once."

It is not true that no one would know. I will know, and in subtle but enduring ways, it may make it more likely that I will violate my code again. Thus my space suit may suffer a small leak that may or may not be as fatal as a pin prick in an astronaut's suit. But my knowing, when productively explored, can lead to further discoveries and amendments to my self-concept.

I started to use a personal illustration here,

> *I believe in traffic control, but I'm in a hurry as the signal changes, and I can see that no other car is close to the intersection. . . . (This was to be finished by saying that I would stop anyway.)*

While that is usually so, on reflection I realized that what I had written was shallow and deceptive. In other words, I was protecting my own self-image of being candid by not being truthful!

Now as I contemplate writing a more truthful example, I am more cautious inwardly and less ready to be displayed in this way. (Recognizing this puts another strain on my self-image, for I like to think of myself as quite open.)

> *I believe in traffic control but if I'm in a genuine hurry as the signal changes and I can see that no other car is close to the intersection. . . . I am likely to check quickly for a police presence, and seeing none, I go on through the red light.*

Now I can say, "I'm a law-abiding citizen, but I'm not a law-worshipping one." Somehow putting that as "worshipping" appeases my self-regard a bit. At this point, I have two, somewhat contrasting feelings. I have been more truthful (that pleases my self-concept), but I was so in a very cautious way (one step down from my pedestal), and by telling all this openly I regain some of the lost ground. Also there is a bit of humor in all this and that gains another step up on a higher pedestal, which evidently I'm still climbing.

Nor are these struggles with the limitations of our self-and-world construct systems only individual. Our families, employers, corporations, institutions all face and respond variously to similar challenges. Publicly known organizations seem almost always to have one image for the world and another for their own members. Public tolerance demands that this duality continue. Yet public appetite hungers for scandals that reveal the truth behind the façade.

To put it differently, one's self-and-world construct system is assailed on one side by the impacts of one's life and environment, and it is threatened on the other side by the absolute vacuum of emptiness pulling always to be filled in some way.

WHAT IS THE *RESISTANCE*?

Viewed in one way, the *resistance* is how we protect our self-and-world construct systems, but it is also true that it is those systems themselves that protect us from disaster, from formlessness. We take them so for granted that we seldom recognize their deeper service. Those who are caught in a maelstrom of anarchy, terrorism, rioting, and similar breakdowns of social construct systems or those facing a psychotic rage are vividly confronted with the ultimate dependence we all have on shared definitions of reality, however arbitrary they may be. Even the adjective "psychotic" implies a major departure from our shared definitions of reality and of our generally practiced agreements about acceptable or civilized actions.

But it is not just such external threats that evoke our need for such protection. We need to feel a stability within our own being. The self-and-world construct system provides a core for that stability. When psychotherapy calls into question some aspects of an individual's construct system, that person will almost certainly—overtly or covertly—resist that therapy. Thus it is essential that the therapist recognize that resistance serves not only an oppositional but also a protective function. The underlying fact is that it is absolutely essential to life that each person has some resistance to protect his or her life and sanity.

Accordingly, the unthinking notion that the client should get rid of all resistance is at once naive and dangerous. Of course, resistance can be—and often is—also counterproductive. It is that aspect with which we are most familiar in therapeutic practice, but we need to remember that some of the resistance we encounter is also necessary and can actually be a constructive influence.

Resistance in therapy may take many forms. Table 8.1 lists some that are familiar. When reading such a tabulation of "resistances," it is important to remind oneself that this is also a list of ways human beings have learned to use to protect themselves and to try to serve their needs. This is not, by any means, a roll call of wrongdoing. That these same patterns may ill serve their users is also true, of course, but it is only part of their significance.

Resistance in the Therapeutic Interview

As we have just seen, there is always resistance in every situation. That resistance may be thought of as holding back primal chaos (as we demonstrated earlier), but it is doing much more as well. The resistance is making possible the productive use of each situation.

When we think of the therapeutic interview as the site in which the client must reexamine, and very likely revise, significant parts of how she identifies herself and the way she is in the world, it should be obvious that a measure of ambivalence is to be expected. That very well-intentioned reexamination must in some measure call into question a client's way of being in the world.

TABLE 8.1

Resistance Forms Familiar In Psychotherapy

Surface Aspects

- Having difficulty finding what to say
- Avoiding in-the-moment emotion
- Trying to please the therapist
- Seeking to be socially approved
- Objecting blindly to the therapist's interpretations

■ ■ ■

Intermediate Aspects

- Trying to be a good (the best) client
- Attempting diligently to produce material the therapist wants (e.g., dreams)
- Making abject confessions with great shame
- Involving the therapist in discussions about therapeutic systems and methods
- Being excessively appreciative of therapy

■ ■ ■

Underlying Resistance Patterns

- Opposition, antagonism, hostility
- Injustice collecting
- Compliance, pleasing, being overly agreeable
- Blankness, "a-void-ing"
- Inertia, excessive dependency
- Overrationality, logic bound

It isn't unusual for a client to become very caught up in the therapeutic work and come to the sessions eagerly and participate readily. During such intervals, a considerable amount of productive work can take place. But there is a sobering truth underlying this "honeymoon" period in psychotherapy. If this mood remains constant, it is appropriate to question whether the therapy is truly working toward significant life change and freedom from dependence on the therapist.[1]

The important practical implication here is that opportunities for major therapeutic gain are dependent on the work's helping a client truly discover more of her life constructs and the ways in which they limit or handicap the client's living. When the resistance interferes with the client's ability to use the therapeutic opportunity, then it needs to become the focus of the therapist's attention. That does not mean that the therapist must immediately make it the explicit topic of the therapeutic conversation. As I will describe in later sections, careful timing of these interventions is one of the key elements in working with resistance.

The therapist, whose only purpose is to get rid of resistance, mistakes the meaning of this universal phenomenon and the values to be had from working *with* the resistance. That process is the central feature of any true "depth" psychotherapy.[2] It is very often the case that when the client's resistance is manifest, an opportunity is presented to get to more core issues than when there is unstressed exchange.

When the client is openly oppositional, it is likely (but not certain) that the threat to some elements of the client's self-and-world construct system is being unperienced and may be, at least in some part, close to consciousness. So it is that when the client is aware of an impulse to counter the trend of the work there is an opening to teach an important perspective to the client.

Segment 8.1
Client (CL)—Chuck Blanchard; Therapist (TH)—Bill Watson

CL-1: You keep bugging me to tell you more, and you never seem contented with what I am doing. Sometimes I feel like just telling you to bug off and let me alone.

TH-1: Sometimes?

CL-2: Well, yeah, kinda anyway. I mean, why can't you just get off it for a few minutes and let me get settled down?

TH-2: But you don't tell me to "get off it."

CL-3: So, get off it, already. Geez! You get your kicks from bugging me, don't you? I must be crazy to pay you all this money just to make me miserable.

TH-3: Are you miserable now?

CL-4: Yes. No. How the hell should I know with you riding me all the time? I mean, will you please just idle back and let me find out where I am?

TH-4: I could do that, Chuck, but I feel like I'd be letting you down if I did.

CL-5: So let me down, for crying out loud. I'm so rattled now I haven't any idea where I am or what I want to say.

TH-5: You're saying it now. You're saying how it is inside of you. You're talking from inside of yourself and not just standing off and talking *about* yourself like you usually do.

CL-6: (*Heavily sarcastic.*) Well, goody for me. Now just shut up a minute and let me find out where I am.

TH-6: I will be quiet, Chuck, in just a minute. But I want you to recognize how much more meaningfully you're talking to me now than you were when you were just reporting on yourself.

CL-7: Okay, okay. I get it. Now, shut up!

TH-7: (*Remains silent, but looks expectantly at client until the latter speaks again.*)

CL-8: (*After a brief interval of silence.*) Yeah, okay. I guess I get it.

TH-8: You "guess"?

CL-9: Oh damn! Here we go again! No, I don't guess; I know it, damn it.

Such a quickly cooperative client! Of course, this is a greatly abridged version of what might take place during most of a session— or even over several sessions. The important point is that the client has become quite aware of his resistance. Subsequently, an explicit dealing with it may be sufficient to move the work to a deeper level. This conscious level of resistance is important and how it is handled will do much to prepare for later engagement with the deeper lying and less conscious layers of resistance.

Therapist Response to Client Resistance

Table 8.1 was roughly subdivided into three sections to illustrate some of the usual modes of client response. The most obvious forms are almost always at least on the periphery of the client's consciousness. As the working relation is ready to support some more active therapist participation (beyond simply facilitating the client's telling her story), the therapist may begin commenting on these forms of the resistance.

Usually it is well to begin with such remarks only occasionally. If the client seems to accept and use them, it may be productive gradually to increase their frequency and pointedness.

When the client has difficulty accepting such interventions, it may be that she is not yet ready for more than occasional comments of that order. In such instances, attention can be directed to how well mobilized is the client's *concern* and especially to the possibility that it is flaccid. Then the client's *pain*[3] has become so much a taken-for-granted matter that it fails to spark any real effort for change.

The purpose of feeding these observations back to the client is dual: to accustom the client to having the therapist point out implicit aspects of the client's use of therapy (rather than dealing solely with

content), and to aid the client's movement from deeper lying levels to
more immediate affective responses.

CL-1: I'm not sure what I want to say today. Have you any suggestions?
TH-1: Is there some reason you don't look within yourself?
CL-2: Oh, I can do that, but I just thought that you might have
    noticed something I ought to talk about.
TH-2: How readily you set aside what's inside of you!
CL-3: Oh no. I guess you don't want to tell me what to talk about; so
    I'll tell you about . . . about my argument with my wife last week.
TH-3: So you have to think up something that seems like it might
    satisfy me. Is that the way it is?

In this short segment, the therapist is trying to help the client turn
inward. If this was the first or second time that effort was received,
as in the sample, the therapist might better stop after his second comment. If, on the other hand, this exchange comes after at least one
previous instance, response TH-3 might be used (although its sarcasm might be inappropriate with some clients).

A further possibility: If this theme has come up before and the
client has bypassed the therapist's observations, it probably would be
well to continue in this vein for at least several more exchanges.

Gradually the insistence (interpersonal press[4]) of the therapist
would increase.

Segment 8.2

CL-11: (*Complaining tone.*) Why won't you ever tell me what to talk
    about? You know me pretty well now, and I don't want to waste
    my time wandering around when you could help me get directly to
    what I need to work on.
TH-11: Biff, you are determined to make me the magic wizard who
    knows more about you than you know about yourself.

CL-12: Oh, that's dumb! If you don't know more about some of my problems than I do, why the hell would I come here and pay you?

TH-12: You're getting pretty angry. How important is it to you to pass the responsibility away from yourself?

CL-13: Well, it *is* your responsibility.

TH-13: No.

CL-14: No? Well, who the hell is responsible for what we're doing here?

TH-14: You are.

CL-15: Then what do I need you for?

TH-15: To tell you that. To remind you that it's your life and that you've got responsibility for it.

Now the work is going forward to a second level (as described in Table 8.1) in which the client is seeking to involve the therapist in a discussion about therapeutic purposes and methods. In this particular passage, we get early indications of the probable path that will involve the therapeutic partners in working with the client's dependence on opposition, antagonism, or even overt hostility in his relations (i.e., third-level resistance). It is, of course, far too soon to make this relationship connection (transference) explicit. That is truly important to recognize.

The point to note is that the client has come toward what is undoubtedly a key theme in his way of structuring his life, and he has arrived at this important point out of his own impetus, not because the therapist instructed him to deal with it. In other words, the therapeutic engagement is "live action" or *actual*, not abstracted from the client's life and not brought into the work on the therapist's initiative.

Resistance patterns such as this are seldom much alleviated by explicit identification or instruction. Whatever benefit is likely to accrue is most apt to be the product of the resistance being acted out in the therapy hours and then being met and engaged by a firm and consistent working through with the therapist. To illustrate, we will jump ahead some months (or perhaps a year) to visit briefly the same (hypothetical) therapy partners.

Segment 8.2 (continued)

CL-101: You told me the other day that my temper was my way of getting along in the world. Well, I've thought a lot about that, and I think you're 120 percent wrong, as you. . . . (*Breaks off and sits glumly staring into space.*)

TH-101: You just cut yourself off. How come?

CL-102: Oh, it wasn't important. Anyway I want to know just why you are always. . . .

TH-102: (*Interrupting.*) You're awfully anxious to bury whatever it was that you started to say. C'mon, you better get it out where we can deal with it.

CL-103: (*Uncomfortable, moving restlessly.*) Aw, it wasn't anything really.

TH-103: Shall we spend the next 20 minutes arguing about this unimportant but aborted bit?

CL-104: Oh, shit! (*Pauses, gathers energy.*) I just started to say "as usual." You know, I was just kind of wound up. I didn't mean anything by it.

TH-104: What was "as usual"?

CL-105: You don't stop, do you? (*Pause, waiting.*) Oh, all right, I had just said you were wrong. . . .

TH-105: "120 percent."

CL-106: Yeah. So you did hear me.

TH-106: I always try to hear you.

CL-107: (*Soberly.*) I know you do.

TH-107: Yes.

CL-108: I didn't really mean it. I just got carried away.

TH-108: (*Looking directly at client.*) Yes.

CL-109: I just. . . .

TH-109. I know. You have depended on being tough and angry for so long that it's hard for you to be any other way.

CL-110: (*Subdued.*) Yeah. (*Pauses, looks down, then at therapist.*) You know, I'm getting sick of it.

TH-110: (*Soberly.*) Yes.

One should not be deceived. This is not the end of the therapeutic work with this client; indeed some of the most important work is yet to come. The client will be supported through his efforts to find other ways of relating and then through his inevitable failures and disappointments. But the corner has been turned by the working through of an important element of the resistance.

DEEPER RESISTANCE PATTERNS

Our second interview segment (just shown) presented an instance of a client caught up in a resistance pattern that was apparent both to him and to the therapist. Often the countermotivation is much less overt.

Segment 8.3
Client (CL)—Gloria Johnson; Therapist (TH)—Helen George

This client is a woman in her early 40s who conducts a small book-keeping service out of her home. She is married and has two children. In therapy, she has followed a pattern of reporting on herself dispassionately and then seeking the therapist's approval or instruction. She seldom is very involved emotionally in what she describes and seems chiefly to want approval for "standing up for (her)self." The therapist has decided that the alliance is strong enough that she can begin disclosing the resistance.

CL-11: (*Concluding a long "he said–I said" and quite explicit report of an argument with her husband.*) And so I told him that I wasn't going to put up with his always being late for anything we wanted to do together. (*She is silent, looking expectantly at the therapist.*)

TH-11: Uh-huh. (*Pause.*) You're looking at me as though it's my turn to talk.

CL-12: (*Slightly discomfited.*) Well, yes. Don't you have anything to say about what I told you?

TH-12: No.

CL-13: Shall I tell you more about our argument?

TH-13: Why would you do that?

CL-14: Well, I. . . . Well, I wonder what you think about what I told you.

TH-14: I think it doesn't seem to matter much to you.

CL-15: (*Startled, silent briefly.*) What. . . . Why do you. . . . What do you mean?

TH-15: Just that. You tell it like you're talking about someone you know, but not very well.

CL-16: I didn't realize you wanted drama. (*Pauses, adopts a hurt look.*) Well, it does matter to me.

TH-16: You're making a face. What does it say?

CL-17: I don't know. (*Pauses, obviously waiting for the therapist to speak. When the therapist remains silent but continues to look at her intently, she moves restlessly, starts to speak, stops, then finds her voice.*) Well, aren't you glad I didn't let him just not pay attention to my needs?

TH-17: Do you think that's what you did?

CL-18: Well, I told him that I. . . .

TH-18: You've already told me what you said to him.

CL-19: Well, . . . Well, I think he ought to be more considerate of my feelings.

TH-19: (*Silent.*)

CL-20: (*Impatiently, then petulantly.*) Oh, come on, Helen. What do you want? Why won't you talk to me?

TH-20: Gloria, I just want you to pause a minute and find out what's going on inside of you rather than wasting our time arguing about my wanting "drama" or talking about your making speeches to your husband as you have so many times before and with so little follow-through by either of you.

CL-21: Well, you said. . . . (*She sees the therapist's unresponsive expression.*) Oh, all right! (*Pauses.*) Well, I just don't know why you're talking to me this way when I was just trying to tell you about. . . . (*Her tone is whiny, complaining.*)

TH-21: (*Interrupting.*) No, Gloria. You can do better than that about checking inside.

CL-22: Well, . . . Well, I don't know. I feel kind of angry, and. . . . And I'm puzzled by the way you're acting, and. . . . (*A longer pause. She checks therapist's face several times.*) Well, I . . . I wonder if I made you mad, because I didn't mean to, and. . . .

TH-22: It's hard for you to really get inside of yourself, Gloria. I can see that. But it's very important for you to try to do so. Coming here and just telling me stories about your life isn't going to change things.

CL-23: I don't know what you mean, "telling stories." (*She waits, then hesitates.*) Well, aren't you going to tell me?

TH-23: No, I'm not going to tell you about things you will know about when you can let yourself really listen inside rather than just telling *about* yourself.

CL-24: I don't know what you want me to do. (*Waiting.*) I feel like you want something from me, but I don't know what it is, and that makes me sort of uneasy and. . . .

TH-24: (*Very promptly and encouragingly.*) Yes! That came from inside of you, Gloria. That's beginning to discover something right now, rather than just reporting the old, familiar stuff.

CL-25: (*Surprised, partly pleased, partly confused.*) What did I say? (*Pause, questioning look gradually fades.*) I mean, what should I do now? (*Another questioning look, then a complaining tone.*) Why don't you answer me?

TH-25: You sound distressed.

CL-26: (*Hesitating. Then gathering force.*) Well, I am. I am complaining. You just sit there and let me get more and more confused and don't help me at all.

TH-26: That's the first time you've said you're confused.

CL-27: Well, I am! (*Pause, watching the therapist closely.*) I am confused, and I don't like it.

TH-27: Now you're really talking to me right here and now about what's in you right here and now. That's a very different thing than just telling me about someone you know who happens to have your name.

CL-28: (*Wailing tone.*) Ohhhh, I don't know what you mean. Do you just want me to be miserable?

TH-28: No, but if you are miserable right now, then say that, as you almost just did. I know this is hard for you to understand, Gloria, but it is very very important.

CL-29: (*On the verge of tears.*) But I don't understand.

TH-29: That's why it's so important. Here's a whole part of your life that you don't recognize or understand. When you just tell me about yourself in ways you already know very well, it doesn't help you reclaim that other big part of you—the part of you that you don't know very well or understand very well.

CL-30: You mean when I cry that's the other part of me?

TH-30: That's part of it, but there is much, much more that we need to get to also. Now, before you say anything, listen inside yourself and see what you can find that is very alive in you right now.

CL-31: Well. (*Considering.*) Wait. . . . I don't know (*She suddenly sobs.*) I really don't understand. I don't understand! I feel just awful.

TH-31: Yes, Gloria, I know you do. You feel awful, but you're really doing your work right now because you're finding out what's alive inside of you right at this moment, and you're saying it right now while it's happening inside of you.

An opening, not a resolution, not the end of the story, but a landmark or reference point that the therapeutic partners will be able to return to many times in the future. Spurred by her immediate distress—which, in turn, is the product of her avoidance of responsibility and, therefore, of what is *actual*—Gloria has broken through that resistance, at least briefly. That event in itself will not change her life, but as a brief glimpse of the unrealized part of herself, it may be a crucially important experience.

So begins the real work of helping this client get *actual*, get into her own innerness where there is the possibility of significant and lasting change. This is just a beginning (and, even then, a quite abridged example) and much more work—often going over the same ground—will be needed to help Gloria find her own inner vision.

Gloria's resistance is quite unconscious, and her puzzlement is genuine if superficial. The real resistance is at several levels. There is, of course, her detached reporting at the most surface layer (CL-11). Beneath that is a sheen of usual social expectancy for two people to take turns speaking—Gloria is making therapy just another conversation (CL-12)—and then there is the first hint of her affective and present tense experiencing as the therapist fails to follow the expected form (TH-14). This break with the expected projects Gloria into more awareness in the present moment [in contrast to her more automatic following out of a social form (CL-17)]. Now Gloria's affect is stirred, and she wants to protest, but can't seem to find more than a rather plaintive tone. By CL-24, she is beginning to be in touch with her *actual*, in-the-moment experiencing. The therapist reinforces this (TH-24). From that point to the end of this excerpt, Gloria is dealing, although still only shallowly, with what is actually going on in her and in the session.

Resistance as the Path to Life Changes

The interview segments of the work with Chuck and with Gloria provide brief illustrations of the central importance of the resistance in the effort to bring about major life changes. Each of these clients brought into the consultation room something more fundamental than an explicit "problem." Each brought a central part of the way he or she was alive in the world. The work of therapy required that these receive immediate and *living* or *actual* attention.

The focus on the very stuff of one's life may be thought of as "character" exploration. Attention to how we have enduringly formed our lives is intended to help us make more lasting changes. Yet that, too, is a realm in which character resistances will be more pronounced.

This level of work is a process radically different from that of logically examining a "problem," then getting its history, and then working out a plan for remedying the situation.

WORKING THROUGH A CHARACTER RESISTANCE

What follows is an abstraction of an idealized working through of character resistance. **No actual therapeutic work should be patterned on such a program.** It is presented here to illustrate some of the elements of a process that helps the client to move from the illusory space of resistance toward the vitality of the actual.

Encourage clients to tell their stories in their own way and until they lose energy or begin to be repetitive. It is most desirable that the client has the sense that she has, at least once, had "her say" and that the therapist truly understands at an explicit level why therapy is being sought and what distress is being experienced. This importance does not imply that a client may say whatever comes to mind about her concerns. Indeed, a frequent (and often unconscious) resistance of the anxious client is to endlessly express her "complaint" while avoiding genuinely grappling with it.

When the client has made adequately clear what she thinks the reason is for needing psychotherapy, it is time to look beyond the immediate presentation. Of course, throughout the therapeutic course, there is likely to be additional information, recovered memories, further associations, and much else that is reported and that is worthy of some amount of serious attention. Yet such material must not be allowed to so preempt the therapy hours that no other work gets done.

Allow clients to continue in their own way while the therapist takes note of recurring patterns. As the telling of the client's story begins to lose its initial impetus, some amount of repetition is probable, but almost always the client will find additional information or concerns that seem to need relating.[5] While this is happening, the therapist does well to begin to note and call attention to recurrent patterns through which the client—often unconsciously—maintains control of the direction and intensity of his participation.

Concurrently, the therapist occasionally reflects back to the client some manifest process aspect. The therapist will have been noting these patterns to himself and now must begin to identify them to the client. The key perspective is to identify in the client's protocol that which is evident but unregarded by the client.

Examples:

1. You hesitated just then.
2. It's sometimes hard for you to show your feelings.
3. You seem to be asking me for something now.

Generally, it is well to begin with observations about patterns that are quite evident (such as in the first example). If these are received by the client without precipitating some kind of confrontation, observations dipping a bit below the explicit level (as in the second example) may begin. Only when these preliminary steps have accustomed the client to therapist reflection are interpretations helpfully linked to the relationship (third example).

Clients, of course, vary widely in their readiness for the therapist to move along this sequence. Clinical sensitivity is required, and no set of explicit cues can replace that necessity. With many clients it will not be possible to use this third example frequently until a number of interviews have built sufficient confidence. Of course, there are wide variations in this timing (from very early in the work to requiring many contacts and even to never being able to do so).

The therapist selects the most persistent and obvious resistance pattern to focus on with repeated identifications. By now, it is to be hoped, the working relationship is strong enough for more interpretative feedback to be used. Therapist participation no longer needs to be so closely linked to overt or explicit client input. These examples are roughly ranked but the sequence is not dependable because now we are dealing with much more subjective material.

Examples:

1. Showing your feelings seems to be a no-no for you.
2. You hesitate whenever you get to your anger.
3. Again when you want something from me, you ask for it very indirectly.

The therapist watches for secondary resistance layer—that is, the way a client responds to the repeated identifications of the previous step. When it is repeated sufficiently, the therapist switches to identifying it whenever it appears.

Examples:

1. You want to explain about what you said *or* you feel a need to justify what you said.
2. You're distracted by *or* switching your attention to *or* reacting to what I just said.

3. You have a lot of feeling about what I said *or* you are angry *or* sad *or* amused by what I said.

The next two steps in the sequence vary greatly in their frequency and in how far they need to be carried:

1. The therapist follows this sequence as far as it goes clearly, but avoids forcing any connection, and instead keeps alert to whatever replaces it.
2. The therapist gives prompt recognition and implicit approval whenever the client gets more immediate in self-disclosure.

There are wide stylistic differences among therapists in using them. (For these reasons, it is not possible to provide examples without having more context. Later sections will provide these.)

Characteristics of Effective Therapist Disclosures of Resistance

In carrying out the work outlined above, therapists naturally follow quite varied modes; however, it is possible to suggest three characteristics often present in the more effective instances:

1. There is an incremental development, beginning with the most obvious and explicit (to whatever extent available) and moving to the more implicit.
2. The evolution from concrete and immediate to abstraction or generalization is paced by the client's demonstrated readiness to recognize the pattern being identified.
3. The therapist avoids argumentation and instead treats the client's rejection of identification as itself a resistance.

A word of caution is needed: The foregoing section has offered a reasonable and orderly succession of steps with examples of manifestly desirable interventions. This is fiction.

There is a dangerous seduction in such materials. It suggests that a therapist can learn "the system" and then use it with confidence that the results will be as desired. More fiction.

The systematic "steps" and the examples are ways of pointing at what cannot be captured adequately with words. Much depends on the grounding, maturity, and subjective approach of the therapist; on the readiness, insight, and growth motivation of the client; and on the history of these two people working together, their expectations, and their current relationship.

CONCLUSION

Work with the resistance is one of the most reliable distinguishing characteristics of deeper, more life-changing psychotherapy. Much effective counseling and supportive psychotherapy can be conducted with only shallowly dipping into this realm. However, without bringing to the conscious surface patterns that are entrenched but essentially invisible to the client, it is much less likely that therapeutic gains will be widespread or continuing.

NOTES

[1]Much useful life-support counseling may be carried out under conditions as pleasant as here suggested; however, there is value in distinguishing that engagement from those efforts that are ultimately directed toward the client's attaining autonomy and that may be termed "psychotherapy" or even "depth psychotherapy."

[2]Edgar Levenson maintains that the truest psychoanalysis is when client or patient and therapist both confront and work through their mutual transferences (resistances) together.

[3]*Pain* is one of the forms of *concern*. The importance and forms of client and therapist *concern* are described in Chapter Eleven.

[4]See discussion of interpersonal press in Bugental (1987).

[5]This is a point in the work that requires a difficult judgment from the therapist. The amount of material latent in the client is, for all practical purposes, infinite. Quite unconsciously, the client may be fending off deepening the inquiry or getting to frightening or guilty material. The therapist must be alert to flagging energy, repetitious content, incompletenesses, and other cues to shallow investment that are typical when the client is unconsciously distracted from her presentations of herself.

9 TWO EYES ARE BETTER THAN ONE

We Need Both the Objective and the Subjective

The central work of depth psychotherapy occurs in the therapist's engagement with the whole person of the client. This calls for the therapist to be aware of both the objective responses that express that person's life and the subjective experiencing that is the core of the person's living. Although much in our current culture tends to emphasize the objective, attention to that realm must not displace recognition of the subjective core's greater importance to the individual's being. When it sees persons as generally interchangeable objects, psychotherapy betrays its mission. Yet approaches that consist of heedless fostering of the client's self-preoccupation are also contratherapeutic and professionally irresponsible.

"In the kingdom of the blind," it is said, "the one-eyed man is king." This is not so.

In the kingdom of the blind, the one-eyed man is in the mental hospital. Since he is seeing things others cannot see, manifestly he must be insane and hallucinating. In the same way, in the kingdom of the one-eyed, the two-eyed view is apt to be rejected—even attacked—as deluded and lost in mysticism, or dismissed as just plain wrong.

Currently, much of our living is in the kingdom of the one-eyed. Announcing an unfamiliar perspective about human beings is likely to earn opprobrium, not approval. Following is just such an announcement.

149

Our human lives have both objective and subjective aspects.
Our inner experiencing is the main site of our living. What is
solely objective has no meaning for us until its subjective impli-
cations are brought into effect in some way.

The objective elements environing our experience include such influences as the physical dimensions of ourselves and our world, spatial movement of all kinds, and vision, audition, and similar sensory potentials. These all can have immense impacts on us, but for the most part the full significance of those impacts is chiefly through their subjective arousals or consequences.

Our subjectivity is made up of many elements, among which the most familiar and significant are feelings and emotions, ideas and understandings, implications and intentions, solitariness and relationships. It is in terms of these primary elements that we experience our lives.

To be fully human means to be alive and aware in both realms[1]—the subjective and the objective—but the former is directly or indirectly the more crucial in most of our living. Stories of persons who, although badly handicapped physically, economically, socially, or otherwise, overcome their objective limitations to make outstanding objective[2] and/or subjective achievements are frequent and demonstrative.

It is customary to think of much of our early and overt learning as concerned with the objective world of things, surfaces, actions, and bodies. Yet, beginning earlier and continuing all through our lives, we are also implicitly attending to the inner world. Although learning the names of these experiences may not come for some time, long before we have words for them, we learn to recognize and respond in relation to feelings, thoughts, meanings, intentions, and much else.

Some of us (e.g., stereotypical engineers and sports promoters) apparently have come to believe that most or all of what matters is the objective world; for others (e.g., equally stereotypical religionists, artists)—and usually fewer in our culture—it is chiefly the subjective life that is deemed to have significance. Both proponents try to manage life by blinding one eye; they differ only in the eye they choose to maim.

Healthful full living requires vital participation in both elements. Many of our times' distresses can be traced to the "one-eyed-ness" of so much in our lives. Thus at this point we do well to remind ourselves of the centrality of our inner experiencing.

When we attempt to get at the immediacy of our lives in the living moment, it may be a surprise to realize that the true site of experiencing our lives is, in fact, our subjectivity. No matter how much we insist that we are objects, that very insistence is itself an inner event, subjective.

Recognizing this reality and attending to that inner realm, we find that our subjectivity is a rich, multidimensional, constantly evolving, and fertile realm. And, paradoxically, while it is private to each of us, it is also the place of what we may experience in our deepest sharing with others.

IMPLICATIONS OF ONE-EYED-NESS FOR OUR TIMES

Today the subjective is mistrusted in many venues. By its very nature, it is covert; with the best intent, it still can only be verbalized incompletely; its forms are truly protean and can never be predicted with surety. It is worth noting that these same attributes make it the site and source of creativity and deep and lasting relationships. Likewise, even we who deem ourselves psychologically sophisticated, who supposedly know our own subjectivity, must recognize that we do not by any means know all that is within our own subjectivities.

Back of all these sobering recognitions there is yet another that we may sense but that some seek to deny: *Ultimately, the human subjective is the most powerful force in the world.*[3] In the subjective of some humans lies the ambition and ruthlessness of a Hitler, the creativity and dedication of those who created the atomic bomb, the zealotry of the Hutus or other murderous and rampaging tribes, and much else that may enrich or threaten our lives.

Of course, it is also true that in the subjectivity of humans resides the exquisite voice of a Debussy or a Brahms, the fertile creativity of a Hemingway or a Raphael, the genius of an Edison or a Pasteur, the humane vision of a Ghandi or a Martin Luther King.

Objectivity is sometimes deemed an ideal, uncontaminated by human emotions and needs. (Of course, terming it an "ideal" is already identifying a *subjective* evaluation.) A prime example of narrow devotion to the objective is the ideal of a government of laws, a government above and heedless of individual circumstances, with justice blindfolded (so that what is unique in those administered will not be taken into account) and virginal (so she is not contaminated by human passions).

And how has this ideal proved out? The courts are arenas for special interests (subjectively motivated), for theatrics (designed to influence the subjectivity of witnesses and jurors), for bitter antagonisms fought with legalistic maneuvers (to inflict hurt on the opposition almost without regard for the ultimate verdict). Well in advance of the actual trial, specialists write specifications for jurors who will be most likely to vote as desired—specifications designed to bend the subjective to objective ends.

I propose we send the virgin back to Sunnybrook Farm and replace her with a mature woman of the world who has known the passions and heartbreaks of life. She would not long tolerate the perversions of supposedly objective justice now so familiar and so often evoking dismay and feelings of being helpless in the grip of a system spinning out of control.

The impossibility of living according to the ideals of a truly objective justice system becomes the perverse justification for doing "whatever works." And the same degradation of abstract ideals may be found in the legislatures, the executives, the administrative offices of government, as well as in the rest of the culture. The splendid ideal of democracy is being traduced by the subjective greediness of competitive and objectively focused capitalism.

Commerce centered on the dollar, the arts having to prove themselves marketable to a wide public—these emphasize the objective. Indeed, it is thought meritorious to have stripped all subjectivity from most walks of life except the arts, entertainment, and sports. As a result, each of these is now being objectified in some measure. Works of art are chiefly newsworthy for the high auction prices they elicit. Entertainment increasingly seeks to shock with violence, nudity, and sexuality—not for themselves as human and subjective experiences, but as a way to set new box office records. Sports, too, have become more objectively oriented, with immense monetary and other rewards to be had by employing blunt brutality. Shades of the Roman Colosseum!

Imagine this scene:

Father: Willie, did you do your math homework?
Willie: No, Dad, I got caught up in listening to music.

What should Father do? What will the teacher expect? Of course, Willie should do the homework in math. . . . Well, very likely he should. Of course, he just might be better able to use his talents for all humans if he stayed with the music. (How was Beethoven in math? Gershwin? Jerry Garcia?)

But that's not the point now. The point—as is most often the case—is the overt, the objective, the getting-ready-for the-competitive exam). "Willie, turn off that damn tape player and get crackin' on them there books!"

In our public education systems, we are taught to regard ourselves and others as objects, chiefly as *things*—things to be stuffed with objective information. The notion of learning simply for the satisfaction, even joy, of knowing is likely to be seen as ridiculously romantic or out-of-date. "C'mon, get real. What are you going to do, sit in a corner musing about the agricultural products of South America"?[4]

We learn to see ourselves as *things* competing with other *things* for the good *things* of life: grades, promotions, teams, recognitions, rewards. . . . The list goes on and on. It is chiefly a list based on limitedness: There is only one first place. "Winning isn't everything," it has been said. "It's the only thing."

It is not so! Losing is much more common. Winning is the unusual. Losing must be accepted by all, and except for a very few, it is by far the most frequent competitive experience for almost everyone. When some of the few winners finally lose—as they inevitably must—they often are crushed (in some instances, even suicidal).

So much of our experience is that of being things, defeated things, things trying to do better to win more; yet so much of our training is only for winning and so little of it is for losing!

Still, feelings and emotions, hopes and fears, satisfactions and disappointments, relationships, and a whole range of subjective experiences are emphasized in news accounts, in radio and video reports, in advertising in all venues, and in everyday talk among friends.

Overtly and explicitly, the objective is featured. Implicitly and pervasively, the subjective is the focus of our concerns.

Because I insist on the importance of the subjective realm, it may seem that I devalue the objective. I do not. Preoccupation with the subjective manifestly can be erroneous, unwise, even deadly. I don't want to ride with a driver who gets lost in daydreams or in the music on the car radio.

SO WHO OR WHAT AM I, ARE WE?

A *New Yorker* cartoon of some time ago showed a family consisting of a mother, a father, a small boy, and a baby in a stroller, walking in the park on a Sunday outing. The little boy asks, "Mother, are we live or on tape?"

What a poignant question! What a profound question!

When speaking to audiences, I have shown this cartoon and asked people chosen at random how they knew they were "live" rather than "on tape." The almost unanimous answer is something such as, "Because I feel things, have things going on inside of me." One's subjectivity is readily recognized as the essence of being alive.

Occasionally we read of some person who, due to illness or accident, has lost consciousness and is being kept alive only physically. It is a disturbing question as to whether his state within that physical shell should be called "living." Sometimes, after years, such a person regains consciousness. Some, but not all, who do so report having been aware of what was going on around them in the hospital but being unable to communicate in any way.

For most of us, that report answers the question: Clearly they were alive! Why such certainty? Because they were aware. Life, we say, was there after all. The equation of life and consciousness is again made explicit. Our lives, as we are aware of them, consist of this internal river of awareness. Without that subjective awareness, we can only imagine death. It is for this reason that a sentence of life in prison without the possibility of parole is deemed to be less threatening than the death penalty.

WHAT IS THE SUBJECTIVE?[5]

What is the subjective? In something of an oversimplification, we can say that the objective world is that external realm which is perceived through our senses, whereas the subjective is immediately given without an intermediate process. I know I am cold because my hands feel uncomfortable, but in anticipating being with my love this evening, I *am* delighted. Feeling cold and feeling delight are very different processes.

My senses make it possible to navigate in the physical world. My feelings and thoughts (and much else that is subjective) give me reasons for and guides to my doing so. Without the subjective, we would be but machines in an impersonal environment. Without our objective sensing, we would be inert and helpless.

The human task is to incorporate both dimensions; to keep alive to the possibilities, opportunities, and threats they present; and to learn wisely to balance their sometimes competing impulses.

Is Subjectivity Centering an Encouragement to Selfishness?

On a less monumental scale, the subtle but pervasive mistrust of the subjective causes some to say, "We should avoid encouraging the subjective. People are too subjective now. They just think of themselves and forget that other people have needs and rights also." This view equates *subjectivity* and *selfishness*, an ironic mistake since narrow grasping for unfair advantage is most typical of those lacking true subjective centeredness. When one is disproportionately driven outward to try to find meaning, value, or identity, then that person is likely to be cut off from a centered feeling of self-worth and genuine relatedness.

I have listened for literally thousands of hours to people struggling with their own needs and whatever awareness they have of the rights and needs of others. Although, beyond question, there are some who have little or no recognition of or regard for those others, I can say with surety that they number no more than a tenth of those I've seen— and probably even that is an overestimate. When they become more fully aware of their inner and subjective seekings, they find—sometimes to their own surprise—caring and empathic feelings for others.

It isn't that we humans are unaware of others, it is the iron rule so much taught and obeyed these days: "Do others before they do you." This is not a world for the naive, for the gullible, for the self-neglectful. At least for most of us, it is not. We are *things* in many ways, but the tragedy is that we become things to ourselves as well and blind to the non-thingness potentials of ourselves and of *all* others.

In so many ways, our culture teaches us a *we–they* outlook, and *they* are objects whose feelings can't be allowed to matter. "If we let ourselves worry about our competitor's feelings, we couldn't do what we need to do for ourselves." Inevitably, the result is that we see ourselves as things also, valuable only for what we achieve objectively.

It is not unusual for people to come to psychotherapy[6] because they feel incomplete, life lacks meaning, and their achievements are savorless. When the therapy goes well and they are able to discover their subjective potential, they often experience it as a "coming home" to their truer selves.

When someone begins seeing with two eyes, then that someone begins seeing things that many others do not see, or, if they should catch a glimpse, they devalue or dismiss it as irrelevant, confusing, or pointless. In actual fact, it is anything but pointless. Human beings who would know life fully must be dwellers in the two realms—the shared objective world and the individual subjective world. Then they will discover that although it is individual, it simultaneously has the potential to be enriched by sharing with others.

To be unaware of either the power and value of the subjective or the influence and necessity of the objective is to be seriously handicapped. Yet it is a handicap widely shared. Thus the kingdom of the one-eyed is perpetuated unwittingly.

From the 1950s on, encounter groups developed rapidly and today their progeny are multifold: support groups of all kinds— men's groups, women's groups, prayer groups, executive sharing retreats— these are only a tiny sample. Some of these are leader-centered, some leader-phobic; some chaotic, others disciplined; some are growth facilitating and some are embryonic cults.[7]

For many who participate in such groups, the magnet is their astonishing and reassuring discovery that others have full subjective lives also and that these can be shared—that the loneliness of objectification is not inevitable.

Still, the subjective is denounced in some quarters because it is individual, elusive, changeful, transverbal, emotional, the source of intentions, and because it resists open observation and direction from the outside. And those charges are true. The subjective not only is private, it is the seat of our individuality, our lives as persons.

Some people are able to have strong connections in both realms—combining their objective activities with strong investments in a loving relationship and family life or in religion or a civic organization, for examples. For many of us, it is an implicit ideal that we attain only imperfectly. For still others, astonishingly, the ideal is to be utterly free of any subjective concerns and thus to become totally objective; that is, machines in human form. But even then, that sadly bizarre goal is, itself, an expression of the subjective.

OBSERVING INTERACTION OF OBJECTIVE AND SUBJECTIVE

Perforce, I have spoken of the objective at one point and of the subjective at another. Thus a necessary distortion results, for objective and subjective are always present in each of the therapeutic partners. Thus they help to define each other—as "right" is defined by its contrast to "left."

Reporting the explicit words spoken by a client is apt to be so incomplete as to easily mislead the reader: "The client said that his mother was an outspoken person." So?

A. The client frowned as he said that his mother was an outspoken person.
B. After a long and tense silence, the client said that his mother was an outspoken person.
C. With a fond smile, the client said that his mother was an outspoken person.

There is, of course, an infinite number of variations that can be imagined. The use of objective cues helps to understand the meaning of the explicit words, and those meanings reside in the subjective.

Skillful and sensitive psychotherapists learn to recognize and to use this palette of possibilities. With a matured therapeutic alliance, it is sometimes possible to enlist the client's understanding.

> *The client had from time to time spoken of having "butter-flies in the stomach" when the work touched areas of marked emotional significance. This phrase provided the partners with another dimension of understanding. From time to time, as the client was exploring within, the therapist would softly ask, "How are the butterflies now?" and the client would briefly reply, "They're quiet now," or "They're getting uneasy," or even, "That last thing I said has made them go crazy."*

This kind of alliance is very productive, but it is most likely to be possible when the key phrase or image is derived from the client's own experience.[8]

SUMMARIZING: THE SUBJECTIVE AND PSYCHOTHERAPY

As the client talks of his concerns, the therapist does well to be particularly attuned to *how* the client tells of his life. This does not mean that the *what* of the account is neglected, but only that it is accepted in a kind of tentative manner while the *how* is noted.

Betty-1: (*Speaking in a businesslike manner.*) I have thought of coming to psychotherapy for a long time. Now, at last, I can afford to be here. Well, what would you like to know about me?

The words suggest a culmination, an achievement; the manner is that of a detached observer. How can this be?

Betty-2: (*Sobbing, wiping her eyes, hardly seeing the therapist.*) I've wanted to get help, get therapy, for so long. Finally I'm here and

. . . (*A new burst of weeping.*) I've been so unhappy. Can you help me? Can anyone help me?

The therapist starts to speak, but she cuts the therapist off to weep some more and to emphasize repeatedly how glad she is to be in therapy, how much she needs it. The therapist's questions to Betty about her distress, what she tried to do about it before, and what seems to aggravate it are barely answered with a few words as Betty-2 floods with more distress and insistence on how relieved she is to be finally with a therapist. How can this be?

Betty-1 and Betty-2 present exaggeratedly evident instances of *how* the client presents herself speaking as "loud or louder" than *what* she says. In actual contacts with new clients, the contrasts between the self-description and the self-presentation may be more subtle; nevertheless, it is essential to be aware of that contrast.

This is, of course, another aspect of our attending to what is *actual.*

It is the therapist's responsibility to provide feedback to the client so that he may access deeper and more influential levels of his experiencing and consequent actions.

Following are some of the attributes of client self-presentation that usually accompany valid expressions of client immediate subjectivity.

- It is now, present tense, immediate.
- The verbal aspect conveys more than explicit meanings, and that more arises from a subjective or experiential substratum.
- Its manner of delivery and emotional intensity suggest that it might go on and on as one thought or percept leads to another and that to yet another (i.e., spontaneous and unwitting "searching" is going on).
- A sense of intentionality, of concern about what is or will be actual (rather than a preoccupation with reporting what is already past).

- The client is expressing what are manifestly matters of personal significance in the very moment of their expression.

Of course, not all of these attributes will be present each time a client talks of his concerns, but the more that are evident, the more likely it is that the client's account is authentically self-expressive and thus therapeutically meaningful.

In contrast, some attributes of client accounts suggest a lack of genuine presence and a subtle objectification (a "talking about" rather than a "talking out of").

- It tends to be illogical in the implications it draws. Conclusions are ill-related to their explanations or justifications.
- The client takes a stance of detached observation or explanation—commenting, as it were, on himself from a distance.
- Much effort is spent in describing others or circumstances in a "scene-setting" manner.
- The client's affective experiencing is accompanied by covert watching for the impact on the therapist.

Of course, our clients come to us and present us with mixtures of both valid and inauthentic self-descriptions. Indeed, it is in these very combinations that the roots of a client's distress and of the client's recovery reside. Our task is to winnow these to work through the negative and foster the contributions of the more positive.

Yet even that is an oversimplification, for so often some of the positive "signs" listed above are mixed with the negative, and much that confronts the therapist is not easily categorized.

WORKING TO INCREASE SUBJECTIVE PRESENCE

The therapist's task is to aid a client's own self-exploration and self-recognition. This means that those ways in which the client objectifies himself during the therapy hour are important resistances that must be addressed sooner or later. Therapeutic change often requires dealing with the client's *actual* life concerns and disclosing conscious and unconscious efforts to avoid confronting painful life issues. It is usual that an internal conflict is being acted out, and, once recognized, may thus be more available for therapeutic attention.

Following are some therapist ways of participating that are particularly helpful in forwarding the client's being able to present himself as genuinely as possible.

- Avoiding dependence on questioning. Questions subtly move the energy locus to or toward the questioner.[9]
- Deferring response to client questions while assuring the client that he is doing what needs to be done by continuing on his own.
- Calling attention at judiciously chosen points to such indications of the client's mood and implicit stance as physical posture, tone of voice, and facial expressions.
- Waiting patiently but expectantly when the client pauses, and, in general, adopting a posture that implies that the client is the primary speaker.
- Pointing back of the explicit to the underlying intention, emotion, or concurrent experiencing of the client as he or she is speaking (when the manner of the client's self-presentation makes it obvious that the client is becoming detached).

CONCLUSION

Humans are dwellers in two planes of experiencimg—the objective and the subjective. Yet much in our culture emphasizes the objective. In psychotherapy as it is here being described, we recognize the *actual* fact that only the subjective is directly experienced.

We can do much to aid our clients to gain better self-direction, less disappointment, and more fulfillment in their lives when we help them learn to recognize, attend to, and more fully actualize their inner living. Far from breeding greater isolation or self-centeredness (as some fear), this adaptive shift almost always will help clients relate more effectively and satisfyingly to others and to their external worlds.

NOTES

[1] It was Aldous Huxley who introduced the metaphor of our being amphibians, dwelling in the vast reaches of the subjective, the water world, and on the smaller, apparently solid land of the objective. To actualize our amphibian nature as completely as possible is to realize—that is, to recognize and to make real or actual—these potentials that life offers.

[2] The astonishing achievements of Stephen Hawking despite his extreme handicaps provide an exceptional example.

[3] See further discussion of this point in Chapter 11.

[4] There is a relatively small but growing counterforce to this preoccupation with the objective. Typified by the Waldorf Schools, these are islands of humane concern in which teachers are trained to be evocative of the subjective potentials of their students.

[5] In the late nineteenth century, the exciting developments in physical science came close to overwhelming the religious tradition for many of the educated. No longer did one cite the *Bible* to found one's argument. Empirical, objective modes were the new religion, and they were paying off wonderfully. This

mode of thought has persisted, produced a never-ending stream of physical miracles as it dominated twentieth-century knowledge.

Inevitably, the baby went with the bath water, and all subjectivity came to be scorned and neglected. Thus even today the charge of subjectivity is likely to be sufficient to have the thesis so labeled be discarded or at least given less concerned attention.

It is time to seek a more balanced and whole perspective, and happily that is beginning to occur. See a striking example in the writing of James Hillman (1995).

[6]See Bugental (1976, 1990).

[7]See A. Deikman (1990).

[8]Very rarely it may emerge from a deep and trust-based suggestion by the therapist. Overeager therapists sometimes try to teach clients one or more code terms to use in monitoring and communicating their subjective work. The results are likely to be confusion as the objective words of the therapist cannot reach the true subjective of the client.

[9]This may seem paradoxical, since the person responding to the question must speak. However, the impetus during a series of questions clearly moves to the questioner—as is likely to be manifest when the questioner does stop questioning and the answerer waits.

10 DEVELOPING AND TUNING THE THIRD EAR

Attention to the Implicit Discloses the Experiential

What should therapists listen to and watch for as they attend to their clients' self-presentations? The answer, of course, is problems, emotions, intentions, and as much of the client's inner processes as is revealed or can be inferred. But these words are so gross, so encompassing, that they offer little guidance.

Trying to become less abstract is an adventure in speculation, a voyage on a sea of possibilities so deep that no anchoring postulates can be sure of a firm bottom. In the following pages, I will hazard such an expedition. Readers must pick up the responsibility of continually adapting my speculations to their own way of working.

Long ago, theaters were converting from live action to the new "movies." Still, for some years, vaudeville continued in the time slot later taken by a second feature picture. There was a wide range in the types of performers trained animals, magicians, singers and choruses, dancers, and acrobats of various but always astonishing skills. One act that impressed me at an age when riding my two-wheeler was itself an achievement, as well as a source of freedom, was a performance by two unicyclists, a man and a woman.

Seated considerably above the wheel, they kept upright by continually pedaling and turning with their feet, thus leaving their hands free. Now began a pantomime of courtship. The man pretended to knock on the woman's door, she greeted him, they embraced—almost losing their balances, of course. Then, still pedaling, she enacted brewing a pot of coffee, using an actual coffeepot. Soon she brought her friend an empty cup, then filled it, went for cream and sugar, and added them. With his needs taken care of, she wheeled back to obtain a cup for herself and went through the same sequence. Usually, at some point, one of the couple would apparently lose track of the whereabouts of the other and thus add hilarious mistakes and near falls. Finally, once more steady, they clinked cups, raised them in salute, and then drank.

All through this routine, they were pedaling, sometimes in a leisurely fashion, and sometimes frantically as they appeared to be on the verge of falling, but they always somehow managed the tricky process of pouring, adding the flavorings, passing utensils and cups back and forth, and then drinking with much show of satisfaction.

I am reminded of this act when I think of the task confronting the client and the therapist. Each must maintain his or her balance while contributing to their conversation. Sometimes they seem to lose contact or one may be close to falling. Sometimes they meet in harmony. But always they are moving, never is there a time when either is unchanging. What passes between them also is continually changing as they are moving along endlessly.

FIVE ZONES FOR THERAPIST ATTENTION

As the therapist attends to the client's self-presentations, he is confronted with an overwhelming array of material, far too much to attempt to observe, assess, and incorporate all of it. At this point, some guides to therapist attention can be helpful.

The explicit content, of course, usually draws the therapist's initial concern. It is important, to be sure, but it itself has many facets. What is conveyed about the client's affective state, attitude toward the therapy and the therapist, intentions in the immediate moment and over the longer range? What is disclosed about the client's readiness to deal with more threatening material, the evolving relationship with the therapist, the client's hopefulness or despair about making needed changes, and so on, and so on?

Manifestly, we must always be selecting and attending more to some aspects than to others. Recognizing that no absolute rule is either possible or desirable, I suggest five categories that may guide our attention:

1. intentionality
2. coping
3. affectivity
4. relationships
5. expectations[1]

These—both explicitly and implicitly, consciously and unconsconsciously—may serve as touchstones for the therapist's concern. I will enlarge briefly on each.

Intentionality. This zone draws our attention to the forward thrust of a person's life. What does that person want, seek, yearn for, or resist, avoid, and withdraw from? In the therapeutic interview, the professional does well to keep alert to this dimension as it is explicitly announced, to be sure, but even more to how it is intrinsic to the client's account, life choices, and deepest goals. For convenience, we can think of intentionality as being composed of "intentions."

Coping. Coping with conflict, both intrapsychic and interpersonal, is an important testing ground of a personality. No life escapes conflicts; some of us seem to thrive on them while others apparently wilt, and most of us adapt with mixed success and failure. The individual's self-assessment is typically manifested in how that person responds when obstructed or challenged. Similarly, the readiness to accept or displace responsibility is here revealed. In our discussion, we think of coping as manifested through times of conflict.

Affectivity. This category interrelates with the other four experience zones, and for many new therapists it is the primary focus of attention. With experience, we learn that affect is always present in some form and to some degree, but that the meanings of such feelings are very much dependent on the other four elements. A setback that may lead to despair for one person who has few meaningful relationships may be taken in stride by another who is richly supported by a caring network to which she also contributes. The familiar and general term "feelings" provides a name for the experiences of this zone.

Relationships. As the comment about affectivity made explicit, one's relationship network may be crucially important in determining how life's inevitable setbacks are received. Similarly, conflicts borne alone can be very different than those which we confront with knowledge that we have dependable supporters. "Relations" is a familiar term for instances of relationship.

Expectations. I began this list with intentionality, the forward-looking aspect of our subjective life. I end it with expectations, a closely related notion but one that is an important ingredient in the individual's reality testing. What one conceives as the likely outcomes of the present situation are, of course, primary ingredients of that person's attitude about her life and efforts in her own behalf and those of others. To use a related term, we will speak of "anticipations."

REFINING THE THERAPIST'S SENSITIVITIES

Learning to receive and communicate meanings about the subjective is a difficult and demanding undertaking. The literal meaning of the words we use is essential, but also may be misleading.

Knowing that each living person is constantly changing in some measure and in some ways, how shall we grasp our clients' deeper meanings and how shall we communicate what we hope will be therapeutic?

The answer to this quandary is that we must look for patterns of client action rather than dwelling on particular instances. When a client reacts with intense anger to a perceived slight, it is important to take notice, of course. However, if this is an exceptional instance, it may be well simply to take notice and reserve focused attention for more typifying instances—while always being alert to other occasions of breakthrough impulses.

We cannot see patterns directly, but our moment-to-moment observations may permit us to infer them. We infer them from the client's emotionally invested accounts of incidents and from the client's self-presentation in the therapeutic room.

Patterns are in the therapist's conception, not in the client's mind. They are neither items of self-knowledge nor capsules of insight awaiting discovery by the therapist. By repeatedly pointing out patterns in the reported incidents, we can help clients become aware of them. Thus, although the therapist's insight cannot be transmitted intact to a client, it may lead that client to her own further insights.

The client may have some awareness of her own patterns, but these generally will not be identical with the patterns apparent to the therapist. In encouraging the client to explore subjectively whatever patterns she is aware of, the therapist will foster greater self-awareness and, therefore, increased choicefulness on a client's part. Concurrently, the therapist will increase his grasp of that client's self-and-world construct system[2] as it is disclosed through these patterns.

When we encourage a client to "stay with" a subjective theme or experience, it is with the intent of fostering the opening-out process that is *searching* and that will bring the client (and the therapist, in most instances) to a deeper and broader grasp of the matter. This may mean helping the client learn a truth about herself that she has not previously recognized, although that is not its chief (or only) value.

In the searching process, the elements of client patterns are made evident, and the possibilities for seeing life issues in fresh ways are brought out.

The key point is that incidents disclose patterns, but the patterns are themselves invisible and inferential.

Much of the foregoing is concerned with the client's self-presentation as a source of insight into the client's subjective makeup. This is basic to recognizing patterns and to knowing what to do when they are recognized.

REPRISE ON LIFE AS CHANGE

Life is a flame. It burns each moment, and while burning, it is changing. How, then, shall we work with life?

To grasp life and meaning, we assume constancy where it does not exist. We name experiences, emotions, and subjective states and assume that what is named is as enduring as its name. Human beings, blessed and cursed with consciousness—especially consciousness of their own being—think in terms of names, words, symbols. Thus, the words remaining the same, humans think of themselves, each other, and their worlds as constant or as only changing in manifest and obvious ways. That illusion costs us much in the way of our ability to understand and direct our own lives. Psychotherapy—especially a psychotherapy that intends to work with what is actual—must get behind the illusion of constancy and attempt to grasp[3] and work with unending flux. This changefulness is the true human condition.

Obviously, our task is to refine our receptivity not only to *what* the client says, but even more important, to *how* it is said. This calls for something a great deal more and other than what even excellent mechanical recording equipment can deliver.

Theodore Reik[4] gave us the useful metaphor of the "third ear," the ear that listens deeper and hears more than words. The path to hearing more than words calls for an orientation to attend to what is *immediate*, what is *actual in the living moment*—and usually that means what is implicit. The potential to develop these sensitivities and skills is latent in all human beings, but counselors and psychotherapists must become more than usually capable in these ways.

Those ways are not the esoteric flora of some mysterious realm accessible only to the initiated. They are ranges of meaning that reside in the implicit and are expressed through many channels—intonation, emphasis, continuity, tone, volume, facial expression, gesture, and all the subtleties of relationship.

Learning to be more sensitized to these cues is not learning a new language; rather it is extending the vocabulary of a language that each of us already knows. From long before we developed speech, we and all humans have had to develop at least minimal skills in understanding this primal language.[5] Even sooner, even as infants, we began to learn to express our needs and emotions in it. Basically what is involved in further developing one's sensitivity to and use of this third ear is simply the intent to expand one's attunement to more-than-verbal communication with those in one's life.

Just as learning to speak a foreign language meaningfully does not fully equate with learning to understand those who speak it, so learning to receive and understand the nonverbal is not the same as learning to express oneself to others in that way.

When traveling in a country whose language we don't know, we are likely to find ourselves in situations in which we need to communicate despite this handicap. Then we rely on gestures, pantomime, nonverbal sounds, and similar means to make our needs known and to understand the person with whom we are engaged.

Although that can be an interesting—even instructive—experience, we are likely also to be very aware of the constriction of our communication. So much we'd like to say, so much we'd like to hear, and so limited our encounter.

In the psychotherapy office, we have a potentially similar situation. We can collect information—the more objective, the more readily obtained—but much more is required than information alone. Now we need to be perceptive, receptive, and expressive in nonverbal modes.[6] Of course, even so, differences in understanding may occur, some of which may trip us up when we too hastily assume commonalty.

The languages of psychotherapy are both verbal and nonverbal. The third ear must be attuned to both.

Psychotherapy of the *actual* is work that must, to an important degree, be individually adapted to each client—indeed, to each client–therapist pairing and, ultimately, to each session of their work together.[7] Just as the client must learn how to avail herself of what therapy can offer, so must the therapist learn how to adapt his skills and draw on his knowledge to make them maximally helpful to the client.

The central implication of these requirements for the therapeutic partners is that the most impactful work will be concerned with what is occurring immediately in each moment in the client's experiencing. This has the further implication of reminding therapists that each client is in important ways unique.[8]

A point sometimes misunderstood: To say that each person is unique is not to deny that there are commonalties among all people. It is simply to affirm that how each person shapes his or her way of expressing those shared characteristics is a primary and particular datum for the psychotherapist's[9] attention.

While every person experiences motivations toward certain acts, relations, bodily states, and much else that make up the human experience, the manner or content of how each sets about satisfying those motivations is unique to each individual.[10] For example, while all are born with the potential for relationship, some make a great many acquaintances, friends, lovers, and companions of all kinds; most of us enjoy some relationships and yet only limitedly engage with others; and still others invert this impulse and become isolated, with only minimal human contact.

A VERBAL EXAMPLE OF A NONVERBAL PATTERN

Many in our culture are reluctant to speak about significant (and especially personal) matters in direct, unqualified fashion. Instead, there is much use of "verbal insulation": "It seems. . . . Perhaps. . . . I suppose. . . . " and "kinda. . . . " are familiar examples. These sorts of verbal excelsior are abundant in many conversations. In psychotherapy, such obfuscation of one's experience is counterproductive, and the therapist often needs to direct attention to it as soon as the alliance and context will support doing so.

When the therapist begins pointing to this subtle but important intrusion on the work, an appropriate opportunity for teaching the client more about how to use the therapeutic opportunity is provided.

CL-1: I think I've always wanted to be a doctor. It just seems like I might make a good one, you know?

TH-1: You sound tentative.

CL-2: No. No, I really do kinda feel that way.

TH-2: Even that's only "kinda."

CL-3: Oh! Oh, I didn't mean I had any doubts about it. I guess I've thought about that goal for at least ten years now.

TH-3: And even now it's a "guess."

CL-4: Oh, did I say "guess"? (*Laughs.*) Well, I guess I. . . . Oh, I did it again, didn't I? It's just a habit I've gotten into. I don't think it's important.

TH-4: It must be important to you some way since you use these qualifiers so much.

CL-5: Well, maybe so, but I can't see how or why.

TH-5: You said that so quickly that I didn't get any sense of your having checked it out.

CL-6: (*Chuckle.*) Well, I hardly need to take time on something as dumb as that, do I?

TH-6: Does it interest you?

CL-7: Not really. (*Pauses, waits, watching the silent therapist expec-*

tantly.) Well yes, in a way. Why do you think I do it?

TH-7: I don't really know, but I notice that it makes whatever you say"sort of" or "kinda" vague and lets you avoid being pinned down.

CL-8: Huh! Yeah, I can see that. I guess it does, doesn't it?

TH-8: There it is again!

CL-9: I'll be damned! You think there's any reason for me to do that so much? I mean, I don't know whether it's worth using our time on, but perhaps it might be. Oh! (*Recognizes the "might."*) Oh, I don't know. (*Disgustedly.*)

And so the work goes forward. The client is a bit confused about the therapist's paying so much attention to what seems a very trivial matter. If, however, the therapist returns to this pattern fairly frequently, there is apt to come a time when the client makes an effort to reduce dependence on such verbal sawdust.

CL-11: You know, I've been thinking about all those "kinda's, sorta's," and "guesses" that I seem to use all the time, and I kinda . . . Imean, I *want* to give them up . . . at least for a while.

TH-11: (*Smiling.*) Sounds like you just used a variation on the same theme.

CL-12: (*Ruefully.*) Yeah, it does. Damn it, I mean it: I'm sick and tired of sounding so wishy-washy. (*Pauses, reflecting.*) You know, I almost said "I think"! Geez!

TH-12: That need to qualify everything really has hold of you, doesn't it? It's likely it's more than just a bad speech habit. What do you think?

CL-13: (*Soberly.*) Yeah, I guess so. Oh, damn it!

TH-13: It annoys you that somehow you persist in being so indefinite.

CL-14: Yes. (*Pause.*) But it annoys me even more that you keep making a big thing out of it and so it seems like we don't get on with my therapeutic work.

TH-14: It's hard for you to see any connection between your need to qualify whatever you say and what you think of as your "therapeutic work."

CL-15: Well, no. . . . I mean, probably there is some, but I . . . don't . . . I mean, I can't. . . . (*He pauses, looks exasperated.*)

TH-15: What's happening right now?

CL-16: (*Angrily.*) Oh hell! Yes, I suppose I can . . . I mean. . . . I mean, it's happening right now, and I want to be definite with you, and. . . . I mean, I thought I knew this was. . . .

TH-16: Mmmmm?

CL-17: I think I see. . . . Dammit! I *do* see how it's part of why I'm here. There! Are you satisfied now?

TH-17: Are you?

CL-18: Yes. I mean, no. (*Pause, miserable.*) How the hell should I know? I don't know anything for sure about myself!

This example has been quite simplified and condensed, of course, and many other productive therapeutic tasks could well be going on throughout the time synopsized here. This sort of work is important as it does several things at the same time:

- It begins to teach the client that the therapist will be paying attention, not just to the client's words, but to the many ways the client wittingly and unwittingly presents himself and uses the therapeutic opportunity.
- It encourages the client to listen to himself in a new way and one that will be important throughout the therapeutic course.
- It evokes the client's concern to be active in bringing about changes in his life—listening to himself with his own "third ear."

UNDERLYING SOURCES OF IMPLICIT PATTERNS

Attention to such seemingly trivial matters as the client's hesitation to speak definitively as in the example above usually leads to other subjective concerns that are by no means trivial. Here is an abridged example.

CL-21: After our last session I was thinking about what we were talking about, and I got to remembering what a bitch of a time I had actually proposing to my wife. It took her demanding that I "put up or shut up" to get me to do it. You know, it seems that maybe I tend to be overly cautious about things.

TH-21: "Maybe. . . . "

CL-22: Yeah, maybe. I don't know for sure. But sometimes it sure seems that way.

TH-22: Uh-huh. (*Pause.*) "Sure" but "maybe" and "seems."

CL-23: Oh, damn! I don't sound sure, do I? But the funny thing is that I'm really getting to see how I always sort of keep my fingers crossed. Gotta have an escape hatch, you know.

TH-23: It's important to you not to get pinned down, huh?

CL-24: Yeah, I guess so. Oh damn it! I don't "guess so." I know damned well that's so. Ugh! It makes me mad to sound so vague, and I really wish I would get off it.

TH-24: Do you think you will?

CL-25: I don't know. (*Complaining tone.*) Oh! That's the same damned thing, isn't it? But, you know, I really do get kinda antsy when I feel like I have to say something flat out that way.

TH-25: You still haven't said it.

CL-26: Well, I . . . (*Slight pause, forceful voice.*) I am going to stop all this vague shit. (*Pause.*) At least, I'm going to try to stop it.

TH-26: (*Silent, looking at client intently.*)

CL-27: I even pulled that back some, didn't I? (*Pause.*) I can't believe how uneasy I feel trying to just say it straight and letting it stand. (*Pause.*) I want to try to figure out why I'm that way, but I know that that's simply a way to avoid feeling like I do right now. (*Another pause.*) Oh, damn! You wouldn't believe how much I want to take back what I said.

TH-27: What did you say?

CL-28: (*Forceful voice, erect posture.*) I'm going to stop always qualifying everything I say. (*Pauses, reflects.*)

Of course, this piece of the work neither ends the client's tendency to qualify excessively nor works through the underlying hesitation to commit in his life that is its root. Yet the struggle the client goes through in the room is essential to those further steps. And it is likely to go more readily than would be the case were an effort made to explore the biographical roots of this pattern.

For our purposes here, it is apparent how the therapist's attention not only to the words (the qualifiers) but to the underlying protective purpose they served was the product of third-ear listening. As the client gradually moves to the recognition of his dependence on this pattern, the therapist's task is to sense how much to press[11] and how to keep the confrontation supportive but persistent. That is accomplished through the use of silence (TH-26 is most evident, but the waiting pace throughout was important) and quiet reconfrontation (especially in TH-24 and 25). Crucially important also, but less explicit, is the quiet—internal and external—presence of the therapist and his clear support of the client's doing his own work (CL-24 through 28).

It is important to recognize that this work is work with the *resistance,* and that what is being resisted is not the therapy or the therapist, but self-confrontation.

OTHER RESISTANCE PATTERNS

Our examples thus far have been focused on the client's resistance to making definitive personal statements. Among educated clients this is a fairly frequent pattern—perhaps in some part because proper academic and scientific writing often eschews definitive statements, except for demonstrated facts. It is also—as the client comes to recognize—a way of avoiding being "caught" or pinned down and, implicitly, having to defend a statement or position.

Responses 14 through 18 demonstrate how the client may catch himself if he is helped to be aware in each moment of just what it is he is manifesting, as well as what it is he is saying.

STRATEGIC SEQUENCE: A SUGGESTION

It is often useful to develop work such as that illustrated in a paced sequence of interventions. Thus the first phase would consist of repeated identifications of a frequent resistance pattern (e.g., avoiding a definitive statement). When this has continued for a while and the client has become aware of it (and, desirably, concerned about it), then it is productive to find a simple key word or phrase to remind the client of the pattern. (Thus the therapist in the example would repeat only the key word—e.g., "maybe.")

Meanwhile the therapist begins to teach that the pattern is motivated (7 and 12). Most clients will do one or both of two things at this point: they may begin to speculate about the need for the pattern, and/or they may question the importance of concern with it (6, 9). Therapists should recognize that both of these responses are, in essence, further layers of the resistance. This recognition can only come when the therapist has developed an appreciation for the client's process and needs. Then it is likely to be well timed and helpful.

SIMILAR RESISTANCE PATTERNS

The argumentative client who rejects attention to a pattern such as that we're considering here presents an added and somewhat more aggressive resistance layer. Similarly, the client who makes light of such interventions is using apparent humor as an avoidance. Both may, wittingly or not, be attempting to move the locus of the work from the client's own inner processes to the relation with the therapist. The unwary therapist may find the therapy sidetracked for some time while this diversion is dealt with and may become himself caught in extensive and fruitless justifying and persuading.

A generally similar but more difficult pattern is that presented by the hostile, belittling client. These ways of responding often portray a person who feels so alienated that she despairs of making positive relations and turns to attack as a first or early means of relating. The therapist needs to handle such situations with discrimination. Careful reflection on the impact of this client's responses often reveals the seemingly angry client is not genuinely angry at the therapist but simply has given up hope of ever winning genuine understanding or support.

In other instances, angry client responses may arise when the client only feels really seen when there is strength and persistence in therapist's responses.

The presence of anger in the exchanges between client and therapist signals an important juncture. At such times, there is, of course, the possibility of a disruption of the alliance. But there is also an opportunity for a deepening and strengthening of the bond between them.

The therapist needs to recognize that there are clients who only feel really seen when the therapist manifests strength and persistence in confronting them. Even with such a person, however, the therapist should not pretend to have feelings she does not truly have. But rarely is that a problem. Clients who need to experience anger to feel genuinely seen are likely to be provocative. Yet, surprisingly, at times they may express hurt and resentment when their own anger is responded to in kind.

Obviously, it is essential for the therapist to maintain her own centeredness, to proceed with discipline and judgment. This is a demanding event. Here is a fictional and greatly condensed illustration of
how this might play out.

CL-51: You're always telling me that I'm doing something wrong.
(*Voice rising.*) I think you are wrong, and you just won't admit it.
When I tell you about how hurt I was, you're suppposed to help
me feel beter; instead you pick on me some more! (*Face red and
angry.*) Well, I just won't stand for it anymore!

TH-51: You feel really hurt when I don't accept that you had no part
in bringing about that scene. Well, I still don't buy that you're helpless, and. . . .

CL-52: (*Interrupting.*) There you go again! I'm always doing something wrong, and you. . . .

TH-52: (*Speaking quickly and firmly when client pauses.*) Hold on a
minute, Helen. I know you're mad right now, and I'm not so cool
myself, but that's all right. We're doing what we need to do and
doing it in the only way we can do it.

CL-53: You mean you're supposed to be mad at me? I don't think. . . .

TH-53: (*Forcibly.*) You're worth it!

CL-54: (*Angry tone.*) Well, I. . . . (*Stops, registers what therapist has
just said.*) What did you say?

TH-54: I said you were worth our getting angry about. This isn't some
detached, academic matter. Your way of being alive is what's involved.

CL-55: (*Startled, anger abated.*) I don't. . . . I didn't. . . . I thought
you were mad at me.

TH-55: I was. I was mad at how you sell yourself short. You don't
need to be such a pushover for such trivial incidents as you let set
you off all the time.

And so the work goes forward.

Sometimes related patterns can also be manifested by clients with
quite different motivations, so the therapist must proceed cautiously

until some further understanding of the client's need to oppose is attained. The client who minimalizes may be angry, but just as often may be someone who feels despairing of anyone ever fully understanding his or her needs. Sadly, this resistance pattern may lead to therapist actions that serve to confirm this expectation.

These varied instances do not by any means exhaust the range of client responses when anger is triggered—nor, of course, does this description cover all possible therapist reactions.

Finally, there are two other patterns that may be encountered and that may have quite diverse motivations: the dependent client and the client who relies on flattering and complimenting the therapist excessively (but, usually, shows little grasp or use of what the therapist offers).

With either of these patterns, consistent feedback of the pattern usually results in the client's bringing forth a secondary layer of the resistance, which is likely to take one of the forms described.

THE BOTTOM LINE: IN-THE-MOMENT EXPERIENCING

Impactful therapist interventions are those that are addressed to the immediate experiencing of the client—that is, the *actual*. In contrast, too often psychotherapy becomes a "who dun it" exercise in which the client and therapist collect clues and compound information in an effort to *understand* what the client's symptoms or problems express and how they came into being. When this happens, the work becomes cut off from what is *actual*, and it may lose its power to produce genuine and lasting changes in the client's living.

It is hard to overemphasize the necessity—yet difficulty for many therapists—to recognize and focus on what the client is experiencing and to let information assume the secondary role of being the form but not the substance of the client's immediate living.

CONCLUSION

The truth is that psychotherapy is damned hard work. It is so because it requires us to go beyond the relative simplicity of working with explicit issues, working out reasonable interpretations, and teaching obvious explanations.

A psychotherapy of the *actual* must confront the endless ambiguity of human existence, the shading of meaning and emotion that words can only incompletely convey, the ambivalences aroused by our addressing the very life structures upon which the client has come to depend, and our own and the client's emotional bond, which we both know must ultimately be dissolved.

NOTES

[1]After preparing these comments, I discovered, to my pleasure, that the initial letters provided a useful acronym.

[2]See Chapter Seven.

[3]This effort is beset with contradictions: I have the intention of getting back of my client's despair in this moment, and so I address her underlying wish to have less pain in her life. I take note of the despair and recall the wish as I say to her, "You're having a lot of pain just as you're trying to change your life." In this way, I acknowledge both aspects of her being in the room. I do not address her particular report of a rebuff by a friend or recall her recovery from a previous painful episode. Those particular events are transitory, but the struggle and the wish are processes and thus are, to some extent, less bound to a particular time. The principle is: *Give priority attention to process while attending to incident.*

[4]Theodore Reik (1949).

[5]See J. C. Pierce (1985).

[6]Vaughan, Frances (1979). *Awakening Intuition.* New York: Anchor

[7]And still we have only sketched the broad outlines of the continually shifting human situation in which we choose to work. When we focus on a particular

client, we see that the client is very different on different days or in different circumstances. Bill Smith at intake impressed the interviewer with his reserve, his balanced way of describing his life, and his lack of urgency for treatment. Bill Smith in his first actual therapeutic interview became acutely depressed, and the therapist was concerned to get a suicide contract before allowing Bill to leave her office. On his third interview, Bill became mute and hospitalization was decided upon. At the hospital, Bill. . . .

And so the story goes. Change, constant change. The unfinished sentence, "At the hospital, Bill. . . . " Bill what? Committed suicide? Made an astonishing recovery?

[8]It is no surprise to recognize that engagements in the consulting room are as varied as the weather. A significant parallel! Chaos theory teaches us that the only way to describe (not predict) weather patterns is by repeatedly including the actual data from one period in the computations for the next, thus ensuring continual variation in any derived pattern. I am far from being qualified to speak at any length whatsoever about this exciting new conceptual paradigm, but the little I do grasp seems remarkably appropriate to the understanding of human actions and experience.

[9]It is well to pause to recognize that it is not only our clients or patients who are continually different, but we, the therapists, each presents a spectrum of differences as well. Even graduates of the same training program who profess adherence to the same values and postulates are far from identical in manner, relating, dependence on formal learning, or ways of working with patients. Further, any one of us—despite efforts to the contrary—will inevitably and continually vary in our own presence, accessibility, expressiveness, and personal relationships—from client to client, from day to day.

[10]Of course, our diagnostic categories attempt to deal with these differences and to highlight commonalties within identified groupings. Yet but a little clinical experience soon teaches how different are two patients who carry the same formal diagnoses.

[11]See Chapter Four of *The Art of the Psychotherapist* (Bugental, 1987).

11

THE RIVER THAT IS THE SUBJECTIVE

*Much of Our Inner Living Is Important but
Neglected*

Our culture has put great emphasis on the explicit, the overt, and the objective. This tendency has been a by-product of the astonishing and literally world-changing achievements in the physical sciences in the twentieth century. Now, as that remarkable period is entering a time of transition, we need to recognize the costs it has exacted: the individual person has become a unit in mass statistics, an interchangeable buyer and consumer, a target for advertising and propaganda, and an unexceptional instance in designing "human service" programs, campaigns, and agencies.

And the tragedy is that often even to himself the individual person is scarcely unique. What individuality survives is almost entirely in the subjective—a subjective manipulated or scorned by mass marketing, broad social movements, and, tragically, even much psychology and psychotherapeutic theory and practice.

Thus the subjective, the ultimate home of each individual, is threatened but never destroyed, is the focus of manipulative efforts but never completely subverted, and is the basis for our hope for therapeutic change.

Just what is the subjective realm? Fundamentally, it is the true psychological realm. It is the rich, many dimensioned, constantly

185

evolving, and fertile inner world that is private to each of us, but which is also the basis of whatever we share deeply among ourselves. It is the chief site of whatever lasting changes psychotherapy may achieve.

Within each of us is a river, a continually flowing process, the conscious aspect of which we call awareness or consciousness. Viewed in larger context, this is our subjectivity.

CLINICAL OBSERVATIONS ABOUT OUR SUBJECTIVITY

The psychotherapy that I practiced for a half-century provided me with powerful lessons about how crucially important to anyone's life is one's inner experiencing. However, one need not be a therapist or a client of a therapist to grasp the meaning I'm going to describe here. It is applicable to every life.[1]

Here is the way it is: When a new person comes to my office for the first time, I am confronted with mystery—limitless mystery. Moreover, I know that three years and 300 interviews later, when that person bids me a final good-bye, there will still be much that I will never know about the client and his life.

All of our professional skills and humane empathy fall back before the immensity of any one person's life. This is especially so when we consider each person's subjective living. Each is a planet, which we can only see at a distance, and which we can never fully explore.

Illustrating this point is a letter I received from an experienced psychotherapist who had volunteered to be interviewed by me in front of a class of therapists. Shortly after our conversation, she borrowed the videotape of our talk. After viewing it, she wrote to me of this experience:

> *I was fascinated watching the tape, observing my own experience from the position of an outsider. I was aware of how little*

*access we have as therapists to what is actually occurring within,
so many twists and turns of subtle emotional surges, so many
images to follow in my imagination, in my recollection of how
it was for me. Yet what a relatively obscure portion of that is
truly accessible to the therapist. It reinforces in a different way
how much we as therapists need to trust and encourage the
client to do her own work.*

The writer of this letter manifests a courageous and matured perspective. Too many therapists become convinced that they know all
they need to know about their clients—and, therefore, they know
what the clients should do with their lives. Having such an illusion
reveals someone with a dangerously shrunken view of human nature.

Each of us is, in some measure, a mystery to each other person
with whom we interact. Mothers, despite popular sentiment, many
times do not know their children fully—to their frustration, and,
often to the children's relief. Lovers eager to gobble up everything
pertaining to their adored ones still are limited by themselves and
by the mystery remaining in even the most naked of relations.
Biographers soon realize that there are serious holes in their grasps
of their subjects, and sometimes resort to fiction to remedy the
story, and at other times confess their limitations, giving their crit-
ics fodder.

And so it is. The fact remains that each person is—at least in
some important measure—a mystery to every other person, whether
therapist, spouse, lover, parent, child, sibling, or whatever. We are
mysteries because each of us quite literally dwells in a separate
world. Consciously or not, each lives most truly and fully in his
inner and irrevocably private (subjective) world. While our separate
worlds have much in common and rich communication and sharing
are possible among them, in important ways, they also each remain
unique.

Yet there is a paradox here: Our commonalties are mostly objective, our individualities are principally subjective, and yet deeper in

the subjective there resides a more subtle connectedness among all persons, perhaps even all life.

The mystery that is each person adds interest to a relation, frustrates and tantalizes lovers, humbles therapists, and may be crucially important when we encounter it in another person. It was just such mystery that killed my friend, a psychiatrist: A patient of his called him to his office door. When my friend started to greet the visitor, the patient shot my friend dead.

Our professional skills cannot penetrate all mystery and thus we cannot count on them to save us from the disaster that may issue from that mystery. Yet it is from that same depth that unexpected strength and understanding may emerge.

I am not using fanciful language when I write of "mystery." I am recognizing the deeper nature of each person, that which no words can fully capture. Yet each of us, if we learn truly to listen, can intuit it within ourselves and can sense it in those with whom we are in some measure of genuine relationship. Nor does that only hold true with positive relations. Conflictful bonds can also make us aware of unfathomable depths in an opponent.

It is this mystery that those bound to an objectivist perspective reject as superficial; that manipulative therapists, teachers, and other authorities are likely to dismiss as irrelevant. Even if they have some sense of the innerness of those with whom they are engaged, they insist that they can't take the time to worry about it, that it is too variable to matter, and—if they're candid—that they really don't know what to do about it anyway.

THE CONTENTS OF THE SUBJECTIVE

To speak of "contents" of the subjective is to use a clumsy fiction, a way of bringing together a variety of human functions that are importantly related and yet in everyday experience often seem separate. That is useful; what is not useful is to see the subjective as some kind of container separate from what it contains. Perhaps one can think of the "elements" or "ingredients" of the subjective as another way of designating this important cluster of our inner activities.

In looking at such a list as is shown in Table 11.1, it is important to keep in mind two characteristics of the subjective: (1) The range of the subjective is, effectively, infinite; and (2) subjective awareness—especially when we attempt to capture it in explicit words—is often characterized by ambiguity, incompleteness, and uncertainty rather than by the seeming precision of the objective.

An Incomplete List of Subjective "Contents" or "Elements"

It will be evident that this list is incomplete and that little effort has been made to organize it. This is partly because categorizations of inner experiencing may do as much to obscure as to reveal the richness of the inner realm. Indeed, many standardized (and "objective") questionnaires and tests have tried to insist that important human experiences be forced to fit a very limited array[2] of possibilities. The consequence has been a loss of validity of results obtained from such Procrustean distortions. It is a demanding but important challenge to attempt to preserve subjective experiencing in its true qualities while communicating about such experiences so that different people can recognize some degree of sharedness.

TABLE 11.1

Partial Listing of Ingredients of the Subjective

The general listings are followed by examples.

- The self-and-world construct system
- Intentionality: wanting, wishing, willing, intending
- Interpretations of perceptions: meanings
- Forward looking: anticipations, apprehensions, fears, hopes
- Learning: memories, reminiscences
- Affiliative emotions: joy, liking, pride, self-esteem
- Oppositional emotions: anger, antagonism, hostility
- Stress: anxiety, pain, distress
- Disappointment: shame, guilt, fear, regret, blame
- Imagination: creativity, innovation, adaptation
- Relationships: love, friendship, parenting, companionship
- Eroticism: sensuality, sexuality, sadism-masochism
- Competition: lust, envy, greed, playfulness
- Betrayal: treachery, distortion, seduction
- Play: humor, amusement, entertainment
- Drive: ambition, earnestness, competition
- Dedication: faith, steadfastness, loyalty

Another evident implication of this list is that the qualities that make a person attractive or despicable, productive or inert, are these subjective characteristics.

If one reflects on the experience of attending to one's inner process, this *river*, it will be apparent that it usually takes at least a brief instant to translate into words what one discovers going on there. This is so because the subjective is prereflective, preverbal, preobjective. In fact, it is much larger than can ever be put into words. Attempting to do so requires that we radically reduce—and often distort—what we can sense is immeasurably larger.

Intentionality

A major aspect of our subjectivity is intentionality, the capacity to have wishes, wants, and purposes and to carry them through or to change or even relinquish them. Intention is the operative concept in self-direction. Implicitly, most therapists seek to enlist clients' intentionality to help in the discovery of what truly matters to them, to reexamine cherished attachments, or to explore possible courses of action.[3]

These thoughts may remind us of the recognition[4] that in all of these undertakings we are working with the most powerful force in our known world: *human subjectivity and its thrust, which we name intentionality.*

If the notion of intentionality being the most powerful force seems exaggerated, a reexamination of one's understanding of this power is in order. Our known world is the world we know because of human intentionality. There is no other. The mode of our being conscious of anything is how we constitute world. It is the world revealed by consciousness and structured and interpreted by our subjectivity. What we can do with, or in, the "world out there" is limited by our subjective awareness and intentions. Human intentionality continually strives to master all other forces and powers—nonhuman as well as human. Indeed, *power* is the ultimate currency or faith of our world, as Hillman so eloquently elaborates.[5]

Our lives are carried forward on the river of subjectivity. Indeed, as we have seen, our lives *are* our subjectivity. If we let ourselves become completely caught up in the world of objectivity, we come to treat ourselves as objects, as things. When that happens, we become powerless meaningfully and satisfyingly to direct our own actions and experiences.

Making humans into objects is the black plague of our time, literally crippling, and sometimes actually killing, vast numbers of people who are unable to be self-aware and self-directing because they treat themselves or are treated by others as objects.

Objects have no power. They are moved solely from the outside. A battery-operated toy or a space vehicle must have its directions and maintenance from a living consciousness. Sometimes that consciousness is much more aware of the *thing's* needs and potentials than it is of its own!

So here it is directly in front of us—no, directly within us—even right now as I write and (a different) right now as you read. Here it is, one of the most profound of all the mysteries with which we are confronted: our own subjectivity. How little we know its nature, its limits and powers, its transformations and ultimate potentials! How readily we write and read such sentences as the last half-dozen and then move casually on to the next matter! That at times we allow ourselves to become unaware *things* needs no further demonstration.

Subjective "Contents" Differ from Objective

The "contents" of the subjective are in important ways radically different from the contents of a file cabinet or of a computer disk. Here are some of those differences.

- The "contents" carried on the river of our subjectivity have many layers of meaning, shifting and multiple images, and ranging emotions that come into focus, then fade, and disappear or may return in changed form. These inner processes express much that is unavailable to usual consciousness. Of course, this is true whether we are awake or asleep—although we are less accustomed to recognizing how much of waking consciousness partakes of these same qualities that are familiar in dreaming.
- The most important of these conscious and unconscious contents have to do with what we think/feel really matters in our lives, that is, our *concerns.*[6] As we saw in Chapter Four, *concern* is a name for a pattern of feeling and think-

ing about some matter that we believe may make a significant difference in our lives—either favorably or unfavorably. Our ability to access our concern and then effectively to act on it is much impaired when we make objects of ourselves or allow ourselves to be made into objects.

- Only a small part of such "contents" exists in verbal form. Instead, they are in pre- and transverbal constellations of cognitive, affective, and intentional elements, which are continuously flowing and interacting.

- These constellations do not have clear boundaries but "bleed into" each other and are influenced by input from the outside so that the possible combinations and permutations are very likely infinite. It is this very potential of the subjective that constitutes creativity of all kinds. This is an instance of the incessant activity of the subjective, which we term *searching*.

- The contents of the subjective may be infinitely "opened out" to bring into awareness materials not previously recognized as being related to the initial entry point.[7] As we focus on some life issue while being open to the ranging of our subjectivity, we find new combinations, fresh possibilities, and unexpected solutions.

Psychiatrist Roger Walsh has written how he discovered his own inner process and its importance to him: "I began to perceive more clearly a constant flux of visual images. . . . These images exquisitely symbolized what I was feeling and experiencing in each moment. Here was a previously unsuspected gold mine of information about myself and the meaning of my experiences."[8]

Subjective Dynamics

There is no "how-to" in the subjective: This is a point too often unrecognized by those who work with the subjective. As a result, many who seek to be helpful are likely to end up frustrated. Then they rely on verbally explicit instructions or other dubious substitutes. Explicitly specifiable procedures are only possible in the objective realm (or to the extent that subjective material has been *reduced* to objective or explicit form)—"You need to get some new friends," or "Quit expecting miracles," or "I'll tell you what to say to him the next time."

What this means is that there is no valid way to answer such questions as, "How can I decide what I really want to do?" "How can I discover what made me so upset yesterday?" "How can I get deeper into myself?" We can provide directions for turning on a machine, for following a street route, or for looking up a word in a dictionary, but no similar step-by-step recipe can be detailed for a person's questions about inner processes.

Intention is the source or basis of our subjective activity. While we cannot give "how-to" answers, we can help those who ask them to explore their aware and unaware impulses in relation to whatever matter concerns them at that time. Saying it differently, if one's subjective intention is single, unconflicted, and energized, one will find oneself already carrying out the desired subjective process. The difficulty in doing so is usually a subjective conflict or a lack of focused concern or feelings[9]—each of those in itself an appropriate focal point for further searching.

It is important to recognize that this is very different than the kind of mindless yielding to impulse with which it is sometimes confused. It is, rather, a mindful and demanding confrontation with one's own intents and values. Only when hindering and conflicting impulses are confronted and worked through can one move into action with the immediacy of focused subjectivity.

Creativity and the Subjective

In recognizing the endless combinations of subjective contents that are possible and that the search process is likely to explore, the point was made above that this is the source of creativity. The conclusion might be drawn from this that a high-powered computer could then be as "creative" (or more so) as any human, for surely such a computer could make all possible matching more thoroughly and much more rapidly.

So far, so good. But which matchings will prove creative? Enter the subjective? Not yet. Humans instruct their computers to look for matchings that meet certain specifications. And where do those specifications come from? They come from prior experiences, whether mechanical or human, but "experiences" at some point, not just printouts.

The infinitude of possible matchings is not the issue here. It might explain a breakthrough in physical (objective) problems, but it would scarcely account for Mozart's Symphony No. 40 or Shakespeare's *Hamlet* or their current equivalents.

But there is still a question hidden here. Are all eventually recognized creative products the result of blind matchings of this kind or are there some crucial elements in some cases—elements that come from the subjective of the creative person?

To come at this from a different angle, consider that a newborn infant brings into our familiar, objective world an incredible range of potentialities. But these are only potentialities. Actualization of all-that-could-be is impossible. What-will-be is selected from the tremendous storehouse of the possible by many influences[10]—the parents of the infant, other family members, playmates and schools, the culture of which that family is a part, the period of history, the economic conditions prevailing during the emerging person's life, and, inevitably, blind chance.

And by the infant, the child, the person himself.

What does that mean? It means that the person is something more than the sum of heredity, plus environmental influences of many kinds. That's nonsense, say the mechanomorphs. Where would that something more come from, wonders conventional wisdom.

Therein lies a betrayal. We have no problem accepting that many external influences mold the plasticity of the new infant. We are stopped when we say there is anything within the infant that participates in this fateful process.

This is the stance of those who see humans in the image of the machine. Only that which is put in it from the outside in some manner is significant, is even imaginable, they insist. They fall silent or talk in circles when asked to account for an Einstein, a Beethoven, a Whitman, a Martin Luther King, a Sun Yat Sen, a Steve Jobs, or anyone else who has come from the ranks of humanity to manifest unusual power in any form.

It is a mystery—one of the many mysteries in which we live. How to account for our individual differences, which are as multiple and as marked as our commonalties.

The simple answer is that we don't know. But we won't get any closer to understanding them when our energies are devoted to insisting on an empty-container view of humans. That sort of superstition has always tried to stop explorations of the unknown.

Subjectivity and the World Macroproblems

The same denial keeps us from realizing that all the world macroproblems are, at root, problems of the subjective. They pose questions of human intention, motivation, values. It's time for the human sciences to address the subjective; accept that knowledge in that realm is always ambiguous, incomplete, and uncertain[11]; and still proceed with the tasks of saving our world. We can make *observations* but we cannot discover eternal *laws*.

Indeed, even the most objective of sciences, astronomy, is teaching us that we can never truly see what is "out there," that always we see only ourselves. Whatever the subtlety of our instruments, however many intervening devices we introduce between ourselves and the objective world, we still are limited to what our sensory apparatus can discern and our minds can fathom, that is, to the subjective.

Our culture places a high subjective value on objectivity. We believe that the many wonders of physical science and technology demonstrate that quality's excellence and productivity. As we do so, we overlook the array of personal qualities that are equally manifested by those achievements.

Without the vision, the determination to go past defeats, the willingness to attempt the seemingly impossible, and the many personal qualities of the scientists and technicians who bring these marvels to us, they would not exist.

A major subjective element in all creativity is the choice to attend to one's own inner processes—call them hunches or intuitions, persistence, even "playing with" ideas and possibilities.

For many new psychotherapy clients, and indeed for many therapists, the expectation is that information will be collected, organized, then interpreted and fed back—thus to produce the desired outcome. This pattern only can be used effectively with short-term work, with issues that are largely on the conscious level, and with limited goals.

Many, if not most, of the issues that bring people to psychotherapy are products of multiple and subtle influences affecting the individual over the course of life. It is unlikely that any collection of information about a client could ever approach completeness. Moreover, when the influence of emotional blocking is factored in, what is readily (objectively) available is almost always distorted, as well as incomplete.

CONCLUSION

Once the human was deemed the center of the universe. The gods dwelt among us, intruded into our lives, envied our mortality. Heroes and heroines moved through the world in pride, fought great battles, won glorious victories, died in terrible tragedies. Humankind was splendid in its own eyes (even as the average man and woman lived brutish lives).

Now much has changed. Expelled from the Eden of the center of the universe, we have repeatedly let ourselves be pushed toward the edge of the drama of the cosmos. Some of us seem to take a strange pleasure in recording our meanness and inconsequentiality. It is time to recall Pascal's words (1670):

> It is dangerous to show [humans] too often that [they are] equal to beasts, without showing [them their] greatness. It is also dangerous to show [them] too frequently [their] greatness without [their] baseness. It is yet more dangerous to leave [them] ignorant of both. But it is very desirable to show [them] the two together.

We live in a time of great pressures to make ourselves into objects, things. Not only mainstream human science, but many social and cultural influences press upon us to yield up our subjectivity, to deny our inner sovereignty, to go along with the popular and approved trend[12]—in Pascal's terms, to yield to our baseness and become but beasts. To do so is to betray our heritage, our potential, our very nature, and our species' future.

Tragically, much of psychology and psychiatry, which should form our first line of defense against objectification, has become some of the most persistent influences demeaning human nature. For too many psychotherapists, "subjective" is equivalent to "error." This equation derives, at least in part, from late-eighteenth-century efforts (e.g., Wundt, Fechner) to make the subjective objective. Then the main intent was to extricate psychology from philosophy and religion; subjectivity was not valued for itself.

Today we are coming back to philosophy. Concern with the spiritual is also becoming intellectually respectable after long being abandoned to the dubious mercies of the naive.

What must be recognized (but is usually suppressed) is that the so-called objective is irrevocably a selection from the universe of the possible—*a selection made by subjective considerations.* This is not a popular recognition in many precincts and is greeted with much subjective intensity.[13]

At long last, we appear to be coming home to our own nature, to our own promise.

NOTES

[1]And most certainly my own.

[2]One is tempted to say "straitjacket."

[3]Bugental (1987, Chapter 11).

[4]In Chapter Nine.

[5]See Hillman (1995).

[6]Bugental (1987, Chapter 12).

[7]This is, of course, the basis of Freud's *free association,* of Gendlin's *focusing* (1978), of Wellwood's *unfolding* (1982), and of what I prefer to call *searching* (1978, 1987).

[8]Walsh (1976).

[9]This is a point on which many otherwise empathic and subjectivity-oriented therapists will disagree with me. I insist that any gains made from giving clients instructions about "how to" work in the subjective—"just quit worrying and get busy on something positive," "you keep coming back to that same theme again and again; it's time you went on to something else"—will prove to be short term and at the cost of the client's sense of autonomy and life potency. That cost will be manifested as the client returns again and again for further guidance. Indeed, this is one factor that contributes to clients continuing in therapy for many years—one factor, but not the only one.

[10]Some are saying that even before conception there are latent influences that will be important in the formation of the child's life.

[11]All knowledge is partial knowledge, is provisional. The "hardest" sciences are always in process, evolving, and never able to make *the final* statement on any matter.

[12]Deikman (1990) presents a remarkable and thorough documentation of how we subvert our own being in this way.

[13]It is distressing to recognize that other views may not accord with one's own—particularly if one's career and reputation are based on that view.

12

A CLIENT'S-EYE VIEW

Psychotherapy Follows a Unique Path with Each Client[1]

In the following protocol, I try to portray the general shape and some representative content of the course of the therapeutic engagement with one client. This fiction is based on several actual clients, but it is not an account of any one client. The advantage of fiction is that it more readily lends itself to condensation and abridgments. In the preparation of this scenario, I have generally tried to illustrate situations other than those already exemplified in earlier sections of the book.

Client (CL)—Stanley Dodge; Therapist (TH)—Bruce Graham

(On the telephone.) I would like to make an appointment to see Dr. Graham . . . My name is Stanley Dodge. I was referred by Ann Halstad. . . . I'd like it to be fairly soon. I mean, it's not an emergency or anything, but. . . . But the sooner the better. . . . Yes, Wednesday at four is fine. . . . Thanks, I know where his office is.

INTERVIEW 1

TH-1.1: *(In the waiting room.)* Mr. Dodge? I'm Dr. Graham. Would you like to come in now?

CL-1.1: Yes, thank you. *(Enters office and takes chair to which Dr.*

201

Graham points.) Uh, I've never done this before. Is there anything you want to ask me?

TH-1.2: You indicated on the phone that you wanted an early appointment. Has something happened recently to make you feel that way?

CL-1.2: No, (*Pause.*) Well, yes, kind of. I mean it's nothing special, but. . . . I guess, it *is* kind of special, . . . in a way, I guess.

TH-1.3: Mm-hmm? (*Questioning tone and manner.*)

CL-1.3: I mean, I have been feeling kind of not really myself for a while now, but then last week. . . .

TH-1.4: Last week . . . ?

CL-1.4: Last week I was in the middle of teaching a section of the introductory course—I teach American history at City College. Anyway, I can't remember what I was talking about now—it was the lecture on the Federalists and . . . and suddenly I saw this girl in the second row. I haven't any idea what her name is or anything. The intro course gets such big enrollments, you know. Anyway, something about her, the way she turned her head, I think maybe, and suddenly I just realized I'd stopped talking and was just staring. . . . I had just stopped talking! And the class just sat there for . . . maybe a minute, and then they began to get a little restless, and I woke up, you know. I wasn't sure just where I was in my lecture, so I switched to talking about Jefferson's attitude toward something or other and then wound up the class and stopped ten minutes early. I don't think anyone thought much of anything about it, but I went back to my office and shut the door and sat there, and I was trembling! I really was. My hands were shaking a little bit, but inside of me in my gut I felt the trembling even more.

TH-1.5: Mm-hmm.

CL-1.5: I thought maybe it was my heart, but I knew it wasn't.

TH-1.6: Not your heart.

CL-1.6: No. I knew it wasn't physical, but I thought I ought not take a chance, so I called Harry Emerson, our family doc. Do you know him?

TH-1.7: I don't think so.

CL-1.7: Anyway, he had me come right over to his office, and he checked my heart and asked me about my health and things like that, and then he said there was nothing he could find to account for that reaction.

TH-1.8: So . . . ?

CL-1.8: So I called you. And here I am.

TH-1.9: And . . . ?

CL-1.9: I know you can't tell me anything yet, but you can see why I thought I ought to talk to you as soon as . . . as we could work out a time, you know.

TH-1.10: Sure.

CL-1.10: So. . . . How do I begin?

TH-1.11: You've already begun.

CL-1.11: Hmm. (*Pause.*) I see. Well, is there anything you want to ask me now?

TH-1.12: Why don't you just fill me in a bit on who you are and what your life is like these days?

CL-1.12: Fine. I'm Stanley Dodge . . . Oh, you already know that! Yes, well, I am 48 years old, married, two children: Roy 18 and Janis 15. My wife, Miranda—she's called "Mira"—is 48 also, and she and I were both married previously, but we've been together for 21 years now.

My own first marriage was a brief, teenage pregnancy-based matter that ended shortly after the child was born. It only lived a few months and then it and its mother died in an accident while I was off in the East, trying to work out how to go to college and support my family at the same time. Friends said it was tragic but fortunate, that I wasn't ready for marriage and needed to finish college. I guess they were right. Helen and I had been so much in love, but today I wonder if it was chiefly the sexual excitement—we were both first lovers.

TH-1.13: I see.

CL-1.13: Like I said, I teach history at City College—American history, that is. I've been there for 14 years. It's a good job, and I like the kids. Every other year in the summer, I can take off with Mira for a trip someplace for a month or so. This year we're supposed to go to Greece, but somehow I've put off making the arrangements, and instead, I'm just sort of mooning around, not accomplishing much.

TH-1.14: Just mooning around.

CL-1.14: Yeah. So I told Ann Halstad I was off my feed a little. Ann and her husband, Ben (he's my golfing partner), have been our friends for a long time. They both have had therapy and they are always telling me I need to get into psychotherapy. As I guess you know, she's a missionary to what she calls the "untheraped." They both always see therapy as the answer to everything. I didn't think I was the type, but after what happened, I thought a visit or two might not be a bad idea.

TH-1.15: What do you make of what happened?

CL-1.15: I don't know what to think. And I've tried to puzzle it out again and again. Something about that girl.

TH-1.16: Mmmm?

CL-1:16: Something she triggered for me. I've thought and thought, and I can't imagine what it might have been. (Pauses, perplexed, sighs.) I think I saw her in the bookstore yesterday, and I just looked right at her, but nothing. It beats me. She's nice looking. Nothing special. Kind of cute the way most of the younger women are these days, but she doesn't start any bells ringing in me or anything.

TH-1.17: No bells for you.

CL-1.17: No, nothing. I asked myself if she reminded me of anyone, but couldn't come up with anything. I wondered if some way I had the hots for her—once in a while I'll have a student who sets me to daydreaming for a bit. . . . But not with this girl. I checked my class list, but I couldn't figure out which name was hers. I really am baffled. What do you think? How can we figure this out?

TH-1.18: Sounds as though you've been trying the "figure it out" route pretty well already, and it hasn't panned out.

CL-1.18: Yeah, that's so, but. . . . (*He waits expectantly.*)

TH-1.19: You're wondering how I can help.

CL-1.19: Yeah. What do we do now?

TH-1.20: Well, think of it this way. You've gone straight at the question, and it hasn't given you an answer. Maybe it's going to require that you come around behind the question, so to speak.

CL-1.20: How do we do that?

TH-1.21: Well, let's think about what happened in the context of what's going on in your life generally.

CL-1.21: Yeah . . . I see . . . but that sounds like a big job, might take a lot of time.

TH-1.22: Yes, it can do that.

CL-1.22: Well, the college has a faculty health plan, and I think they'll give me five or six sessions.

TH-1.23: Stan—is that what you like to be called, "Stan"?

CL-1.23: Yeah. Sure.

TH-1.24: I'm Bruce. (*Pause, checks Stan's face.*) I'm going to make a little detour for a minute because it's about a matter that could be trivial or could turn out to be important to our working together.

CL-1.24: Okay.

TH-1.25: As I said, it may be just a minor point, but it's important to recognize that the health plan doesn't "give" you anything. You've worked for any benefits you get; you've paid for them already. They belong to you already. Recognizing that, you should know that in many plans, if you need them, you can have more sessions than what they try to say is your limit.

Now in one way, we're off the main point of your being here, but I feel an obligation to you to be straight about this since so often these plans are deceptive.

CL-1.25: Yeah. I've heard about that. Thanks.

TH-1.26: You're welcome, but actually no thanks are necessary.

CL-1.26: Anyway, I think you're telling me this isn't going to be something we can take care of in just a few sessions, huh?

TH-1.27: That's probably so, although I can't really say much about it yet. In the long run, it's going to be up to you how far you want to go.

CL-1.27: (*Distractedly.*) Yeah, I suppose so. (*Pause, starts to speak, stops, takes a breath.*) Do you think it will take very long? I mean, Ann's been coming here for several years. Do you think I might have to do that too?

TH-1.28: Stan, I really don't know how long you'll want to come. In the long run, only you can say. I can tell you that I don't think five or six sessions are going to accomplish much. What you've told me makes it obvious that there's a lot going on in you these days, and that means we have to have time enough for you to use this place to get a handle on things.

CL-1.28: (*Preoccupied, he stirs himself to reply.*) Yes, I see. . . . I guess I better give it a try. You know, I've had a pretty normal life, no big traumas or anything. I mean, I don't see what we'd talk about after a couple of times. I suppose that's something we'll find out about as we go along, huh?

TH-1.29: Yes. (*Pauses, waits for Stan to digest what he has said.*) Our time's about up today, let's talk about how often you will come and when.

CL-1.29: Uh-huh. Well, today's Tuesday. Can I come every Tuesday at this same time?

TH-1.30: Yes, that will work okay. But I'd recommend that to start with, you come at least twice a week. It takes a bit of time to learn how to use what we do here so you can get the most from it.

They arrange a schedule of two sessions a week and take care of other details, and then Stan leaves.

INTERVIEW 3

Stan arrives promptly and seems eager for the interview, entering briskly, taking the client's chair, and exchanging greetings. He is obviously ready with a question.

CL-3.1: One thing I wanted to ask you, have you any idea of what sort of thing it might be that could cause me to have such a strong reaction— like I had to that girl? By the way, I figured out who she is—I mean, her name—Beverly Campbell. (*Pauses, reflects.*) I mean, I've never had anything like that happen before. What sort of thing are we looking for do you think?

TH-3.1: Well, I can give you a general sort of answer, but it probably won't be much help. Think of it this way: We all have a lot of emotional experiences in our histories and many of them are in some way incomplete. When events in our current living match up to some of them, we get a subjective experience that is partly current and partly out of the past.

CL-3.2: (*Vaguely.*) Yeah, I . . . uh . . . understand the idea, but. . . .

TH-3.2: Think of it like a big safe with two or three turns of the dial that have to be set at the right numbers for the safe to open. Most of the time, when you spin the dial, they don't get the right combinations, but once in a while by chance you do, and then there is suddenly something unexpected happening.

CL-3.3: That means that unless you've know the combination, it's a long drawn-out process of working out chance efforts. Do you know the combination?

TH-3.3 No, but you do—in a way. You don't know it consciously the way you do your phone number, but you know how to get it the same way you know how to get the phone number of a friend in another city. You have to track it down, so to speak.

CL-3.4: How do I do that?

TH-3.4: You had this experience last Tuesday, right?

CL-3.5: Uh-huh.

TH-3.5: So some way inside yourself, you've been touching on material emotionally important to you. Now you have to follow your inner feelings and thoughts so they'll lead you to what you're trying to get open inside.

CL-3.6: How do I do that?

TH-3.6: You've already begun. When you ask about this with that sense of concern that I heard in your voice just now, and off and on during this time we've been together, when you have this feeling of something mattering to you but you don't know what it is yet—then you've begun. Be open to that feeling. Let it take you wherever it needs to go.

CL-3.7: I don't know what you mean.

TH-3.7: So . . . ?

CL-3.8: (A bit irked.) What do you mean, "so"?

TH-3.8: You don't know what I mean; so what happens inside you when you don't know what I mean?

CL-3.9: I get confused. I feel as though. . . . I don't know what you want me to do.

TH-3.9: So . . . ?

CL-3.10: (Irritatedly.) I feel like you're teasing me, and. . . .

TH-3.10: And. . . .

CL-3.11: And I don't like it! Do you want to make me mad?

TH-3.11: Stan, I'm going to stop what I was doing just now to explain something, but I won't always stop because that will defeat the work you need to do.

CL-3.12: I don't get it.

TH-3.12: I know that, and that's why I'm stopping to explain to you now. Very likely there will be other times, if we continue to work together, when you'd like me to stop, and I may not.

CL-3.13: You mean you want to get me pissed off?

TH-3.13: Yes and no. I want to help you get inside of yourself where you live more fully, but to get there in a different way than you're familiar with. A way in which you are less self-conscious about being in a somewhat formal and business relation, and, instead, you are more immersed in what's happening inside of you and what you're experiencing there. That's the only path by which you can find the real combination to open your inner life and discover what's going on, and going on at a level of which you're not usually conscious.

CL-3.14: Can't I just tell you about it without all this playacting and stuff?

TH-3.14: Tell me why you had such a reaction to that girl in your class last week.

CL-3.15: (*Pauses, reflects.*) Yeah . . . yeah, I think I see what you mean. You're saying that I can't tell you because it's some place inside me that I'm not conscious of? Couldn't you just hypnotize me and find out?

TH-3.15: It might work, Stan, but if I find out that you had that reaction for reason X and I find that out by bypassing your conscious mind, what then? Suppose you reacted that way because she reminds you of a cousin you knew when you were 14. So what?

CL-3.16: So then wouldn't I be free of that reaction and not have it happen again?

TH-3.16: No.

CL-3.17: No? How come?

TH-3.17: Because in our inner lives all sorts of things are interrelated, like all the ingredients of a soup, and you can't just pull one out—like trying to pull the carrots and their flavor out of a vegetable soup without disturbing the rest of what's in the pot. Go back to my example of a minute ago. Do you, in fact, have a girl cousin?

CL-3.18: Yeah. She's older than I am, though.

TH-3.18: That's okay. Now let's suppose that you had the reaction to that student because she reminds you of that cousin. So what? What will you do with that information right now?

CL-3.19: Uh. . . . Uh, wait. (*Pondering.*) I don't know. It's hard to imagine. I mean I can sort of think up ways of making her connected in some way but it's just a kinda fake thing.

TH-3.19: And that's the point. You need to have a whole lot more inner experiencing to make it meaningful.

CL-3.20: Yeah. (*Dispirited.*) I don't know. Maybe I should just forget the whole thing.

TH-3.20: Can you?

CL-3.21: I already tried, and. . . . Oh, shit, I don't know what to do.

TH-3.21: Stan, let's set aside that whole thing about the student and your reaction to her for a little while. Okay?

CL-3.22: I guess so. Yeah.

TH-3.22: How are things in your life more generally these days?

After a minute or two of "shifting gears," Stan describes his life as generally "okay" and his relations with his wife and children as "really good," except for some problems in setting limits for his 18-year-old son. Then slowly, Stan begins disclosing a change that has been coming over him lately.

CL-3.23: For some time now, maybe six months or more, I've been restless, preoccupied, and sometimes kind of irritable. I don't really know why. Maybe approaching the big "five-O"—I'll be 49 in November—maybe seeing the kids coming toward the time they'll leave home, maybe Mira's moodiness as the "change" hits her . . . maybe all of these. I don't know.

TH-3.23: Lots of things going on in your life these days.

CL-3.24: Yes . . . lots. Do you think this thing—you know, with that girl in my class—has anything to do with these changes?

TH-3.24: Yes, but all I'm really saying right now when I say they're related is that they are parts of all that is going on in you and in your life, and that tells us that there are links among them. We don't know now what those links are or even whether they are important to investigate now. That's what our work will show us as we work together.

CL-3.25: It sounds sort of vague, doesn't it?

TH-3.25: Yes. That's usually the case when we're just starting our work together.

INTERVIEW 6

Three weeks later: Stan has begun to understand about how their work is conducted, but he is still unsure of his own and the therapist's roles in the process. Today he arrives just at the scheduled starting time.

TH-6.1: (*Opening the door to the consultation room.*) Hi. Stan. Come on in.

CL-6.1: (*Winded, entering and flopping into the client chair with exaggerated breathing and relief.*) Whew! I made it. You know, I was sure I was going to be late. (*Breathing heavily.*) How are you?

TH-6.2: Okay. You were sure you were going to be late?

CL-6.2: Yeah. I was so tied up with student interviews that I didn't notice the time until suddenly I did, and. . . . But I made it, after all!

TH-6.3: Uh-huh.

CL-6.3: Yeah, yeah. It was close though. But I got here!

TH-6.4: (*Soberly.*) Stan, I hear how you're repeating about your having made it after all. It seems important to you to get that message over to me.

CL-6.4: (*Surprised.*) Oh, no. It's just that I had these interviews and. . . .

TH-6.5: (*Interrupting.*) Wait, Stan. Take time to check inside. You sounded as though there was something you wanted me to know.

CL-6.5: (*Puzzled, starting to protest, pausing.*) Oh, no. Well, wait a minute. Yeah, I can kinda see what you mean, but. . . . But really it's no big deal, and. . . .

TH-6.6: I'm going to interrupt you again, Stan. I hear you about to reassure me and to say that what was going on inside of you was not really important.

CL-6.6: Well, yeah, maybe. . . . Did you get something I'm missing? I just thought that. . . .

TH-6.7: There's something you're missing, I'm pretty sure, but that's past now. But there's something else that you're missing that is right now, and it's that I want to help you recognize.

CL-6.7: Okay, sure. (*He seems almost to caricature the obedient pupil.*)

TH-6.8: What's going on inside of you right now? Wait! Don't answer too soon. Take time to really find out.

CL-6.8: (*Pauses, face intent, eyes down, starts to speak, stops. Then his face relaxes a bit, and he is quieter. Finally, he looks up.*) Uh, I'm not sure. I mean, I just have a whole lot of different stuff going on inside. I can't remember for sure what we were just talking about.

TH-6.9: Go back inside. Just go slow. It's hard to do at first.

CL-6.9: Yeah. (*He's intent on his inner thoughts, face impassive, breathing shallow. After an interval, he looks up, catches his breath, opens his mouth to speak, and then pauses again.*)

TH-6.10: (*Very quietly.*) Take your time.

CL-6.10: Yeah. . . . Yeah, like you say, there's a lot going on, but I have trouble when I try to put it in words, you know?

TH-6.11: Yes. It is hard at first.

CL-6.11: Do you think it's important? I mean, a lot of it just seems to be kind of dumb stuff that doesn't seem to go anywhere.

TH-6.12: (*Speaking deliberately and insistently.*) It *is* important, Stan. It's your own life, your life going on right at this moment inside of you, and you need to know a lot more about it.

CL-6.12: Yeah, I guess so. (*Still partly immersed.*)

TH-6.13: (*Silent, intently watching client.*)

CL-6.13: (*Sort of shaking himself out.*) So that's what you've been trying to get me to be more in touch with, huh?

TH-6.14: Yes. That's the door to what's inside you.

CL-6.14: Uh-huh. Yeah, but a lot of it just doesn't seem to make sense or help me with what I need to work on here.

TH-6.15: Boy! It's so hard for you to value your own inner life, isn't it?

CL-6.15: Well, it's just not very practical. I can sit and daydream on my own and not have to pay a bunch of bucks an hour to do it.

TH-6.16: You've decided it's not practical without really getting very far into it. You're like someone who turns down a book because the cover doesn't please him.

CL-6.16: No, really. I can do that kind of thing any time. While I'm here, I need to work on my real problems.

TH-6.17: Like?

CL-6.17: Like why I'm so jumpy lately or what triggered that reaction when I was teaching a couple of weeks ago. By the way, I've watched that same girl several times since, and nothing . . . zero. (*He yawns mammothly.*) Oh! Sorry. . . . I don't know what happened that day, but it's over now, and I don't want to waste any more time on it.

TH-6.18: How quickly you dismiss something that had you very troubled only a few weeks ago

CL-6.18: (*Another yawn.*) I suppose so, but so what? (*Pauses, rubs his eyes, fights down another yawn.*) I mean, it's past history, why dredge it up? I . . . uh . . .

TH-6.19: Looks like you're having a hard time staying awake.

CL-6.19: Yeah. (*Yawns.*) Oh, I know why: didn't have my coffee yet today. Trying to get here on time, you know.

TH-6.20: Uh-huh. Think it could be anyway connected to what we're talking about?

CL-6.20: No, it's just that I never function well until I've had my morning coffee.

TH-6.21: You seem very positive.

CL-6.21: Yeah. Anyway, I want to tell you about my interview with the department head. . . .

And so the session continues with Stan talking about the pressure from his department head for Stan to publish more professionally and about a recent disagreement with his son. Several times, the therapist points to

Stan's emotional involvements in what he is describing, but Stan seems to have decided that this is just some idiosyncrasy of the therapist, and at the most he simply acknowledges the observation and moves on to more description.

Knowing the importance of Stan's having the sense of having "told his story" at least once, the therapist listens without interrupting, in the meanwhile becoming familiar with Stan's way of being in himself.

INTERVIEW 17

CL-17.1: (*Entering, slumping into his chair moodily, avoiding looking directly at therapist.*) Yeah, hi. (*Silent, eyes downcast. Several minutes pass. The therapist is looking at the client expectantly but silently. Then Stan makes a visible effort to rouse himself and sit up, finally looking directly at the therapist for the first time in this interview.*) Why don't you ask me some questions?

TH-17.1: What's happening in you right now?

CL-17.2: Nothing much. (*Tone is flat, distant, almost sullen.*)

TH-17.2: (*Earnestly but not angrily.*) The hell you say. You're brimming over with feelings of some kind right now.

CL-17.3: Yeah, I suppose so, but they're not important. I don't want to waste any more time here, so ask me something so that we can get some place.

TH-17.3: You *are* some place right now—some place you clearly don't want to be, but some place that I'm pretty sure is important for us to explore together.

CL-17.4: Yeah, I knew you'd say something like that, but it's no use. I can't do what you want me to do. I just don't. . . . (*His voice trails off as he falls silent again.*)

TH-17.4: (*With moderate urgency.*) I know it seems that way to you,

Stan, but it's not so. You're doing important work inside yourself right now, and we must not waste it.

CL-17.5: It sure doesn't feel that way to me.

TH-17.5: I know that; that's part of what makes it important. You're in a place that you don't like and that keeps you from doing what you need to do. That's precisely the place you're here to do something about. So you're doing exactly what you need to do when you bring it in here.

CL-17.6: (*Bitterly.*) Well, hooray for me.

TH-17.6: Doesn't feel like much to hooray about, does it?

CL-17.7: (*Rousing himself a bit, but still with a bitter quality.*) It sure as hell doesn't. So (*pause*) what do I do now?

TH-17.7: You're doing it. Just tell me whatever comes into your awareness and just as it comes.

CL-17.8: Nothing. Nothing comes.

TH-17.8: You said it. Right then "nothing" was what came to you, and you said it. (*Pause.*) Keep going.

CL-17.9: Same thing. Nothing and nothing and. . . . And it doesn't do any good to keep saying that.

TH-17.9: And so you stopped saying "nothing" and told me that it wasn't doing any good.

CL-17.10: Well, it isn't! (*Tone suddenly firmer, edging on anger.*)

TH-17.10: Something more came in this time. Something with more emotional thrust to it.

CL-17.11: (*Exasperated.*) Look, I don't want to play silly games with you. This isn't doing anybody any good. (*Pause.*) Why don't you try to be some real help to me?

TH-17.11: I am. And I don't agree that you're not doing anything. You're really letting me see another part of you that you don't seem to like very much, but that is part of you nevertheless.

CL-17.12: Well, I don't see how it can help me to bellyache at you about something. I need you to help me get out of that place, not encourage me to stay in it.

TH-17.12: You're already in a different place than you were five minutes ago. It seems hard for you to see how continuously you're moving along inside right now.

CL-17.13: I'm in a worse place. I feel lousy, and you aren't helping me. You just sit there telling me I'm doing something when all I'm really doing is spinning my goddam wheels. For crying out loud, . . . (*Pauses, searching inside.*) Whatever the hell your first name is. Are you just getting your kicks out of seeing me sweat?

TH-17.13: My first name's Bruce.

CL-17.14: Yeah. (*Silent, considering.*) Okay, Bruce, so you think what I'm doing now is useful, huh?

TH-17.14: (*Nods.*)

CL-17.15: Well, I strictly don't get it. Really don't see any use at all in what I've been doing today. Seems like a real waste of time.

TH-17.15: I know it does.

CL-17.16: (*Waits. When therapist doesn't continue, moves restlessly.*) So how's about telling me how it's anything but a waste.

TH-17.16: I hear you trying to get into another place emotionally now, but I notice that you haven't taken any time to try to answer your own question. How might what you've been doing today be of any use to you?

CL-17.17: (*Dejectedly.*) Oh shit! You're putting it back on me again! Really, I need some help right now, not Socratic questioning or whatever you're doing.

TH-17.17: You're really angry and disappointed when you have to grapple with your own feelings and what they may mean.

CL-17.18: No! . . . Yes, . . . I guess I am. . . . That's why I come to you and pay you all this money. (*He waits.*) Well, aren't you going to say anything?

TH-17.18: Still all your attention is on me.

CL-17.19: Yes, of course, it seems to me. . . . (*A long pause, his eyes averted. Then his tone changes, is more reflective.*) It seems to me that I'm wasting my time here, and yet you keep telling me I'm not.

When I try to think about that I get all mixed up inside. I want to be angry with you . . . or with myself . . . or with someone or something, but. . . .

TH-17.19: Being angry would be a kind of relief.

CL-17.20: Yes! (*Reflects.*) Yes, it would, but. . . . But it would also get me away from . . . from. . . . I don't know what, but. . . .

TH-17.20: (*With some positive energy.*) You're doing it, Stan. You're listening to yourself more than before. Stay with it.

CL-17.21: (*Uncertainly.*) Yeah, yeah. (*Considering.*) Yeah, I think I know what you mean. (*Pause.*) I. . . . I don't know. . . . I think I lost it.

TH-17.21: That's my fault. I was in too big a hurry to encourage you. But for a minute there you really were in yourself in a different way, and that's important.

CL-17.22: (*Hesitantly.*) Uh-huh. I mean, I think I know what you mean. It's all kind of confused inside me right now.

TH-17.22: That's okay. That's where you are right now. Be with your confusion, . . . and tell me whatever you can.

CL-17.23: Mmm. Well, I think about what you said . . . about its being important, and I guess I kinda wonder why or . . . or just how it is important, and. . . .

TH-17.23: Can you feel the difference now?

CL-17.24: Yeah, . . . I mean, I guess so.

And that's pretty much as far as the work gets today. However, an important reference point has been established.

INTERVIEW 37

In the four and a half months Stan has been in therapy, he has gradually come to a pattern of working in which he takes time at the start of the session to make the transition from his outwardly directed concern to attend to his inner promptings. He fluctuates in his attitude about this change. Today, he came early so that he could sit quietly in the waiting room for about ten minutes before his session started. This is a new addition to his work in therapy.

CL-37.1: (*Entering and getting settled in his chair.*) I tried coming early enough to have a few minutes to myself before we got started. (*Reflecting.*) I think it's a good idea. . . . It's hard for me to get away from campus quickly enough to get here that way. . . . I'm uncomfortable telling you all this, and I don't know why. (*Complaining tone.*)

TH-37.1: Mmm-hmmm.

CL-37.2: I'm losing it. (*He leans back in his chair, shuts his eyes, doesn't speak for at least two minutes.*) Damn! It's gone.

TH-37.2: It's gone, . . . but you're here.

CL-37.3: Yeah. (*Tone brighter, looking at therapist.*) Yeah, it's gone now, but for a little bit there I think I was really in touch with myself . . . inside, you know. I've been trying to get there when I have a little break in the day. Mostly, it's too noisy in there, too much going on, or something. . . . Anyway, mostly I don't. . . . I don't seem to get any big insights or anything, but every once in a while. . . .

TH-37.3: Every once in a while. . . .

CL-37.4: Yeah, I get a feeling like I'm more in . . . more in . . . myself, I guess you'd say.

TH-37.4: (*Agreeing.*) That *is* what I'd say.

CL-37.5: Yeah. (*Reflecting.*) Yes, more inside myself. (*Pause.*) It's funny, but it seems like I should always have been inside myself and like I should be now, but I'm not, and I haven't been. I'm not even sure what I mean by that, but I guess you know.

TH-37.5: I might know, but *you* don't know right now.

CL-37.6: Yes. (*Coming to focus more on therapist.*) Oh, am I putting it all on you again? I didn't mean it that way. I was just thinking about how you helped me see that there was more stuff inside of me than I ever realized.

TH-37.6: I understand.

CL-37.7: When I get inside that way I feel as though I know more about what I want than I usually do, but I find it hard to put in words what I know.

TH-37.7: Uh-huh.

CL-37.8: Why is that? Why is it so hard to say what I mean? I tried to tell Mira about it the other night, but I felt clumsy and dumb, and she didn't get it at all. Made me kind of mad at her . . . and at myself and. . . .

TH-37.8: And . . . ?

CL-37.9: Yeah. Why is it so hard to say what I mean?

TH-37.9: Like right now?

CL-37.10: Right now? Oh, no, I think I can say what I mean now. Why? Did you see something?

TH-37.10: When you can't say what you want to, it makes you "kind of mad" at Mira and at yourself and at. . . . You stopped abruptly at that point.

CL-37.11: Did I?

TH-37.11: You did.

CL-37.12: Well, I don't know. (*Uneasy.*) I mean it probably isn't important. Just ran out of gas.

TH-37.12 Or hesitated to finish the thought?

CL-37.13: (*Reluctantly.*) Yeah, I guess so. I mean, it wasn't anything important, just a passing thought.

TH-37.13: You seem anxious to dismiss it.

CL-37.14: Oh, you know what I was doing. I meant I felt a little bit pissed at you for showing me how I didn't really listen inside. You know how that is. It's no big deal.

TH-37.14: Yes, I know what you mean, Stan, but I disagree. I think it is a very big deal.

CL-37.15: Oh, come on. I'm not really mad at you.

TH-37.15: I know that. But that's not the big deal. The big deal is that you feel there are times when you can't say here what is really happening in yourself. That's a serious leak in our system.

CL-37.16: Hmmm. (*Reflecting.*) Uh-huh. I see what you mean. I hadn't thought of it that way.

TH-37.16: (*Very earnestly.*) This has got to be a place where you can say it all, where you don't have to edit and censure what you discover in your inner self.

CL-37.17: I can see that. (*Pauses, then speaks with more energy.*) I really do see it!

TH-37.17: You sound surprised.

CL-37.18: Yeah, I am. I don't know why it hits me so hard, but it does, and. . . .

TH-37.18: For some reason . . . ?

CL-37.19: (*He is silent for several minutes, face concentrated, attention inward. Gradually he brings his attention back to the room and to the therapist.*) Hmmm! Well! I don't know what happened. I was thinking about what we'd been talking about, and then it sort of faded out, and it was almost as though I was going to go to sleep. Well, anyway, I guess I've said all I need to about that. And now, I. . . .

TH-37.19: And now . . . ?

CL-37.20: Now, I . . . I guess what I want to talk about is the interview I had with the dean yesterday, and. . . .

TH-37.20: You're changing the subject pretty fast, aren't you?

CL-37.21: No, I don't think so. I think I've said everything I have to say about . . . about whatever we were talking about. Why? Is there something you want to ask me about?

TH-37.21: What *were* we talking about?

CL-37.22: Oh, let me see. It was about how this needs to be a place where I don't have to be careful with what I say. See? (*Teasing manner.*) I do remember it.

TH-37.22: Yes, you do. What do you think about that recognition now?

CL-37.23: Oh, I agree. Absolutely.

TH-37.23: Okay, then stay with that a bit more and see what comes up for you.

CL-37.24: Yeah. (*Briefly silent.*) Uh, nothing. I mean I think I said all that I had to say about it already. Just that it seems a good idea to have this sort of a "safe haven," you might say.

TH-37.24: Not so fast. Just stay with it for a bit longer, and keep aware inside for whatever comes along.

CL-37.25: Okay. (*Briefly silent.*) No, nothing.

TH-37.25: For some reason, you're awfully fast in dismissing this.

CL-37.26: (*More soberly.*) Yes, I was. (*Pause.*) A "safe haven," ummm. I like the thought of that. (*His voice changes, becomes softer and more reflective.*) Mmmm! I feel kind of sad, almost like I might cry or something. . . .

TH-37.26: Go slow.

CL-37.27: (*Reflecting inwardly.*) I can't seem to get anything except this sort of sad feeling. . . . It's fading now.

TH-37.27: Your feelings surprise you, but they also are getting closer to the surface. That's progress, Stan. Don't push, but just keep aware.

CL-37.28: Yes. Well, there was sure something more there, wasn't there? How did you know?

TH-37.28: I didn't, but I do know there is always more and when you're in such a hurry to get away from where you are, something's cooking. We never can get to the end of all that's inside of us.

Although they spend several minutes more on this unexpected emotion,

Stan gets no further with it today. Instead his thoughts move on to the conversation with his departmental chair and the pressure he feels to produce professionally.

No matter what has been said on any issue in one's life, there is more that can be said. Exchanges 21 through 28 in Interview 37 show a different facet of this open-endedness of our inner processes. It is my belief that it is impossible to exhaust all that is potential within a person's subjectivity. Whatever the entry point, if one persists, more will be found. Moreover, the very searching process itself (which is, of course, what is involved here) would continually produce more awarenesses.

The recognition that the client attains in Interview 37 is notable for the way it keeps opening up. Its influence is evident throughout the remaining sessions in his therapy. This central theme to the client's life was brought out by the therapist's restrained participation as it aided the client's finding his own way to an important and previously unaccessed discovery.

INTERVIEW 67

Stan has now been in psychotherapy for almost nine months. He is familiar with the routine of the work and has developed a pattern of coming 10 or 15 minutes before his session time in order to sit quietly and make the transition to the therapeutic process. He also often stays in the waiting room for an interval of reflection before leaving.

During this time, he had a serious dispute with his wife over the discipline of the children, especially his son, who is now 19 and who insists on being free of parental control. Also during these months, Stan has begun to write a piece for a professional journal in his field.

CL-67.1: (*Nodding a greeting and going to the couch.*) Okay if I use this today? (*He was introduced to its use some time ago and now employs it whenever he feels an impulse to try to work more deeply.*)

TH-67.1: Sure. Like I told you, it's a tool for you to use when you want it.

CL-67.2: (*Getting settled, kicks his shoes off, lies down, stretches. All of this time his eyes are unfocused and his attention is manifestly inward.*) Mmmm. Yeah, uhhh. I'm chewing on something, Bruce, but I don't know what it is yet. (*Silence.*) Argument with Mira. Chuck giving me lip. No. No, that's not it. Damn! It's hard getting down, stopping all the chatter, all the thinking about what I *should* be talking about. (*Silent again.*)

TH-67.2: (*Quietly.*) Take your time.

CL-67.3: Getting old . . . body changing. . . . Some of the girls in my classes wear shorts or minis, and they can be distracting. (*Pause.*) No, that's not it. Sure I like looking at them, might like to do more than look, but that's not what I'm stuck with right now.

TH-67.3: (*Gently.*) Slowly. . . .

CL-67.4: You know, I've always wanted to write a book . . . a novel really . . . about American history. . . . Really about Fort Sumter. That's where the Civil War began, you know. Only I'd call it "The War Between the States." That's the way the South thinks of it. (*Pauses, shifts position on the couch to get more comfortable.*) I want to tell the story from the South's side and then tell it again from the North's view and then have them come to the crucial confrontation that. . . .

Oh, wait! I don't want to get into all that. What I need to talk about is different. . . . (*Silent, shifting position again.*)

TH-67.4: (*Reflectively.*) What you want to talk about is. . . .

CL-67.5: Is. . . . Oh, no wonder I'm getting so lost. Well, not really lost but. . . .

TH-67.5: (*Voice quiet, insistent.*) Stay with what matters to you.

CL-67.6: Right! But it's sort of embarrassing to say it out loud. I want to write a novel. . . . I mean a big novel, one that will make me a million . . . or at least a pile of money, and will be made into a blockbuster movie. You know, like *Gone With the Wind*, or some of the others. I suppose it sounds silly. . . .

TH-67.6: (*Still soto voce.*) You're breaking faith with yourself.

CL-67-7: Yeah, . . . but dammit, I do. I do want to write a novel that shows the good will on both sides and the ways it all went wrong and the terrible cost and the bravery and . . . and all that. And I want it to be big. . . .

TH-67.7: (*Softly echoing.*) Really big!

CL-67.8: (*He is silent, motionless; then his voice is low and self-conscious.*) Oh, I know, every half-assed history prof in the country wants to write another *Gone With the Wind*. I suppose I sound pretty silly having such ideas, and. . . .

TH-67.8: (*Interrupting.*) You keep breaking faith with yourself. How hard it is for you to stand with your hopes and. . . . Slow down and listen inside.

CL-67.9: (*Embarrassed.*) Yeah. . . . Well, I do sound pretty grandiose and inflated, don't I?

TH-67.9: You're double-crossing yourself right now.

CL-67.10: Yeah. (*Pause, shuts his eyes, takes a deep breath.*) I'm just embarrassed to be so . . . so naked. I mean, this has been my plan . . . (*Stops, shifts on the couch.*) My hope, I mean. . . . No, damn it! I mean, my "plan." It has been my plan for most of my adult life. (*Stops, seems to be listening to the echoes of what he has just said.*)

TH-67.10: Mmm-hmmm. (*Confirming tone.*)

CL-67.11: I've never told anyone. I've always kept it a secret so no one would laugh and no one would know if I failed, if I didn't make it. Now, I've told you, and maybe that will jinx it, make it so it will never happen.

TH-67.11: Maybe.

CL-67.12: (*Waits, hardly breathing, listening inside intently.*) I'm glad I told you. I don't care what you think. Still I'm glad I said it . . . at last.

TH-67.12: At last.

CL-67.13: I'm surprised. . . . It seems like it takes a load off. I'm feeling relieved! I'll be damned! I *am* relieved. It's like I . . . I don't have to do that any more. . . .

TH-67.13: Relieved.

CL-67.14: (*Softly, musingly.*) Yeah. It's strange. I thought I'd be crushed, be miserable . . . if I ever let anyone know that that was who I was in secret. . . . I had to do it first, win the Academy Award or whatever . . . had to do it before anyone knew. . . .

TH-67.14: Now I know.

CL-67.15: You know, and I don't care! I don't have to do it!

TH-67.15: Don't have to.

CL-67.16: That should be a relief. (*Hesitates.*) It is. And yet, somehow it isn't. I don't know why not, but. . . . I'm trying to. . . . (*Silent for several minutes, eyes shut.*) So much. . . . So much but there is something more. I can feel it, but I can't name it . . . yet.

TH-67.16: (*Softly.*) Stay with it. You're doing your work.

CL-67.17: I want to do something like that . . . something creative . . . something . . . I. . . . (*Sighs, opens his eyes.*)

The rest of the hour passes with Stan's gradually returning to a more everyday way of being, occasionally reflecting on the "secret"—sometimes with interest, sometimes with a wistful quality. At the end of the hour, he gets up from the couch, smiles wryly at Bruce, and leaves with no further words.

The next three interviews all take place within ten days.

INTERVIEWS 68 AND 69

In these two sessions, Stan finds little or no opportunity to return to his "secret." Instead he is preoccupied with concern about his son and the struggle that he and his wife are having in trying to be understanding and patient while the son appears driven to challenge them in every way pos-

sible. Stan, in his own words, is "all over the lot" with the boy–man, sometimes blasting him and sometimes filled with love and concern for him, and most times struggling to keep control of himself and be helpful to both his wife and his son.

INTERVIEW 70

When Stan arrives for the 70th hour, he enters and takes the chair with only a casual greeting, obviously full of an intention to go to work at once.

CL-70.1: Well, I've been thinking a lot about the last several times I was here.

TH-70.1: Uh-huh?

CL-70.2: Yeah. It has been quite a trip! First my big "secret" and then this battle with Ted. It was a trip indeed!

TH-70.2: *It* was, huh?

CL-70.3: Yeah. Quite a trip. (*Reflecting.*) Yes, I know I said "it." It seems like it was almost someone else that was here. I know I said all that stuff about a big secret, but. . . .

TH-70.3: Sounds to me that you're pulling out on the you who was here the other day. Kind of keeping your distance, aren't you?

CL-70.4: Oh, no. . . . Well, yes, in a way, but. . . .

TH-70.4: But . . . ?

CL-70.5: But. . . . I don't know. It was pretty heavy stuff, you know. I mean, I'm not pulling out on what I said, but I think I got kind of carried away, you know?

TH-70.5: I know you're sure keeping yourself detached right now.

CL-70.6: Well, yes, I suppose so. But. . . . But, I mean, I never talked about any of that stuff before. For crying out loud, I had hardly thought about it since I was maybe 20 or so. I've been too busy with reality to spend a lot of energy on dreams. You know how it is.

TH-70.6: It seems important to you today to downplay the work you did here about wanting to do something big.

CL-70.7: (*Sobering.*) Yes, I guess it is. I feel kind of shook-up about that whole secret dream, you know. It's embarrassing. Here I am, almost 50 years old, a professor, a married man with children, and. . . . Well, anyway, it seems so . . . so juvenile. You know what I mean.

TH-70.7: Do you want me to join you in belittling what you were able to get to and in denying the significance of what you described?

CL-70.8: No! I mean, yes. . . . No, I mean, "No." (*Angrily.*) It was important, and I don't know why I have to deny that and act like it didn't amount to anything. I guess I just was wondering what you thought about it.

TH-70.8: Maybe that would be useful to get into sometime, but right now the important question is, what do *you* think about it? What do you *really* think about it?

CL-70.9: I think it was damned important. (*Stops and considers. Then, soberly.*) It's strange, but I've always known I had that dream, and I've never let myself really know it, really think about it. You know it was so much a part of me I couldn't see it any more.

TH-70.9: (*Very quietly.*) Yes.

CL-70.10: But now I can't put it back in that place in me. I feel like I want to forget it or put it away again—whatever that may mean—and yet I know I can't and . . . and I really don't think I want to.

TH-70.10: Mmm-hmmm. . . .

CL-70.11: You know, just as we're talking now, just now, it comes to me that I don't really have to do it, but that I might.

TH-70.11: You might.

CL-70.12: Yes, I might try to write that novel. I think I'd like to try. But there's a difference. (*Rising tone, fresh recognition.*)

TH-70.12: A difference.

CL-70.13: Yes. . . . (*Listening inwardly.*) Yes. The difference is I don't *have* to. (*Nods with some excitement.*) Yes, the thing was, I had this dream, you know, but really it was more like an assignment, a requirement. I couldn't have my life for myself until I'd done it, until I'd written this huge novel and been recognized and honored and made a pile of money.

TH-70.13: (*Silent, but attentive.*)

CL-70.14: Yes, "had to," had to prove . . . to prove. . . . Oh, I don't know what, but . . . something. Something to do with my father, . . . I think.

Through the rest of this session and the two following it, Stan gradually brings to consciousness the way in which he felt he had to achieve an outstanding success to make his father proud and, even more, to offset his father's feeling of having failed in his own life. This was, it seemed, a kind of assignment he had come to feel must be accomplished to validate his father's being . . . and his own.

These recognitions were important in several ways: First, they allevi- ated the undercurrent of feeling that he had failed his father; second, they let him think about his work and his possible writing with a more spon- taneous attitude (i.e., as his choice rather than as an assignment); and third, they brought into Stan's immediate consciousness the recognition that he was at a point in his life where he needed to, and could, take more charge of his future.

INTERVIEW 95

Stan has been coming to psychotherapy for a little over a year now (vacations and necessarily canceled appointments have meant that the twice-a-week schedule had to be altered at times). He is using the work more effectively now, which means that on some days he is able to be more in touch with his inner living and at other times he finds it elusive.

TH-95.1: How's it going these days, Stan?

CL-95.1: Pretty well, Bruce. I've been thinking a lot about how Mira and I are going to be more on our own in a few years as the kids go off to college or to live on their own. It sometimes sounds like that will be a wonderful, free opportunity for us to do things we haven't been able to do. Then sometimes it sounds kind of scary with just the two of us in the house.

TH-95.2: Uh-huh.

CL-95.2: Then the thought of my novel comes up. I haven't given up the idea, still think it's a good one, has real possibilities. But then some shadow of the old requirement feeling comes along with that. As we talk now, I realize I'm a little afraid that I'll be back into that. (*Pause.*) Yeah, it's still there. Not as strong as it used to be, but. . . . It seems like it is just waiting to come back, and yet. . . .

TH-95.3: Waiting.

CL-95.3: I feel it now. "It wouldn't hurt you to try to do it for your father. It's little enough considering all he's done for you." You know that's my mother's voice! I didn't realize that she'd been part of this too. She was always so patient and so anxious for us to do well and to make our father proud of us. You know, she didn't have much of a life of her own; it was always what Dad wants, what Dad will be pleased about, or what he will dislike.

TH-95.4: You haven't talked nearly as much about her as about him.

CL-95.4: That figures. He was the center of things. But he wasn't mean about it, you know, he just was the one we all . . . turned to and . . . looked up to.

TH-95.5: Your voice changed as you said the last part of that.

CL-95.5: Yeah, I heard that too. Wait a minute. (*He closes his eyes, is silent.*) I don't know. . . . I think it has to do with his being "the man of the house"—that was her expression. I can't seem to get any further with it.

TH-95.6: You're pushing too hard, I think.

CL-95.6: Maybe so. Hold on. (*He gets up from the chair and goes to the couch, gets settled, and then is silent.*) Dad was a teacher too, you know. High-school math chiefly, I think. When he died, a lot of his former students came around or sent messages. He was well liked by almost everyone. I wonder if I'll be thought of that way. If I wrote that book, maybe I would be. Maybe even bigger. Uh-oh, I feel guilty when I think that. Mustn't try to surpass Dad, dear Dad.

Well. (*Voice changes, becomes more assertive.*) He was "dear" to all of us . . . to me. Yes. (*Abruptly he sobs.*) Yes, Dad was. . . . I loved him, Bruce. He was a good father, and. . . . (*Tears overwhelm him, and he is silent for several minutes.*)

TH-95.7: (*Quietly.*) Take your time, but keep aware.

CL-95.7: (*Cries softly, begins to shake his head slightly.*) I didn't know it. . . . I didn't know. . . . (*He rouses himself a bit and now seems to speak more directly to the therapist.*) They tried so hard, Bruce. Really they did. Both of them. (*More tears; not sobbing, just quiet grief.*) I didn't know it, but yet. . . . Yet in some way I did.

TH-95.8: (*Softly.*) Some way. . . .

CL-95.8: (*As the weeping stops, he dries his eyes again, and sits up on the couch, looking at the therapist.*) It's all so confused inside of me. Can't work it all out yet. I know now that they had such big plans, but then things intervened—the war, the recession, I don't know what. And they saw me as the way all their dreams would be realized at last. Little things they said, their reactions— I almost said, "*over*reactions"—when I got recognitions—Boy Scout Eagle badge, honor roll at school—and when I didn't do well. . . . Well, they never were punishing, but somehow I knew I'd let them down, disappointed them. And now. . . . (*He stops, choking on a sob.*)

TH-95.9: Go slow.

CL-95.9: (*Almost whispering.*) Yeah. . . . Yeah. Now, if I don't write that great novel. . . . (*He has trouble speaking, relaxes, then continues.*) If I don't write it, I'll be letting them down again. (*More tears.*)

TH-95.10: Again.

CL-95.10: (*Wiping his eyes, he looks at the therapist wonderingly.*) I didn't know that! (*Nods to himself.*) But of course. Of course, I had to make them feel proud and good. Had to!

TH-95.11: (*Very softly.*) Had to.

CL-95.11: (*Nods to the therapist this time. Dries his eyes, straightens up, but stays seated on the couch.*) Yes, had to. They would never have demanded that, but I still felt that I absolutely must. (*Pauses, blows his nose mightily.*) Whew!

TH-95.12: You've really been there.

CL-95.12: You know it!

The session continues as Stan reviews what he has been uncovering and then adds bits and pieces, but essentially just fills in the picture. His mood is gentle, caring, and subtly sad. When he leaves, he reaches for Bruce's hand and shakes it firmly while saying nothing but looking intently into Bruce's eyes.

INTERVIEW 111

CL-111.1: Well, Bruce, today's the day. As we talked about it last time, I'm ready to leave therapy. . . . No, that's not so. I'll never be ready really to leave it or to stop it. But now I think I can go ahead on my own . . . and I know I can always call you if I get snarled up some way.

TH-111.1: Sounds right to me.

CL-111.2: I thought about making some big summarizing and farewell speech to you, but then . . . I realized that was sort of like writing my great novel: I'd be doing it for you and because it would be a wonderful thing to produce. You know, you'd want it recorded for your next book or something.

TH-111.2: Well, sure. You mean you're not going to do that for me? (*Teasing tone.*)

CL-111.3: Not this time. (*Pauses, considers.*) You know, we never did find out why that girl in my class had such an impact on me.

TH-111.3: An unsolved mystery.

CL-111.4: There are lots of unsolved mysteries in me. I know that
now. And I guess there are in everyone . . . even you.

TH-111.4: You better believe it.

*And so in a rather lighthearted manner, they draw their work to a close.
Stan finds that he has said most of what he wants to convey. After he
hears a few comments from Bruce, he hugs Bruce, concludes the interview, and leaves.*

NOTES

[1]And this is not either.

13

COMMENTARY ON A THERAPY FOCUSED ON THE LIVING MOMENT

Every Client Response Is an Opportunity

Stanley Dodge's psychotherapy with Dr. Bruce Graham as synopsized in Chapter Twelve illustrates exchanges typical of a psychotherapy that emphasizes the actual, in-the-living-moment, experiencing of the client. As such, it contrasts with the frequent practice of collecting and disbursing information about and to the client.

Absent from the account are the many repetitions of interactions and the not infrequent occasions of apparently trivial details and side issues. These are termed "apparent" because a written and explicit report must fail to convey the often more implicit and affective importance of living and working through such times. Saying it somewhat differently, the account omits a great deal of the implicit work of psychotherapy as it chiefly demonstrates some of the pivotal points in the therapeutic series—points at which the crucial elements are implicit.

The client is actually a composite of several different clients with whom I have had the challenge and satisfaction of working over the years.[1] If any of those actual persons should read this account, be assured that it is my intention to provide an only limitedly accurate recounting of our particular work together.[2]

This chapter summarizes the development of the therapy presented in Chapter Twelve by discussing nine segments of the protocol. These segments should not be seen as prototypical for this kind of therapy. Each client–therapist unit must find its own way and tempo.

The participants in the interviews will be identified either by their names or their roles: Stanley Dodge, client; Bruce Graham, therapist.

INTERVIEW 1: GETTING ACQUAINTED, MAKING THE CONTRACT[3]

As is typical of initial contacts, the first interview is devoted chiefly to getting acquainted and agreeing on a first schedule for their working together. In this instance, these matters were readily handled, and a favorable alliance seems likely to develop.

Some suggestion of a depressive tendency appears (CL-1.13) but the client does not dwell on it, and it is too soon and of too little apparent concern to the client for the therapist to pursue the matter now.

From the outset (CL-1.1, 1.9, 1.10) Stan's seeking the therapist's instruction is a prominent aspect of his participation. This is by no means unusual—or in any way inappropriate—as one undertakes a new course of action. However, it is also a frequent focus for the enactment of the client's transference and for client–therapist encounters, which have implications and consequences far beyond the explicit and immediate. At this early point, the therapist does well to take subjective note but direct no explicit attention to it.

When a therapeutic agreement is proposed (TH-1.20), Stan is briefly hesitant (CL-1.21) as he begins to recognize that he is undertaking a significant commitment. This hesitation does not reappear when the therapist proposes a twice-a-week schedule (TH-1.30).

The therapist's interjection of his view of managed-care policies (TH-1.25) may have subtly given the client a feeling of support, but it also implicitly reminds the client of the therapist's greater experience in these matters.

INTERVIEW 3: FIRST CONFRONTATION, LEARNING A CORE LESSON

Exchanges 3.6 through 3.18 are particularly illustrative of the client's confusion *of talking about* his experience with *talking out of* that experience. The former is information directed; the latter is expressive and actuality focused. The therapist in this sequence is mixing explanations with fostering the client's experiencing, and he is doing so at some length to win the client's general understanding. That understanding won't be enough to keep Stan from having an emotional reaction in future sessions (e.g., Interview 17) in which the therapist persists, but it is intended to be sufficient to protect the alliance. When the therapist plunges too abruptly into the *actual* mode, he may evoke strong and conscious resistance much earlier than the alliance can sustain—sometimes with the result that he impels the client to abandon therapy. Thus another client, superficially similar to Stan, might have been made uneasy by the therapist's early transfer to Stan of responsibility for telling about himself without more guidance (TH-1.11, 1.12. 1.20). If the therapist had not dealt with that reaction, the client might very well have canceled further sessions.

Notably, the client spontaneously reports listening to his inner sensing (CL-3.1). This is encouraging since many clients have difficulty doing so or they hesitate to report it. Using this favorable indication, the therapist devotes most of his effort to beginning to teach the client about how to use the therapeutic opportunity (TH-3.7 through 3.21). It is important to note that even this early, some clients—but by no means all—need to begin to experience some frustrations in order to arouse deeper affective layers for the work. This arousal by the therapist, however, is appeased in some measure by fairly prompt explanations at a conscious-rational level. Later that easing of tension cannot be relied on.

The therapist elects to do so with a confrontational approach, although this is rather early for this tactic. (Usually more time needs to be given to building the alliance so that the client won't be frightened or angered and possibly abort therapy.) That the choice works out well is attributable to (a) Stan's troubled feelings (i.e., sense of concern) helping him, at least to some extent, to hang in in spite of his irritation, and (b) Bruce's skillful sensing of when to leave the confrontational mode and provide a supportive rationale that the client can grasp and accept.

This same evidence that the alliance is growing well encourages the therapist to begin to challenge the client's dismissal of his own inner thoughts and feelings. One product of that challenge, which often seems surprising to those not familiar with this work, is the subtle bonding that can occur as a result of helping a person learn to hear and validate inner experiencing.

Not shown in this account are the frequent returns to this sort of confrontation with the *actual* or immediate that will take place in subsequent interviews until Stan can more promptly access his inner awareness and use it in therapeutic searching.

CL-3.23 brings out client concerns other than the presenting issue. Often, as a client begins to settle into a working alliance, other matters begin to press for attention. This can be the sign of a favorable alliance or of diversion from the main work; it's a judgment call. The best course is to try to follow the client's deeper affect.

Of course, some of these issues may be returned to later, while others never will be addressed directly. Some will be alleviated by the work on the main concern; some may continue to be intrusions on the client's life throughout its span.

Psychotherapy cannot deal with all of the issues of a person's life. The idea of a "thoroughly analyzed" person who has no psychological issues or problems is a myth. Pursuit of that myth keeps some people in lifelong therapy. Others continue indefinitely simply because the circumstances of their lives offer no other personal resources for thinking through their experiences.

INTERVIEW 6: FURTHER DISCOVERY OF THE IMMEDIATE

The main therapeutic intent here is to help the client increase his ability to distinguish and attend to what is immediate within himself—that is, the actual *in-the-living-moment* concerns of his life. As it is for most clients, this is difficult for Stan, who is ready to talk *about* himself but tends to regard his subjective as largely irrelevant.

When one pauses genuinely to reflect on Stan's attitude in this regard, surprise is likely to be the response. Stan is an intelligent, well-educated professional, and yet he has learned to devalue and even avoid his inner thoughts and feelings! It is not surprising that he often finds himself unsure of his intentions and unable to mobilize his energies as he wants to.

Interview 6 is particularly and explicitly concerned with helping the client discover the unusual inclusiveness of the therapeutic field. To protest that one has "nothing" in his subjective is to demonstrate a naiveté that must be addressed if the work is to go forward and to go into deeper subjective layers.

In this interview, the client attempts to "take time out" from the therapeutic task and to *talk about himself* detachedly. He has yet to learn that in psychotherapy this is impossible. Life doesn't permit "times out," nor should psychotherapy.

Whatever happens— is said, done, or occurs—in the therapeutic hour is *irrevocably* part of the work, part of the therapy enterprise. There are no time-outs or asides or any other exceptions, for that is indeed the nature of reality. This teaching began in the first interview when the client asked how "to begin" therapy, and the therapist said, "You've already begun" (TH-1.11 and again in TH-3.6).

Actuality, "playing for keeps," recognizing no exceptions, insisting that whatever happens in the session is a legitimate focus for attention—these constitute a unique environment for the therapeutic effort. In all other venues of our lives, we expect exceptions, modifying circumstances, qualifying provisions, or similar social conventions for denying full reality to what happens.

It is often a surprise to the client for the therapist to begin the application of this rule, and it may be uncomfortable for well-meaning therapists as well. The client can't think of anything to talk about, makes a mistake when addressing the therapist, starts to say something and then hesitates, grows irritable about therapist interventions, abruptly needs to go to the restroom, and so on—all familiar instances of which therapists should take note. Then, as the client is deemed ready, it becomes appropriate to call for client exploration of what may subjectively be coincident with or in back of such intrusions.

Many times, at least early in the work, the client simply wants to dismiss such occasions as "accidents" or as otherwise unworthy of much time or concern. It calls for sensitive and determined therapist skill to help the client discover that such simplifications are actually distortions that can be costly to therapeutic effectiveness.

Recognition of this truth is a source of great power for the work. At the same time, it imposes a unique burden of responsibility on both participants. As one client phrased it, "There's no hiding place."

Of course, immediate and full implementation of this basic truth is usually too heavy a demand to place on a person new to this sort of work. It must be brought to the client's recognition in measured portions, and yet throughout it is the essential working condition toward which the therapist needs to be guiding their relationship. There is no hiding place for the therapist either.[4]

This same policy also needs to be in place when an intrusion occurs because of a client's or therapist's involuntary action: The patient sneezes ("Oh, excuse me, I've got this damned cold"); the therapist hiccups (both ignore it . . . at least at first[5]); either of the participants breaks wind ("farts"); the therapist calls the client by the wrong name; the client arrives at the wrong hour; either becomes manifestly ill during the session—and so the list may be extended.[6]

Once the client has come to appreciate the importance of this basic rule, the general policy is to inquire, "What's in your awareness now?" Of course, if the client is deeply engrossed in some work and hardly notes the intrusion, that work has priority.

Outside Intrusions

The inclusiveness of this axiom extends to instances in which attention is distracted by intrusions of sounds, sights, smells, and similar sensory stimuli from outside the therapy room. Of course, such intrusions affect the therapist as well as the client. Thus therapists who pretend not to notice and try to insist on the work's going forward as if nothing inadvertent had occurred are fostering inauthenticity, which may well recur in other and more contratherapeutic circumstances. It is the therapist's responsibility to deal with the issues that make the therapist vulnerable, and not act them out at the client's emotional expense.

To put the matter most succinctly: Therapists must be so in touch with the actual in the therapeutic hour that they can either guide their clients' explorations without intruding their own unresolved issues or can be candid about their own limits and accept responsibility for them.

Such occasions provide important teaching opportunities. Even the client, who has come to understand that his slip of speech has unconscious motivations, still finds it surprising that the therapist calls for inner exploration when something quite external to the therapeutic hour intrudes—for example, a noisy altercation occurs in the hall outside the office, the room temperature drops so that the therapist has to adjust the thermostat, or the waiting room buzzer sounds well before the end of the hour.

The unthinking tendency in such instances is of the order of: "Just ignore that and go on with what you were saying."

Impossible! The best the client can do is to attempt to continue with the same content with which he was engaged before the intrusion. This means trying to "push aside" whatever subjective responses may have been stimulated by the intrusion. It may or may not constitute some loss in exploring the preintrusion subject matter.

The more important loss is the unrecognized "training" the client receives in overriding his own inner process—training much emphasized in this culture and significantly contributing to our treating ourselves and each other as objects and thus to having difficulty in bringing our subjective intentions into overt realization.

INTERVIEW 17: DEALING WITH CLIENT FLIGHT

Sooner or later, not once but repeatedly, and with some clients throughout much of their therapeutic course, there come times of overt opposition, angry or excessively detached questioning, and attempts at withdrawal. While it is usually a sign of progress, at the outset, it is extremely unwise to so interpret it to the client. To do so is to make the client feel belittled and patronized, for it is apt to be experienced as ignoring the genuine turmoil that is almost always going on subjectively when this pattern emerges.

It is here regarded as progress because often it occurs when what was formerly repressed material begins to enter consciousness and there is the threat of loss of one's usual control. This threat must not be dismissed, and—as in the Chapter Twelve protocol—gentle but persistent responsiveness may help the client to greater awareness.

The extent of Stanley Dodge's being caught up in—and somewhat angry with—this inner emergence is manifested by his briefly being unable to remember the therapist's name, although he has been using it for several months now. When Stan begins to get some recognition that his (until-then) growing anger is warding off grappling with his own feelings, the therapist wants to affirm that discovery quickly. In the protocol, he takes responsibility for having acted too quickly. Doing so poses a moot point. Once the meaning of the client's feelings becomes apparent to the client, being met and confirmed can be helpful, but it can also be aborting. The therapist is often impelled by the countertransference to want to relieve the tension, and that impulse may add to the difficulty of making the judgment call.

An appreciable portion of Interview 17 is devoted to helping Stan recognize that "nothing" is actually "something"—something worth therapeutic attention. The therapist begins teaching this lesson with a sharp intervention in exchange 17.2. Thereafter, he continually shows Stan that what he is doing is "the work." Stan repeatedly tries to escape by "talking about" what is going on at a surface level, but the therapist refuses to allow this detour.

This work with direct confrontations to the client can be very confusing (at first) to the client, but often brings important affective material forward. The client who has not really absorbed the point that everything that is said, done, experienced, and otherwise brought into the hour is quite literally part of the business of psychotherapy understandably protests. Then to find that even the protest isn't treated as outside the therapeutic focus can be a transition point in a person's psychotherapy. Clients vary in how readily they can come to recognize and accept this unexpected but essential requirement of depth therapeutic work

Therapists also have their own difficulties coming to appreciate the importance and the power of working in this very direct fashion. It is likely to be uncomfortable for them as well, and the urge to explain or teach the client and avoid the irritation—or even outright anger—of the client is strong. Yet to take that detour will end up reducing the therapeutic impact.

In Session 17, the underlying protective function of *resistance* is evident in how quickly the "nothing" (CL-17.8 and the following exchanges) roll back to a next layer at which the significance of his inner experience is still unrecognized. This is an important learning—important for more than facilitating the progress of the interview. The deeper implication is the need to help the client discover that his or her inner living is always significant. Stan, like so many others, tends to think of it as superficial and transitory.[7]

A point often misunderstood: This psychotherapy isn't *about the subjective*; it is working directly *in the subjective*.

The significance of the rule that whatever happens in the consultation hour may appropriately be examined is not that whatever happens necessarily reveals something otherwise hidden in the client. That is a relic of the "whodunit" view of psychotherapy in which the therapist–detective is trying to get clues to the hiding client–perpetrator's whereabouts (or guilt). Life coaching such as I am here advocating is not trying to outsmart the client; it is instead trying to reinforce (and, sometimes, redirect) the client's own efforts.

Rather than a detective, the therapist working with the *actual* is more like an Olympics coach who is neither an opponent nor a competitor. The therapist, is, in fact, a supporter of the athlete's (client's) own purposes and efforts.

The reason for the absolute rule that "everything is everything" is very simply the manifest truth that when something intrudes on the therapeutic work, it makes waves, it has effects, it cannot be treated as though it did not happen. Therefore, it provides an opportunity to teach the client respect for his own inner processes.

Some additional instances will make this reality more evident. Here is an incident that we'll examine in some detail.

> As the patient begins speaking, an angry voice in the hall outside the consultation room says loudly, "You are a royal pain in the butt! I'm out of here." A door slams.

Assuming that the client is silent after this intrusion, the therapist's question after such an unexpected event is, "What's in your awareness now?" This is a simple question, to be sure, but not one that most clients find easy to answer. Four possible client responses to this question are described in the following.

Client A: "Well, I just was telling you about the argument I had with my brother, and. . . . "

The therapist cuts in, "Yes, but something happened, and it's important to see where you really are *now*."

Clients generally reply with some variation on, "Oh, it's okay, I remember what I was going to say, and. . . . " They are set to pick up the content thread, but again it is wise to use this opportunity for teaching.

"Wait just a minute, Helen. I am sure you remember what you were planning to talk about, but something intervened. If you tell me now about the argument with your brother, you will be in some measure in a different subjective place because you were interrupted, and. . . . "

"No, really. It's all right. I just wanted to tell you how he was. . . . "

At this point, it's a judgment call. To force the point now would be to make a major interruption out of what might indeed be a relatively insignificant event. On the other hand, to let the client repeatedly be so content focused and unaware of inner processes will contribute to keeping the work shallow.

Probably the wisest policy is to reflect on whether this is the first instance of its kind—in which case, just going along with the client's intention is probably indicated. However, one would do well to watch for signs of residues of the intrusions affecting the client as she continues.

If, on the other hand, this denial of the intrusion's impact has occurred before, it is likely to be time to deal more directly with the resistance. One possible path for that inquiry might begin like this.

I know you feel that those sounds didn't affect you, but it is important to explore that more. Your inner experiencing needs to be accessible to you if you are to live fully. This is a place in which we can discover more about times when you tend to shut things out.

Of course, this approach may elicit a variety of responses—protests that she heard but didn't want to get distracted, annoyance that the therapist is interrupting her more than did the outside intrusion, relief that it is all right to have been distracted, curiosity as to what was going on out there, and so on. Whatever the response, the work picks up from there.

Suffice it to say that it is critically important to the therapeutic process to help clients become sensitized to their inner living, for only then can they weigh alternatives and make choices that are truly fulfilling and harmonious to their own long-term needs. Saying that, however, is not to say that the lesson must be taught thoroughly at the first opportunity.

Client B: What might be discovered were the client—as a result of some teaching—more inwardly and immediately aware could be something like the following: "Well, I just was starting to tell you about my argument with my brother, and then it was like I heard my own voice shouting at him. (*She laughs briefly, tightly.*) Although I don't think I ever called him a 'royal pain in the butt.' My, that's quite a phrase, isn't it? (*She is silent.*) You know, I wish I had. Oh, I don't mean just those words, but I wish we had been more honest with each other. You know, our family was always so. . . . "

This is a fortuitous instance. Not by any means does the content always segue so well out of the intrusion. More typical would be the following.

Client C: "I'm annoyed at that loud mouth out in the hall, but what I really want to talk about is the way my brother and I seemed to have this love–hate relation. I remember one time. . . . "

The client continues as though there had been no intrusion. The momentum of her need to discuss this topic is manifest, and the therapist does well to go along with this work—at least this time.

Client D: Other times, an intrusion may bring about some change in direction: "I don't know. I just started to. . . . Wait, let me see: (*Pause.*) I'm kind of rattled. I wish you had better sound insulation. I was going to tell you something about my brother, but right now it doesn't seem very important. What I find inside right now is kind of a general feeling of dissatisfaction. It's like I want to complain about something. . . . "

No lightning stroke of insight, but a useful demonstration of the client's having learned to distinguish more meaningful material from the socially expected, leading to what may be an early indication of transference issues, which will become important. (However, note that the transference issue suggested is still at a "talking-about" level and probably not yet ready for direct attention.)

INTERVIEW 37: MORE LESSONS IN SELF-DISCOVERY AND SELF-ACCEPTANCE

By this point, Stan has learned to use therapy well, and in this session, he has begun to take more responsibility for its progress. It is doubtlessly helpful for him to come early and have time to become centered before beginning the consultation, but it is even more important that he is valuing the work and thinking about how to make it more impactful. The underlying meaning is that he is taking more charge of his life generally.

Stan asks, "Why is it so hard to say what I mean?" (about discovering his innerness). Then he demonstrates an answer in his avoidance of expressing a negative feeling toward the therapist. This is not the only influence contributing to his difficulty, but it is representative of the kinds of unrecognized censorship that handicaps our thinking even when we believe we're just thinking privately.

Stan then acts this out again as he tries to change the subject. However, he is beginning to recognize the signs when he is avoiding, and that will expedite subsequent work a great deal.

In responses 37.8 through 37.17, the therapeutic partners are helping Stan to peel back the layers of his more nearly conscious resistance.

No matter what has been said on any issue in one's life, there is more that can be said. Exchanges 37.20 through 37.28 in this interview show a different facet of this open-endedness of our inner processes. It is my belief that it is impossible to exhaust all that is potential within a person's subjectivity. Whatever the entry point, if one persists, more will be found. Moreover, the very searching process itself (which is, of course, what is involved here) would continually produce more awarenesses.

INTERVIEW 67: SELF-DIRECTED INNER SEARCHING

Stan is now using the therapeutic opportunity well and finding ways of enriching it by coming early, staying after for a "decompression" time, and using the couch from time to time. The payoff of this is evident in his ability to distinguish fairly readily between surface and deeper concerns. This is a skill that is difficult to learn and that, once learned, makes therapy move more powerfully.

In this interview, Stan chooses to use the couch. This aid is linked in the popular mind with psychoanalysis and, by extension, with psychotherapy generally. It is certainly a valuable tool when used well, but it is only that. The associations most of us have to lying on our backs are generally those of lowered vigilance and freer introspection—obviously fostering the inner searching that often is the main avenue of client work in the therapy being described here.

In general practice, I've found it helpful to introduce the couch when the client has begun to search and is ready for the further facilitation that this posture can usually provide. Once the client has genuinely experienced that aid, I usually let the client choose when to employ it, although at times I may suggest it.

Important in this session is the therapist's repeated identifications of the client's not keeping faith with his own aspirations and yearning. This is a crucial aid to freeing up the long-suppressed ideal.

The recognition that the client attains in Interview 67 is notable for the way it keeps opening up. Its influence shows throughout the remaining sessions in his therapy. This central theme in the client's life was brought out by the therapist's restrained participation as it aided the client in finding his own way to an important and previously unaccessed discovery.

In general and outside the therapist's office, a person of average intelligence may be unable to grasp fully and with feelingful recognition the contrast between thinking earnestly and at length *about* a problem and grappling with that same problem in a discovery mode (as Stan is now doing).

Yet, despite his very real gains, another layer of Stan's resistance is manifest in his tendency to stand outside himself and become disparaging of his deeper aspirations. The therapist points out how this self-betrayal handicaps the client's searching, and the client is able to use this reminder to go forward—an example of a well-working therapeutic partnership.

Notable in the latter part of this interview (CL-67.13 through 67.17) is the client's increased ability to sense beyond that which is immediately conscious. This typifies clients who have truly gained more than usual access to their subjectivity. No longer does Stan get one insight and feel he's reached the end of the road. Instead he senses the greater understanding that is still latent.

One hint to what may yet be brought fully into consciousness is the client's "I don't have to." This seems in contrast to some extent with his ambitious image of the highly successful author.

INTERVIEW 70: THE STRUGGLE TO KEEP FAITH WITH ONESELF

In Interview 70, Stan is discovering the many layers of his inner knowing. In a previous interview (67), he had brought to the surface his "secret" ambition. In that session, recognition of what that secret meant to him evolved to some extent. In the next two sessions, it was present, but was little changed from its first surfacing. Now, in the fourth session in which the "secret" is explored therapeutically, there is a further opening as Stan sees its connection to his feeling for his father.

Very often, in depth therapy some incident or item of information will surface and may be worked with to an extent that seems adequate and productive. Yet when the client has learned to be open to his inner processes, it is not unusual for that same matter to reappear and then be the impetus to further self-understanding. Indeed, this may occur a number of times.

It is this familiar phenomenon of longer-term depth therapy that demonstrates so clearly that information itself is not the significant element in the work. Rather it is the exploration of how the client accesses, incorporates, processes, and links the information with other subjective material that chiefly yields the therapeutic result.

This interview is critically important to Stan's psychotherapy (and Stan's life): his initial impulse to distance himself from the "secret" discloses how it is still alive (not just a "closed" memory). There is much—too much—in our culture, particularly in the case of the intellectually invested portion, that favors self-disparagement, dismissing one's attainments, and generally maintaining a calculated distance from such subjective impulses as high aspirations, pride in accomplishments, affection for associates, and similar positive emotions about one's innerness. "Cool" is the key word, and it too often deteriorates to "cold."

This pattern of standing off in self-judgment has proved to be a major part of this client's distance from (*resistance to*) being fully in his living and giving it a more satisfying direction.

In this session, the therapist takes a firm but simple stand in calling for the client to recognize the self-betrayals he attempts and to honor his own deeper values and aspirations. This therapist action expresses a further development in the alliance. While in earlier sessions, the therapist did well to maintain a certain neutrality, now that a solid alliance is in place, the therapist may selectively speak for those parts of the client that have been disclosed and found to be health and growth seeking.

To be quite clear: The point is not whether Stan writes *the* book or any book. The point is that Stan needs to risk staying with—but not necessarily attempting to actualize—his inner reality. Thus the impulse to write the great book is manifestly real, but it is very likely only one prompting competing for actualization with others (which for Stan might include foreign travel, early retirement and devoting himself to some hobby, or becoming a recognized scholar and contributor in his field).

INTERVIEW 95: Searching Goes on . . . and on

One of the important demonstrations of this interview illustrates how searching can continually bring forward fresh recognitions and understandings about our lives. So often we have an unexamined image of our subjectivity as though it were a book in which all we have experienced has already been written. Thus psychotherapy would need only to find the right pages, and we could read what has been recorded. That notion is a total misunderstanding of the nature of human subjectivity, and it undermines much potential creativity and understanding.

Any person's subjectivity is a spring-fed pool from which flows an endless stream of images, memories, emotions, impulses, and all else that bubbles and percolates in our depths. The pool may be dipped into from any points we choose along its perimeter, while the stream that flows from it continually goes on of its own accord. All the while, there are depths that rarely if ever surface, but are essential to the existence and dynamic of both pool and stream.

My metaphor is generally accurate, but it does not fully express that in those depths new combinations and implications are continually latent. The life-important implications: There is no predetermined content or quality to what may emerge from our depths, and there is no finite limit to how much may come into consciousness.

When a client protests, "I've told you everything about (any matter) . . . ," the client is self-deceived. If the client will stay centered and attentive, he will soon find there is much more to be said. Moreover, when the client insists that there is only one way of interpreting some life incident, this is a similar misunderstanding of our nature.

INTERVIEW 111: THE UNENDING END

What has just been said about the openness and mutability of subjective experience makes it evident that the idea of a "completed psychotherapy" is an oxymoron. Stan has come to recognize this, and yet he knows he is ready to discontinue formal interviews. He has the tools now to do much more work on his own, and he knows that he can return to Bruce[8] if that seems desirable.

NOTES

[1]For accounts of psychotherapy with other clients, see Bugental (1976, 1990). Readers may find it interesting to track, through those two books and this book, the evolution in my thinking over the last 20-plus years.

[2]If you, the reader, are a former client of mine and you do read this, know also how grateful I am to you for your patient tutelage of me as a sometimes slow learner.

[3]The term "contract" is widely used and may refer (as in this protocol) to an oral understanding about the frequency and mode of payment, or it may identify a much more formal and sometimes written statement. In the latter instance, it is usually good practice to provide the client with written information about the therapist's policies and the confidentiality conditions (in part, these may be legal stipulations). In such instances, and particularly with regard to confidentiality, it is well to have the client sign a statement that he has been apprised of the limits on privacy.

[4]The therapist who is genuinely present to the work with clients must be accessible—even, at times, vulnerable—to those clients, for only then can the therapist be alert to the nonverbal cues that inform him or her of the client's uneasy avoidance and dedicated pursuit of greater self-awareness.

[5]Elaine May and Mike Nichols, in their days as an improvisational comedy duo, enacted a classic and very funny scene concerning a psychoanalyst with the hiccups and an analysand determined to overlook that fact and continue the therapeutic work while making helpful suggestions soto voce.

[6]The extended list would include the humorous and the tragic, the trivial and the momentous. It would include my own falling asleep during a session, a client's falling totally silent and refusing to speak again, a mix-up in room assignments that paired the therapists with each other's clients, and many, many other so-very-human events.

[7]On reflection, one will be apt to find it remarkable how widespread is this denigration of our subjective living. What should be recognized and valued as the very essence of being an animate being is so often regarded as trivial, fleeting, and without value. When the client learns the centrality and significance of his subjectivity, a major step has been made toward greater self-possession and more effective participation in one's own living.

[8]Or to some other psychotherapist, if circumstances make that preferable.

14 SUMMARIZING THE EXPERIENCING-CENTERED ORIENTATION

Psychotherapy Freshens How We Perceive Our Living

As we near the end of this presentation, it is appropriate to take several steps back in order to view in broader perspective what it is that is the focus of our concern. When we do so, we are demonstrating the very theme we are expressing: Life is lived as a perceptual experience. How we "see" or define our own nature and the nature of the world in which we find ourselves is a crucial element in determining what our lives will mean to us and to those with whom we share this epoch of living.

The opportunity, necessity, and challenge of living are that each of us must create and live out a life. Ultimately, this is an individual responsibility—even though often that may not seem to be the case. Many influences press us to disavow or, at least, to try to delegate this responsibility.

Recognition of this basic life truth of our ultimate self-responsibility is sometimes misunderstood as a kind of "blaming the victim" philosophy, and in other instances is thought to be an absurd "Pollyanna-ism" that promises that anyone can do anything if only she will set her mind to it. Of course, neither of these is sensible, and certainly neither is accepted by the stance here presented.

It is obviously and irrevocably true that we live in a multifaceted reality, which profoundly affects what we experience and what opportunities and obstacles we encounter in carrying out this basic responsibility for our lives.

When and where one is born, whether female or male, healthy or ailing, intelligent or of limited potential, and into what sort of family, society, and times influence our lives' courses.[1] Yet each of these factors—and many others, including some of which we are only partially aware—open out into further arrays.[2]

Literature, both popular and technical, provides many accounts of individuals who overcame crippling environmental and chance-inflicted handicaps to live rich and contributing lives. To be sure, often such stories also recognize how exceptional native talents were called into action and, in turn, facilitated the exceptional outcomes. But it would be naive to attempt to dismiss all such instances as simply products of random gene combinations. Indeed, there is the real possibility that the exceptional talents were in some measure the products of human will as it confronted those very handicaps.

Candidly, if we were to soberly examine our own history, we would be likely to discover occasions on which we failed to use our powers effectively and others when we stretched to go beyond our usual life patterns. Popular idiom says it, "If life hands you a lemon, make lemonade."

Yet by no means does this homily assure a happy-ever-after outcome. We simply don't know the stories of unnumbered men and women of great potential who were overwhelmed by circumstances and, therefore, never realized their potentials.[3]

THE THERAPIST'S MISSION

Our work, as we view it in this book, is to engage with the client's way of grappling with life or, in other words, with the patterns through which the client seeks to be safe, fulfilled, and in relation. To "engage" is not to *learn about* those patterns; "engage" signals a more experiential process. That, in turn, implies that the therapist cannot simply be a detached observer but needs the lived experience of how her client is grappling with his life.

Those patterns constitute the client's implicit conceptions of his own nature, powers, vulnerabilities, and all else that is implicit in his way of experiencing his own being and employing his powers in life—that is, the client's self-and-world construct systems[3] as they are structured to deal with possibilities, hazards, resources, and much more.

What underlies this stance is the recognition that the self is always defined in terms of its interaction with the environing world, and the world is always perceived in terms of its actual or potential effects on the self.

Another aspect of this conception needs to be made explicit: We are speaking here of *perceptions*, of how the self and its attributes and the world and its many aspects are *perceived*. Of course, *perception* here does not mean only visual or even sensory perceptions as independent existants. Although the sensory facets of our perceptions may prove of great importance at times, they always do so in larger contexts.

We live in a perceptual world—that is, in the world that our perception reveals. As we experience our lives, we form percepts about this world's elements and aspects. These become de facto definitions, and rightly or wrongly they do much to determine how we will relate to that which they name.

Is the world a safe place? Can a woman deal with this kind of problem as well as would a man? How will this art authority respond to my paintings? Must I cultivate the big shots to get promoted in my job or will doing a good job be enough?

THE OMNIPRESENCE OF DEATH

The disease that results in 100 percent fatalities is called "Life." Life is lived between the brackets of birth and death, and that very stark reality subtly or openly affects much that we think and do. In earlier years, we implicitly claim immortality, but even then the shadow falls from time to time. As we age, that warning is more frequent and demanding.

Death accompanies life day by day, moment by moment. It isn't an event that *will* occur in the future; it is an actuality in each moment *now*. Each moment's life lives on the dead corpse of the previous moment. My lover today dies in tomorrow's kiss.

Recognizing this, anticipation, apprehension, remembrance, and regret are appropriate, but not if they obscure what *is* in this present moment. The very fact of ending can give vitality to that which is in fact now and, therefore, in some measure accessible, and it counsels action rather than delay.

Psychotherapists need to be aware—and to help their clients to be aware—that the resistance is an attempt to delay the death of possibilities. Becoming genuinely aware of that inexorable fact may impel one to claim the life of what is immediately possible and to avoid the death of inaction.

Searching is the life force (*chi*), being its own nature. Case formulations can so easily become like butterflies impaled on pins and put in display cases.

PSYCHOTHERAPY AND CHANGING

It is time to try to bring together the chief elements of the existential–humanistic perspective on life-changing psychotherapy, as I envision it. Other psychotherapists will, of course, have points of difference, and that is as it should be. We are considering an art form, and, by its very nature, not all art can be captured by any one artist.[4] Thus each person must, perforce, produce a masterpeice, and no explanations can ease that responsibility.

Effective Ingredients in Psychotherapeutic Change

To begin with a synoptic statement of this existential–humanistic perspective: Essentially and experientially, life is subjective awareness. Without awareness, we are not truly alive. The conditions for which we seek therapy (e.g., anxiety, impulse control, meaninglessness in life, difficulties in relationships) may usefully be thought of as likely to be the products of shrunken and distorted ways of being aware—that is, of being alive.

The range and depth of our awareness constitute the settings of our *self-and-world construct systems.* When that system is too confining or too poorly corresponds with the consensual world view, we experience anxiety, pain, futility, or other symptoms that may lead us to seek psychotherapy. In a great oversimplification we may say that the task of such therapy is, then, to explore the client's self-and-world construct system and then to facilitate the client's making needed revisions in it.

This system is the way in which the client survives, seeks fulfillment, and avoids harm, and yet it is this same system that must be investigated and in which changes must occur as a result of the therapeutic work. Understandably, the work of therapy inevitably encounters *resistance* from the client's way of being in the world (i.e., that same self-and-world construct system). Thus psychotherapy must encourage and support confrontation with the negative effects of this system while supporting its positive contributions to the client's life.

The two chief ways in which the therapeutic process carries out this work are through (1) intensive attention to the actual way the client explores and utilizes his own capacities as manifested in the client's self-presentation in the consultation room, and (2) coaching the client to attain improved skill and range in self-exploration in order to better understand his own self-and-world construct system. These tasks are best carried out in a setting of mutual respect and dedication.

This approach to the therapeutic work may be called "life coaching" to contrast it with notions of psychotherapy as repair of injuries or curing of diseases. Coaching seeks to increase the positive life skills of the client rather than to focus on negative patterns as such.

Restating the Central Thesis

From Freud on, we have been governed by the myth of historic determinism. This implied emphasis on the need to try to discover what happened in the past has brought us to today's *information-centered* approach. In so much of our work as therapists we tend to be caught up in collecting and disbursing information *about* the client. Such information may be the client's history, current concerns, relationships, and what the client hopes to gain from the therapy. Our clients soon get caught up in this information-about process.

However, all information is abstracted from the flow of time—that is, the flow of life. The only truly *actual* element is the process of the moment in the client, and yet clients and therapists have come to discount the momentary and seek "the long view."

What is advanced here is that therapists need to give greater attention to what is, in fact, *actual*. This means the subjective experience of the client in the moment. This means (in line with Hillman's[5] views) abandoning the notion of finding *causes*. And this means disclosing to the client her immediate experience.

I do not reject the notion of historical sources of much in our living, but I do insist that while history equips us with habit systems that can be useful (speech, social intercourse, and much else), these habits are at a level similar to that of muscle habits—available, repetitive, continually evolving, incompletely conscious, and only semivoluntary. I can, and at times need to, adapt or override some habits to type these words, to drive a car, to do most of the physical activities of daily life.

I can change and override emotional patterns *when I am aware of them in the moment of their activation.* However, so many of my emotional habits I only *know about* incompletely and after their functioning—that is, as information about myself and information about what is past.

An emotional habit is a set or predisposition to respond in patterned ways to certain situations

What is proposed here is that pointedly identifying in the moment *that which is activated but unregarded* introduces a new element in one's internal governance. When this is done, a change process is initiated that can have far-reaching results.

WHAT IS LIFE COACHING?

Life coaching is a mode of psychotherapy. It is, as the name suggests, a combination of concepts and practices through which a trained and dedicated person may provide a facilitating and renewing perspective and experience to another person. The recipient of this aid may be termed a "client" or "patient," but what is important is to emphasize the centrality of this person's own responsibility and self-direction.

Central to this conception is the conviction that many—perhaps most, possibly even all—of the distresses that bring people to psychotherapy are at their base the products of ineffectual and counterproductive life assumptions and the patterns of action and reaction deriving from them.[6]

A similarly central assumption insists that relief or recovery from such distresses is only to be had when the distressed person comes to fresh perspectives on his life—its assumptions, patterns, and internal conflicts.

REFLECTIONS ABOUT OUR WORK

1. The people with whom we are engaged are living all the time they're with us. They bring that-with-which-they-are-not-content to us. They live it out in our offices.
2. We are not physicians, repairpersons, or substitutes available to direct others' lives.
3. We are coaches for those who are not satisfied with their experiences of being alive.
4. The only change agency that produces lasting results is the change in a person's perception of his self and world.
5. Change will only occur when we help clients to see more fully how they are living their lives right now, right in the room.
6. The only reality about one's self is that which is *actual* in the moment. All else is static, is without power, is only information.
7. Recognition, insight, interpretation, and similar, familiar therapeutic products are often mistaken for the goal. They are useful to the extent that they evoke or express an immediate experiencing.

THE CENTRAL DRAMA OF DEPTH PSYCHOTHERAPY

I will sketch here, in greatly oversimplified terms, the core processes as they are conceived in this orientation. This will permit the review of key terms. It will also, I hope, foster a more energetic or dynamic sense of the therapeutic engagement than I (quite bias-edly) think of as the "whodunit" approach to therapy—that is, those modes in which primary attention is given to seeking cause-and-effect relations among elements of the client's history and complaints and then to teaching those connections to the client in the hope that the complained-of conditions will be eliminated, or at least radically modified.

The basic drama of depth psychotherapy is carried out as a struggle between two opposing forces. On one hand is a sense of *possibil-*

ity in combination with feelings of *concern*. These impel us forward in all venues of our lives. On the other hand, these positive impulses come up against other subjective elements in the form of forces or structures that seek continuity and predictability. These latter influences can be lumped together as *resistances*. As we explore them further, it becomes clear that they are chiefly expressions of our self-and-world construct systems, the very ways in which we define our own nature and the nature of the world in which we live. Obviously, threats to these definitions, at the most extreme, are experienced as threats to our lives.

What is evident from the foregoing is that our lives are lived at the level of perception. How we *see* ourselves, our world, our needs, our powers, our potentials, our experiences—this is the key to our living.

It follows then that psychotherapy must be concerned with perceptions. And, of course, that concern must not be limited solely to the conscious and verbalizable perceptions. Thus in the therapy work described in this book, we attend scrupulously to implicit perceptions as they are manifested in the living moment.

The phrase "in the living moment" is particularly important. It is no exaggeration to say that *the only* reality we have is that of this living moment—the moment in which I write these words and the quite other moment in which you read them.

Even were we talking together in the same room, we would not have precisely the same living moment because of the multiple and contrasting histories we would bring to our engagement. Another implication of this recognition is that when the client tells *about* an experience, it is always a different experience than it was when it occurred.

The particular merit of the perspective I'm presenting here is expressed by references to "the actual." What is actual is what *is* at the very moment; therefore, therapeutic attention and efforts need to be focused on the immediate *now* as much as is possible.

CONCLUSION: A SEMIFINAL RECOGNITION

This book has attempted to summarize my thinking and experiencing about psychotherapy as of 1999. It has fallen short of doing so. Thank the good Lord!

Psychotherapy is concerned with life, with living. That means it is concerned with what is going on, with what is changing and evolving, with what is about to be recognized. A book is much more static than is actual, vital psychotherapy. What I have written has taught me about what I have written. When I rewrite the account of some point I want to express clearly, the point has changed somewhat. When I try to capture the new perception, it has already gone on ahead of me.

That is the way with life. That is the way with our thinking about life. Therefore, that is the way with psychotherapy. We are—and we should be—always running to catch up.

You must excuse me now. I've got to hurry to find out what is next.

NOTES

[1]May, R. (1981). *Freedom and Destiny.* New York: Norton.

[2]Again a parallel to the "Mandelbrot sets" of chaos theory is evident.

[3]It is useful to think of these constructs as composites of relatively enduring percepts about life-significant matters. See Chapter Eight.

[4]Of course, psychotherapy is not only an art form; it demands an adequate scientific or knowledge base in human psychology and related disciplines.

[5]Hillman, J. (1983). *Healing Fiction.*

[6]Obviously, this centers our attention on what are sometimes called "functional" or "psychogenic" complaints. However, it should also be recognized that many organic or bodily distresses may have roots in or be aggravated by purely or chiefly psychological factors.

Life Isn't What You Think

Life is not what you think. Life is.
Does the yolk know the shape of the shell?
Does the foaming crest know the power of the wave?

Life is not what you think.
Life is going on . . . now.
Life is impending even as I write
   and as you read.
Life is experiencing, but not experience.

Life is not what you think.
Life is not future, past, or even *now*
   For even that *now* is now past, now-past.

Life is not what you think.
Life is not what will be in the future
   for when that future has become now
   it will be now and not the now we foresaw.
Life is what is before it becomes what was.

Life is not what you think . . . or what I think . . .
   or whatever it might be
Life is.

APPENDIX

AXIOMS FOR A PSYCHOTHERAPY OF THE ACTUAL

Axiom I: Everything is everything.

I-A: Nothing is something.
I-B: There is no time-out in therapy.
I-C: There is always more.

There are great validity and power in insisting that whatever happens in the consultation room is part of the psychotherapy—even when there is silence, even when there is an aside of any kind and about any matter whatsoever. This policy will surprise most clients—and not a few therapists.

How the client uses the therapeutic opportunity, how the therapist participates (or is inactive), what happens by chance in the room or in some way affects the room, even the time of day and the current weather—all may be appropriate topics to discuss, to take into account, to recognize as having effects, wanted or not.

The third of the corollaries is a statement as much about life as about psychotherapy. Despite our best efforts, there is no final sentence to be said on any topic of any life significance. There is no complete account of a client's subjective experience. There is no total presentation of a therapist's perspective.

Axiom II: Whatever the client does is the work.

II-A: The client is always doing his work.

II-B: The work goes on no matter what the client says or does.

II-C: Attention must be given to whatever happens.

Axiom II is a corollary of the first statement but it expresses further implications (and demonstrates the point) of the first axiom.

For the client to find that whatever he does or says is treated as a contribution to the therapeutic enterprise often means that there is a sobering and deepening of the client's participation. In line with the second corollary, even the client's protests—and the manner of their delivery—about this policy are, in themselves, material for therapeutic attention.

Axiom III: The subjective is the seat of our experience of life.

III-A: Thus it is the central site of psychotherapy.

III-B: Thus an invitation to disclose one's subjectivity is appropriately resisted.

New clients and inexperienced psychotherapists may find it difficult to understand therapists' greater attention to clients' immediate inner experiencing rather than to feelings, thoughts, and intentions. The difference is whether the latter, subjective processes are the subject matter of client reports or are the expressions of a client's in-the-moment experiencing. If the latter, then they are the very stuff for therapeutic focus; if the former, they are treated as detours.

Axiom IV: Life only is possible in the moment *now*.

IV-A: Therapy can only take place in the moment *now*.

IV-B: What is real is what is *now*.

Popular psychology—and more than a little traditional psychodynamic thinking—has popularized the simplistic notion of one-to-one connections between childhood experiences (particularly traumata) and current feelings and actions. This is missing the crucial significance of the *actual*. The client who confesses a childhood offense while weeping and seeking the therapist's reassurance may be protecting feelings about the earlier incident by pressing for current absolution. Or the client may be reenacting a confessional from previous years. Or she may be seeking to draw attention away from current conflicts with her family. In other words, there are numerous possibilities when we adopt a "detective story" approach.

When, on the other hand, this client is helped—by having her resistance exposed—to go more deeply into immediate subjective experiencing, the client can discover whatever prior or concurrent elements are of significance while she works through the immediate distress.

No amount of intellectual insight about one's past can provide for a working-through that can lead to genuine and lasting therapeutic changes.

Axiom V: Psychotherapy is concern with perceptions.

V-A: We're not treating illnesses or injuries.

V-B: We're freeing capacities that are restricted.

V-C: The client needs an experience, not an explanation.*

*Attributed to Freida Fromm-Reichman.

What has just been said about the futility of intellectualized under-standings in bringing about lasting changes in a client's emotions and actions reminds us that we can only work with how and what our clients perceive. We are forever separated from the actual events with which they may be concerned. This is not a recognition of impotence but one that directs our attention to how our clients perceive them-selves and their lives. When we can help clients thoroughly and vitally to express their views of many aspects of life-important situations—their current views, not their memories or what they have learned about a situation—then change of some kind is certain.

Axiom VI: The therapeutic alliance is the central vehicle of the work.

VI-A: Good therapists are not good detectives, and good detectives are not good therapists.
VI-B: Only the client has a compass.
VI-C: The therapist is a companion and interrogator but not a hid-ing place or a tour conductor.

The key to the actual in therapy is, many times, the alliance of client and therapist. Generally, this is desirably a positive relation in which there are mutual liking and empathy; however, that is not essential. Good therapeutic work can go forward with a less-than-ideal alliance if both participants put the task ahead of their feelings about and for each other and are able to be candid with each other.

The meaning of "good therapeutic work" is that the client's needs have priority, that the therapist is able to use sufficient empathy to attune to the pertinent elements of the client's preconscious as she explores inwardly. If the client is finding fresh awareness, if the ther-apist can empathically bring attention to resistances, then the relation may be sufficient. (Indeed, that level of bonding is probably quite frequent for some therapists who still attain reasonably satisfying therapeutic products.)

Axiom VII: Emotion can be facilitating or obscuring.

VII-A: Without concern, nothing matters.

VII-B: Concern is both a compass and an energy source.

VII-C: Confusion is often a signal that the client's usual ways of handling experience are not working, and thus may indicate some readiness to take new steps.

Emotion is a term for a wide range of subjective experiences, and most of them can either help the therapeutic work or hinder it. New therapists and counselors are inclined to think that emotional catharsis is itself evidence of therapeutic progress. This is not so. Good progress often triggers emotions—regret, dismay, joy, amusement, and anxiety, as examples—but that fact in itself does not bring about lasting changes.

Concern, in contrast, is the experience of the affect associated with confronting life issues that truly matter and that are latently or actually affecting the well-being of the client. Mobilized concern (as we saw in Chapter Four) is a power source and a guidance system for good therapeutic work.

Axiom VIII: The therapist needs to be as open as possible.

VIII-A: The client's attitude toward herself often shows the resistance.

VIII-B: Knowing about is not knowing.

VIII-C: Look for what blocks the vital flow.

Just as we encourage clients to openness and unaltered self-disclosures, we need to be as accessible as we can be—although therapist self-disclosure is another matter and should be used only with great discretion.

When the client describes experiences that seem similar to those the therapist has known, the impulse often is to assume that understanding has been facilitated. In many instances, just the opposite has occurred. The therapist's ability to hear what is unique—and, often, what is particularly important to this person (the client)—is obscured by the therapist's own memories and attitudes. More than for other areas of experience, the therapist does well to foster more extended self-description by the client.

As always, the resistance calls for the therapist's particular attention. A useful guide is to note fluctuations in the client's energy as that person participates. As there are hesitations, lack of interest, distractions, incompletenesses, it is useful to explore these quietly, but sufficiently to understand what may have caused these intrusions.

References

Bernard, Theos. (1947). *Hindu Philosopy*. India: Marilas Bararsidass.

Bugental, J. F. T. (1972). Misconceptions of Transpersonal Psychotherapy: Comment on Ellis. *Voices, 8*, 26–27.

Bugental, J. F. T. (1976). *The Search for Existential Identity*. San Francisco: Jossey-Bass.

Bugental, J. F. T. (1987). *The Art of the Psychotherapist*. New York: Norton.

Bugental, J. F. T. (1990). *Intimate Journeys: Stories from Life-Changing Psychotherapy*. San Francisco: Jossey-Bass.

Chaudhuri, H. (1956). *The Meeting of East and West in Sri Aurobindo's Philosophy*. Pondicherry: Sri Aurobindo Ashram.

Deikman, A. (1990). *The Wrong Way Home: Uncovering the Patterns of Cult Behavior*. Boston: Beacon.

Fierman, L. B. (1965). *Effective Psychotherapy: The Contributions of Hellmuth Kaiser*. New York: Free Press.

Gendlin, E. T. (1978). *Focusing*. New York: Everest House.

Goffman, E. F. (1961). *Asylums: Essays on the Social System of Mental Patients and Other Inmates*. Garden City, NY: Anchor.

Hillman, J. (1983). *Healing Fiction*. Tarrytown, NY: Station Hill Press.

Hillman, J. (1995). *Kinds of Power: A Guide to Its Intelligent Uses*. New York: Currency/Doubleday.

Jaynes, J. (1976). *The Origin of Consciousness in the Breakdown of the Bicameral Mind*. Boston: Houghton Mifflin.

Kopp, R.R. (1995). Metaphor Therapy: Using Client-Generated Metaphors in Psychotherapy. New York: Brunner/Mazel.

Kopp, S. B. (1971). *Guru: Metaphors from a Psychotherapist*. Palo Alto, CA: Science and Behavior Books.

Levenson, E. (1995). *The Ambiguity of Change*. Northvale, NJ: Jason Aronson.

May, R. (1958). *Existence: A New Dimension in Psychiatry and Psychology.* New York: Basic Books.

Pierce, J. C. (1985). *Magical Child Matures.* New York: Dutton.

Reik, T. (1949) *Listening with the Third Ear.* New York: Farrar, Strauss & Giroux.

Robertson, R. & Combs, A. (1995). *Chaos Theory in Psychology and the Life Sciences.* Mahwah, NJ: Lawrence Erlbaum.

Sarason, T. (1990). *The Challenge of Art to Psychotherapy.* New Haven: Yale University Press.

Smith, H. (1982). *Beyond the Post-Modern Mind.* New York: Crossroad.

Soukhanov, A. H. (Ed.). (1992). *The American Heritage Dictionary of the English Language*, 3rd ed. (p. 642). Boston: Houghton Mifflin.

Walsh, R. N. (1976). Reflections on Psychotherapy. *Journal of Transpersonal Psychology, 8*(2), 100–101.

Wewood, J. (1982). The Unfolding of Experience: Psychotherapy and Beyond. *Journal of Humanistic Psychology, 22,* 91–104.

Yalom, I. D. & Elkin, G. (1974). *Every Day Gets a Little Closer: A Twice-Told Therapy.* New York: Basic Books.

INDEX

Note: Page references enclosed in square brackets indicate textual references to endnotes.